Robert Newton Flew

1886–1962

ROBERT NEWTON FLEW, 1955
from the portrait by Frank O. Salisbury

Gordon S. Wakefield

Robert Newton Flew
1886–1962

LONDON

EPWORTH PRESS

SBN 7162 0186 0

Enquiries should be addressed to
The Distributors
The Methodist Book Room
2 Chester House
Pages Lanes
Muswell Hill
London N10 1PZ

Printed in Great Britain by
The Whitefriars Press Ltd
London and Tonbridge

TO

ARTHUR MICHAEL

ARCHBISHOP OF CANTERBURY

ut omnia unum sint

Contents

Preface

RECENTLY I was in the company of the head of another Methodist Department and we both said that we would love to meet and talk again with our teachers of old. We felt that we would understand them better and learn even more from them now, and also tell them of our indebtedness and try to assure them that such faith as they had in us had not been wholly in vain.

Such conversation must wait for 'the happy isles' where we may perchance 'see the great Achilles whom we knew', but when six years ago his family asked me to write Dr Newton Flew's *Life*, I was honoured to accept, in part in gratitude for his great goodness to me, which I had not been able to repay by any very remarkable achievements in the schools or in the church.

The work has taken longer than I expected and there have been the usual problems of authorship in a life with many other duties and no sabbaticals. But, also, as Dr Flew might have said, 'There's a special technique about biography'. (He once made this remark at High Table *apropos* broadcasting and was curiously misheard by B. K. Cunningham, the Principal of Westcott House.)

It is important to set the subject in the context of his times and to try to make his contemporaries more than names. This is why I have given detailed accounts of some of the Cambridge, Methodist and ecumenical figures with whom Dr Flew was associated. Because he was an erudite theologian of his period, I have felt it necessary to relate his two most important books to the theological scholarship of the succeeding decades. This means that Chapter 5 is different in style from the rest of the book and will be found heavier going by some readers. Because it cannot be assumed that all will have read *The Idea of Perfection* and *Jesus and His Church*, or have them immediately in mind, I have given detailed summaries of both.

Biography must not degenerate into hagiography and the faults must not be concealed. But they must not be writ large. The reader should be enabled to enter into the subject's mind and world, to see situations from his point of view, and yet to retain his own moral judgement and condemn what is wrong for himself and without the author's perpetual strictures.

When once I told a continental scholar that I was writing a life of Dr Flew, he licked his lips at the thought of all the files, crammed with ecumenical memoranda and lecture notes, which were waiting for me to devour. But Dr Flew did not belong to the age of large secretarial staffs and mechanical aids, nor did he have a card-index mentality. He left few documents (or literary remains), but there are many letters to his mother and some to his friends. He was a brilliant letter-writer as well as a very faithful one, and these, nearly all in his own hand and many somewhat yellow with the years, have been a chief quarry. Otherwise it has been a matter of sleuth-like deduction, a piecing together of facts from people's reminiscences, contemporary books and records, and one's own memories. I hope that there are not too many 'howlers'.

Mrs Flew has been an unceasing help and encouragement. Her patience has been beyond all my deserts and I wish that the book could be worthy of her devotion and elegance. Mrs Strong, Dr Flew's sister, has made helpful comments. The Board of the Faculty of Divinity at Cambridge, through two of its Chairmen, Professors Nineham and MacKinnon kindly allowed me to read the Minutes of the Board during the years of Dr Flew's membership and to reproduce the extract on page 80. The Revd Paul Ellingworth, the Archivist of the Methodist Missionary Society, obtained permission for me to consult certain files relevant to Church Union in South India, which among other things has enabled me to endorse the judgements of Bengt Sundkler in his *Church of South India: The Movement Towards Union* 1900–47. The Oxford University Press has permitted me to quote lavishly from *The Idea of Perfection in Christian Theology*. The SCM Press has let me use the largish passage from Bonhoeffer's *Letters and Papers from Prison*. Routledge and Kegan Paul and Shocken Books Inc. have allowed the excerpt from Iris Murdoch's *The Sovereignty of Good*, and SPCK that from Henry J. Cadbury's *The Peril of Modernizing Jesus*.

Dr G. F. Nuttall has taken great interest, assisted at several stages and brought to the script his impeccable scrutiny. Dr Ernest A. Payne and Dr Marcus Ward have also read the whole, and saved me from some errors. Professor MacKinnon has read Chapters 4 and 5 and generously given me the benefit of his stimulating comments on other sections. The Revd Dr F. N. Davey has been of especial help on Chapter 4. The Bishop of Lincoln, the late Revd C. J. Barker, the late Revd F. W. Beal, the Revd H. R. Hindley, the Revd Reginald Kissack, the Revd Canon Charles Smyth have all assisted at specific points, while Sir Barnes Wallis sent invaluable reminiscences of schooldays and Mr Roderick Macleod has supplied letters. I do not propose to name any old Wesley House men, apart from Dr Ward, for to do so would be invidious and make possible identifications which had better be left unrevealed, but from many, both by correspondence and conversation, I have

learned much and am truly grateful, as I am to the lay
people who knew Dr Flew as a Methodist Circuit
minister or Chaplain to the Forces.

My wife has encouraged and at times driven me to the
work, which has been noble of her, since I doubt if a
mistress could be more demanding than a book and for
long hours and whole days I have been closeted in the
study, at home, yet not at home. Without the superb organisation of my Secretary, Mrs Jean Cumming, I could not
have been sufficiently free of the chores of the office to
have written anything at all, while Mrs Diane Dent of
Woodford Green and Miss Dawn Annan of Brisbane
have helped most willingly in the heavy task of typing
copies fit for the printer.

Finally, may I thank the Archbishop of Canterbury
for the honour he has done me in allowing me to dedicate
the book to him? Dr Flew loved the great Anglican
tradition and was a pioneer of Anglican–Methodist
unity. At times he became disheartened and did not
spare Anglicans his reproaches. But he glimpsed the
grandeur that is the English Church behind its party-
strife and inhibitions and had the deepest respect for the
disciple of Hoskyns and former Regius Professor at
Cambridge, who is now its leader and shares his own
longings for unity in truth and holiness.

Warwick House   GORDON S. WAKEFIELD
Harpenden
June, 1971

I

Foundations

ROBERT NEWTON FLEW was born on 25th May, 1886, at Holsworthy in Devon, where his young father, Josiah, was a Wesleyan Methodist minister. In later years, Newton would write to his mother as 'your unworthy, but Holsworthy son', but since Josiah, according to Wesleyan custom, was an itinerant, 'stationed' by the Conference of the Church for a year at a time, the family had moved on to Salcombe by the time the baby was three months old. Three years later they were in Warminster, followed by Stratford-on-Avon and War-wick. In 1898, Josiah was appointed to Wandsworth and remained in London suburbs for the rest of his ministry.

The family home was Portland, the 'Gibraltar of Wessex . . . that stretches like the head of a bird into the English channel', as Hardy describes it in the last and least of his novels, *The Well-Beloved*. 'Flew', which seems to be of Norman or Breton French derivation, is one of the dozen or so prominent family names of the island. There were Flews on Portland in 1525. In the old Churchyard there is this inscription:

> To Abel Flew, who was buried October 25th
> *A.D.* 1676
>> In life I wroath in stone
>> Now life is gone I know
>> I shall be raised
>> By a stone and B(y)

> Such a stone as giveth
> Living Breath and Saveth
> The righteous from the
> Second death.

To Portland in 1746 came Charles Wesley and the sight and rhythm of the quarrymen's hammers inspired a hymn, 'written before preaching at Portland'.

> Come, O Thou all victorious Lord,
> Thy power to us make known;
> Strike with the hammer of Thy word,
> And break these hearts of stone.

Charles Wesley found a small Methodist society on the island, led by William Nelson, who retained a close connection with the Parish Church and was prominent in the plan to build 'the new Church' of St George. But the man who consolidated Methodism on the island was Robert Carr Brackenbury, Lincolnshire squire and Cambridge graduate, who was given remarkable freedom by Wesley to preach wherever he felt called, and who established Methodism in the Channel Isles. In the autumn after Wesley's death, in 1791, Brackenbury heard of the social problems of Portland, remote and exposed as it was in those days. He settled there for several months and found the usual willing response to Methodism of the socially and geographically peripheral and depressed. From his time, Methodism was secure. One of the earliest members was Thomas Flew of Chesil, a grocer.

Newton Flew's grandfather, Robert (1832–1901), was a prison steward. He began at Portland and was transferred to Dartmoor, but returned to the island to die. He was a Wesleyan Methodist local preacher and also belonged to the Court Leet of Portland, the ancient manorial government. Josiah Flew was at one time Reeve of Portland and was probably the last to hold a Reeval staff, with its strange markings, which indicate the different parts of the island.

Newton Flew always regarded Portland as his home and visited it throughout his life. He would stay in a quarryman's cottage, call on the Methodists who remembered his father and grandfather, take services in the various chapels, and preach in the open air. One of the islanders has recalled how, 'in that cultured voice of his', he would always at some point address his hearers as 'fellow-Portlanders'. On 14th June, 1949, he was at Didsbury College, Bristol, on the retirement of his old friends Bardsley Brash and Alec Findlay. He met a small boy, five years of age, William Gibbs, son of John Gibbs of Cardiff, scion of another old Portland family. A previous William Gibbs had been associated with Thomas Flew in the Methodism of Brackenbury's day. The encounter stirred Newton Flew deeply and he clothed the lad in his own gown, hood, square and spectacles!

The Christian names, Robert Newton, honoured both Flew's own grandfather and Robert Newton, a Wesleyan statesman, partner of Jabez Bunting, four times President of the Conference and an oratorical preacher of immense popularity. His roots, then, went deep into Portland and into Wesleyan Methodism and *pietas* was one of his outstanding qualities. His father, Josiah, seems to have had a close and affectionate relationship with Robert, and Newton loved them both. On 10th March, 1895, he wrote a somewhat blotched note from Stratford-on-Avon to his grandfather, whose Dartmoor house had been burgled:

My dear Grandpa
  We heard of that "Desperate affray at Princetown" and I should advise you for the future to keep a gun and so when any burglar enters your house you may *shoot* him. Twas a very lucky thing Mr Rickard had one, wasn't it?

I am getting on very well at school My favourite lessons are
History, Reading class and Geography though sometimes the
latter is rather hard Pshaw I dont mind that I send my love
and kisses

Your loving grandson
Robert Newton Flew

[There follow eighty-one crosses]

On 10th April, 1896, he sent this to Josiah:

April 10th 1896
From Robert N. Flew to his Father on his 37th birthday
My dear Father
I wish you joy of your 37th birthday
I send you as a petty present this card
It is one of the two I have got
Wishing you a happy time
I remain

Your loving son
Robt. N. Flew.

There follows:

May blessing crown
thy Head
And guard thy 37th
birthday

THIS thy birthday morn
my sweet –
So send I this my dear
to greet –
Ah! me – if I were only this –
I'd greet my darling with a kiss

written all this was on
April 10th 1896 A.D.

Again the paper is smudged but the affection is clear
enough; also the frankness, confidence and freedom

from inhibitions which must have governed the relationships between father and son. Not many Victorian
parents would disclose their ages to their children.

At every stage of his life, Flew would talk of his father
as the one 'who led me to Christ'. He was influenced by
Josiah and inherited many of his gifts. He often referred
to his father's disciplined devotion and how the house-
hold knew when the master wished to be alone in his
study. Josiah Flew published two books, *Studies in
Browning*, the love of which poet Newton shared, and
Saints of Yesterday, a collection of his circuit talks to young
men and women on such worthies as Henry Drummond,
Archbishop Leighton (whom Newton was to quote in his
address to the Ministerial Session of the Methodist Conference in 1946), General Gordon, Robertson of Brighton,
Thomas Coke and many others. Josiah had a remarkable
facility for talking to children. One of his famous addresses
began by asking the children if they knew the meaning of
such abbreviations after distinguished names as M.A.,
V.C., O.B.E. and so on. Then he would inquire if
they knew O.P.K. Their ignorance elicited the disclosure
that the letters stood for 'Orange Peel Kicker' and there
followed a talk on helpfulness and removing obstacles.
He regularly returned to Portland for the Sunday School
Anniversaries which were such a feature of the nonconformist religious life of the period, and this mantle
too descended on his son. Josiah's first sermon, preached
a week before his sixteenth birthday, was on the text
'Thou shalt guide me with thy counsel and afterward
receive me into glory', and this Newton also chose when
his turn came.

It is impossible to tell which was the dominant
influence in Newton Flew's life, his father's or his
mother's. Josiah had married Florence Jones when she
was little more than a girl. She survived her firstborn and
died in 1964 two days short of her one hundred and first
birthday. In his adult life, Newton wrote to her almost

every day with a full account of his doings. From
Rome in 1916, he describes his love for his Mother as
' "the Madonna cult" in my system, which grows
stronger every year'; in the Preface to his Fernley-
Hartley lecture of 1938, he quotes some words of the
renowned Cambridge scholar, F. J. A. Hort, who was
also an ecclesiologist; 'All men's debts to their mothers
are great, and it is folly to imagine comparisons with the
world of sons; but few, I think, can owe what I do.' He
used to say the people attended the lecture to see his
mother, to whom the book, *Jesus and His Church*, is
dedicated. He teased her often. A card inscribed like
this might accompany a present:

> To my *First Teacher in Music* (result: failed), my *first teacher
> in Botany* (result: failed); *in theology* (result: 'Has made a fair
> beginning, should work harder!'): in *letter writing* (result:
> 'eager, but third class; nowhere near the charm of his
> Mother's letters or of his wife's letters'); in *Social Reform,
> especially the morals of the Royal Family* ('a listless pupil, easily
> surpassed by his young Sister') result failure in nearly every
> subject!

From the first fortnight of his Principalship of Wesley
House, Cambridge, he wrote as follows:

Who taught me all my naughty mischief? My Mother!
Who read stories of John Wesley to me when I was a boy of
four till I knew them by heart? My Mother!
Who said – Now Newton that little word O? My Mother!
Who slaved away at teaching the exquisite lyric
    "Now Bobbie if you please
    Let us feed the chickadees
    Let us get some food and make it nice and hot, hott, hottt",
with the felicitous answering rhyme "pot, pott, pottt", thus
nourishing a love for noble poetry? My Mother!

Josiah and Florence Flew had two other children

besides Newton, a son, Howard, who became a chartered accountant very much involved with Methodist finance, and a daughter, Rosalie. The home was one of 'decent poverty', enough money for a maid and for books, but none for luxury or excess. In Warwick, for instance, Josiah's stipend was £197 10s. a year. There was a discipline of money and of time, but a good deal of laughter and a delight in what was then called 'a liberal education', weighted strongly towards literature, ancient and modern, with the Christian tradition in its Wesleyan form the centre but not the circumference of its interests. The family would be as likely to recognise an allusion to the Dickens novels as to the Wesley hymns.

We see, then, an impressionable boy, diminutive in stature, but wiry, heir to Methodist evangelicalism and Puritan simplicity, but also to a Catholic love of family and friends. 'The communion of saints' was a reality of his upbringing. Like his father, he was sensitive both to the present and the past. He needed heroes and people to love and he needed those who adored and loved him.

The boy of eight, writing to his grandfather, was a more accurate assessor of his scholastic prowess than the man of fifty bantering with his mother. In 1897, he gained a scholarship to Christ's Hospital, the blue coat school founded in 1553 by Edward VI in fulfilment of a sermon by Bishop Ridley and the intention of Henry VIII. Among its alumni are Charles Lamb and Samuel Taylor Coleridge.

When Newton Flew entered the school it was in Newgate Street in the City of London, but, in May 1902, he shared in the excitement of the removal to its present site at Horsham, in Sussex. Christ's Hospital gave to the Wesleyan minister's son the whole new dimension of the public schoolboy. He entered his second charmed circle; the school slang—in its milder and less offensive forms— was added to the parlance of Wesleyan Methodism and he reverted to it on occasion for the rest of his life. Josiah was intermittently Pater to the end. It was also the world of competition, described by Charles Sorley as that in which 'one plays before a looking-glass all the time and has to think about the impression one is making'.[1]

He seems to have been happy at school after initial homesickness. There is a letter to his grandfather on 30th January, 1898. The handwriting has improved and there are no blots or kisses. He says that he is 'all right with the exception of a little toothache. I am getting on very well in school. I think that the worst term of my school life is past, but of course one can never tell. That is in the hands of God'. He writes apologetically, 'I am sorry that I cannot say very much in this letter, for I have not much to say'.

He went on to great distinction, for he obtained the Thompson Classical Gold Medal, and the Charles Lamb Silver Medal for an English Essay, and became editor of the school magazine. But it was not only in the classroom that he excelled.

He had the reputation of a strong and uncompromising character. Somewhat unexpectedly, one of his younger contemporaries, Sir Barnes Wallis, the renowned marine and aeronautical engineer, writes 'I never remember him as high-spirited, light-hearted, or gay, though he had, when in the mood, a keen sense of humour. Life was a serious matter, as indeed it is.' The same correspondent tells that, when in Ward 7 at Newgate Street Flew was a monitor and he himself a 'scrub', he used to take delight in annoying his stern senior. One gathers that Wallis was prepared to go farther in 'fooling about' at Flew's expense than with anyone else and often paid the price!

[1] Quoted in *The Art of the Possible*, The Memoirs of Lord Butler (Hamish Hamilton 1971), p.10

In those far-off London days, monitors were free to punish offenders by 'fotches' or 'owls', a 'fotch' being a severe box on the ears, first one side and then the other, while one stood meekly with one's head inclined to receive the blow; an 'owl' was a blow on the top of one's head, delivered with the knuckles of the clenched fist. I literally 'saw stars' when R.N. smote me thus, for he was, even in those days, a very muscular Christian.

Nicknamed 'biggie Flew', because his younger brother was also a blue, he was prominent in athletics. He won the open hundred yards and quarter mile and became secretary of the Rugby Football XV and a very useful forward in one of the best teams ever fielded by the school. But on this, let Barnes Wallis take up the tale:

A most curious change came over our relationship when we all moved into the wonderful new school at Horsham . . . . I think the sheer novelty of our surroundings, the, to us fresh from the cramped quarters of the old school . . ., spacious accommodation . . . the amazing luxury of shower-baths, and basins with hot and cold water, and the freedom of the sweet-smelling countryside were all sufficient to keep my surplus energy reasonably occupied. And with the coming of the first Michaelmas term (1902), R.N. developed an amazing capacity for leadership.

You must realise that at London the whole school of over 700 boys (the Prep. were then at Hertford) had only one playground, known as 'The Hall Play' because it lay between the great gates separating us from Newgate Street and the whole frontage of the mock mediaeval dining hall, in which to play what passed for Rugby football. I say 'what passed for', because, being completely covered in asphalt drained by shallow gutters of cobble-stones, we were forbidden to tackle low – part of the essence of Rugger. To do so one's adversary, who has the ball in his arms, necessarily and intentionally, is brought heavily to the ground. Such a fall is of no account on grass – unless the ground is frozen – but on asphalt invariably would result in broken bones. I have stood gazing helplessly at a boy with a broken thigh, watching the drops of sweat gathering on his forehead, while awaiting the arrival of a doctor hastily summoned from St Bartholomew's Hospital which adjoined the School buildings on the North Side, behind our own grim and grimy infirmary.

A dozen matches, each with fifteen boys on each side, might be going on simultaneously in what to any onlooker must have seemed hopeless and inextricable confusion, so that the skills of dribbling – no easy art with a prolate spheroid for a ball – and passing were practically impossible and therefore unknown to us small fry.

Somehow R.N. realised what a unique opportunity our move provided to weld us into a skilled and coherent team, for every house had two perfect Rugger pitches, all its own, complete with goal posts and even a heavy roller to tame the but recently mown grass. So every day, in every spare minute, he organised a series of voluntary classes for such of us in Peels A, which was the new name for the House into which ancient Ward 7 was transformed, as would join him. He formed his stalwart volunteers into squads to man the huge roller, wherewith we smoothed down the treacherous bumps in our pitch; he taught us how to dribble a Ruggerball; how to pass with foot or hand, how to tackle low – for to fling oneself head foremost at a pair of flying feet does, for a nervous small boy, demand some small degree of physical courage; how to punt; how to drop-kick; how to place-kick; in short all the skills and subtleties of Rugger as it was played when I was a small boy. Where had R.N. learnt it all himself, and what power turned him, with no previous practice, into such an inspiring coach? And, most surprising thing of all, who do you think was his most ardent, enthusiastic and never-failing pupil? ME!!

I shall to my dying day never forget my acute embarrassment, when, one evening he was rebuking the House, assembled in the Dayroom – probably for evening 'prep' – for not coming out in their spare time to practise these things with him, he actually mentioned me by name as a shining example of how the enthusiastic learner should behave.

On 17th October, 1903, R. N. Flew proposed in the
Christ's Hospital Debating Society, that 'Imperial
Federation would be injurious to the unity and best
interests of the Empire'. The motion was lost by 115
votes to what looks like 26 in his note on the programme
card. A fortnight earlier he had been one of the opponents of the motion that 'The Lot of a Barbarian is
happier than that of a Civilised Man', a theme which
doubtless roused him to great eloquence. If it did not
implant, Christ's Hospital nurtured his devotion to the
Classics. To the last he would regard these as the
foundations of learning and would think that, without
them, a scientific education produced barbarians and a
modern arts course philistines. The style of a Methodist
preacher was thus adorned with tags and allusions and
disciplined by the rigours of Latin and Greek grammar.
But he never flaunted his learning among simple people
and he dreaded to be regarded as an academic preacher.
Every now and then his classics would out, but often
humorously, as when, in the nineteen thirties, he told
the congregation at Kew Road Methodist Church in
Richmond that 'The lives of the Greek gods are like the
modern newspaper descriptions of Hollywood' and was
included in the *Twickenham Times* 'sayings of the week'.
But at Christ's Hospital he found a few with whom he
would be able to say, in W. J. Cory's familiar translation
of the Greek epigram, that they 'tired the sun with
talking'. Such were Roderick Macleod, F. W. Stewart,
future Indian Civil Servants, and Edward Geary, later
Dean of Corpus Christi College, Oxford.

In 1905, he won an exhibition, worth £70 a year, for
three years with possibility of continuation for a fourth.
This took him to Merton, one of the oldest colleges of
Oxford University, where he became a Classical Post-
master, as Merton scholars are called. The exhibition was
supplemented by allowances amounting to £50 – '£30 for
Caution Money, Settling Fees etc, £10 for Books' (paid

direct to the bookseller on the Head Master's approval of the books selected) and '£10 for Apparel'.

For the rest of his life Flew was an Oxford man. His poetic and imaginative nature was captured by the older of the two universities and it might be said of him as F. Brittain wrote of Arthur Quiller-Couch:

> Although he was destined to be at Cambridge, more than six times as long as he had been at Oxford, the feeling was not the same. In 1917, in his *Memoir of Arthur John Butler*, he wrote: 'While a Cambridge man reverts to Cambridge as a *place*, gracious and hallowed by the feet of great men as well as by those of his own transient youth, it does not lay on him just that spell which binds an Oxford man to *personify* Oxford, to enshrine and adore her as veritably and ineffably, at once and altogether, mother and mistress and queen – and yet not three goddesses but one goddess.'[2]

Flew always felt that the beauty of Cambridge was cold and scientific; that of Oxford, tender and romantic.

The Oxford which he entered had been open to non-Anglicans for about thirty-five years and he followed a small and distinguished succession of Wesleyan Methodists, notably W. F. Lofthouse, whom he was to encounter frequently throughout the years and whose life's work was done at Handsworth College, Birmingham, and Ernest E. Genner, Fellow of Oriel. The Lady Margaret Professor of Divinity was William Sanday, renowned as the author with A. C. Headlam of an epoch-making commentary on *Romans*. Tractarianism had achieved a powerful position in the University as well as in the diocese. The Puseyite spirit had made the Anglican clergy doctrinally conscious and also conscious of being gentlemen. Ecclesiastical and social superiority had converged and dissenters were carried downwards

---

[2] F. Brittain, *Arthur Quiller-Couch: a biographical study of Q*, (Cambridge, University Press, 1948).

on the flood. Yet the world of scholarship was a grand co-operative society. *Lux Mundi* (1889) had shown that churchmanship had to reckon with Biblical criticism, and *Foundations* (1912) was to go much farther in a Liberal Anglican direction. One of Flew's tutors in Theology was Richard Brook, later Archdeacon of Coventry and Bishop of St Edmundsbury and Ipswich, a contributor to *Foundations*. Another was Henry Newell Bate, later Dean of York. Neither was 'high and dry' in his encouragement of the able young man. There was also Hastings Rashdall, historian and philosopher. Already the liberality which was to launch the ecumenical movement was in being, and scholarship was preparing the way for the long efforts towards ecclesiastical unity.

But Flew went up to Oxford to read Classics. In 1907, he achieved a first-class in Moderations and two years later a second in Litterae Humaniores. He then turned to Theology and gained a first in 1910, which was the harbinger of innumerable prizes in the next five years.

Naturally, Flew made friends at Oxford, although affable and outgoing as he was, his intimates, apart from his family and, later and pre-eminently, his wife, were never numerous. He began a lifelong friendship with W. J. Rose, a Rhodes scholar of Magdalen, and a future Professor of Polish History and Literature at London University. In 1908, a young Wesleyan, C. J. Barker, who in the second world war was to take Anglican orders, entered Christ Church. He has testified to the kindness of Flew's welcome of a junior. 'He exemplified the power of Christian fellowship by overstepping, though not ignoring, the gulf which the traditions and etiquette of the University set between the freshman and his seniors.' At this time, Flew was sharing lodgings with two contemporaries, Leslie Brown and Alfred Codd, in Walton Well Road. He and Barker would go for long walks in the Oxfordshire countryside and Flew would invariably say 'My dear Barker, we will talk of all things in heaven and earth'. He was no longer the stern and serious prefect of Christ's Hospital; he was tremendously 'earnest', but with this were combined great cheerfulness and gaiety of spirit.

He was altogether loyal to Wesleyan Methodism and led a class meeting connected with the Wesley Memorial Chapel in New Inn Hall Street. The Methodists had already organised themselves into one of those denominational societies which were destined to reach the climax of their strength between 1930 and 1965. The society at Oxford began at Michaelmas 1882 as a result of a mission under the renowned Wesleyan, Hugh Price Hughes, then minister in Oxford, whose later condemnation of Parnell caused *The Times* to write of 'the nonconformist conscience'. The original name of the students' society was 'Wesley Union', which had, so it was maintained, 'nothing unworthy or sectarian about it', but was 'perfectly in harmony with the spirit of the age'. In 1883, this was to change to 'Wesley Guild', which lasted for twenty years; but then the Wesleyan Connexion founded a cultural movement with this title and so the Oxford men chose 'Wesley Society'.

Between the lines of the Society minutes it is clear that the Flew who came up from Horsham was the prototype of the later Principal and Church leader, with a winsomeness which tended to the pontifical and made him both the recipient of much affection and the target of, generally good-natured, banter. He must have seemed precocious to his peers and learned far above the norm. We find him intervening in most of the discussions and a frequent proposer or seconder of votes of thanks to the speakers. In these, his literary, social and comparative religious interests emerged. One infers that he was not often contradicted and usually had the last word. In thanking the Wesley Memorial minister, R. Martin Pope, for a paper on *Amiel and Matthew Arnold*, read on

11th May, 1907, he 'alluded with pathos to the far off days when he had listened to sermons and found in them many gems from Amiel'. Who, outside specialists in the literature of nineteenth-century France is aware of Henri Fréderic Amiel now? But the reference is even more interesting in that it reveals the part which the pulpit had played in the education of a young Oxford scholar still a fortnight away from his majority. He had sat in the family pew from earliest years and, like his contemporaries Kenneth Kirk, the Anglo-Catholic Bishop of Oxford, and Bernard Lord Manning, the Congregational historian at Jesus College, Cambridge, he could testify to sermons as a means of liberal education as well as religious experience for the middle classes.

We find Flew defending the position held by the Wesleyan pastor in a debate on Methodist union, which at the time when the Methodist New Connexion, Bible Christians and United Methodist Free Churches amalgamated in 1907, was a topical matter. He replied to a paper read by a young minister of the Oxford circuit, S. E. Beaugié, from Victoria College, Jersey, and Pembroke College, Oxford, on *Buddhism and Christianity*. Flew 'questioned whether Buddhist teaching is as lofty as it is supposed to be and quoted alarming examples from the sacred books to prove his point. Beginning with marriage, apparently with special reference to the reader, he proceeded to dilate on chairs, swineherds, washing bowls, toothpicks and swearing'.

That minute was written by Charles Kingsley Williams, who almost half a century later, published a translation of the New Testament. He too was a Merton man and Flew had once helped him to dry out his bed, sodden with water after a drunkards' prank at the expense of the Wesleyan abstainer.

On 28th November, 1908, Flew himself read a paper to the Society on *The Inspiration of the Bible*. The minutes give the following summary:

Starting from the elementary notion of verbal inspiration, the reader reviewed the various shades of opinion on the subject and defended in detail the subtler modern doctrine held by himself and other eminent scholars.

That is an interesting note. Young Flew speaks with authority; we are not told precisely what his understanding of the inspiration of Scripture is, only that it is 'subtler' than fundamentalism. More than forty years later, A. E. J. Rawlinson, then Bishop of Derby, was to refer to Flew as 'a very subtle theologian'. It would seem that as a newly-fledged graduate he had the ability to synthesise and to advance enlightened doctrines, compatible with the contemporary world-view, without altogether renouncing what his opponents sought to conserve.

The following Hilary term he seconded the resolution of C. J. Barker that an annual dinner of the John Wesley Society be instituted 'to which members of the peerage or other distinguished visitors might from time to time be invited'. This was not favourably received and had to be withdrawn. It reveals a characteristic often evident later and one which was generally remarked with affectionate amusement. Flew liked the company of the great. In extenuation – if this is necessary – it must be added that this did not make him a snob such as was Cosmo Gordon Lang in one of his roles. It was very much a foible of his temperament and time. He needed recognition, just as did the Methodism of his period. But I doubt if in his prime he ever mingled with the leaders of the Churches or the professions without an almost schoolboyish delight and wonder that he, the Wesleyan minister's son, had been brought thus far. One of his favourite texts was I Corinthians 4:7 'What hast thou, that thou didst not receive?'

Some there have always been who have regarded entrance to the older universities as the kiss of death for

English dissenting Christianity. By them, Flew will be seen as a too willing victim on the altar of the great tradition and the prevailing culture of the gentleman. Here is no protest, no rebellion, no gospel which denies the world; rather there is joyful acceptance of partnership in the established order.

At Oxford and afterwards, Flew was the true son of John Wesley and drew much of his confidence from the same source – a classical education. But Flew was no Tory; indeed he became sympathetic to the socialism which was replacing the liberal allegiance of the more progressive Wesleyans. In contrast to the abortive motion about the annual dinner, the Society's minutes show his awareness of social problems and the need for reform, while, in later years, his high Wesleyanism was accompanied by many gestures of friendship towards Methodist people of other styles.

In 1909, he left Oxford for a period at Bonn and Marburg. On 12th February, 1910, he was welcomed back to the Society, which noted that 'his studies had not robbed him of his playfulness'. Our last glimpse from the minute book is of a brief visit from Handsworth College, when it is written that 'he charmed the Society only more with his eloquence than with his presence'.

He studied German at Bonn in the house of Herr Pfarrer Jungst. One of the two sons worked with him. He never forgot the Christmas he spent there. After the war, in 1922, he revisited the house with his young wife. Maria, the daughter came to the door. Recognition took some moments, but then she called upstairs to her father. The frail old pastor came hurrying down as fast as he could. 'Lieber Herr Flev, lieber Herr Flev', he cried, flinging his arms round Newton. Then he took the Flews into the sitting room to see his wife, who also welcomed them with joy. On the mantelpiece were two portraits of soldiers. Both sons had been killed in the war against the allies. The Flews and the Jungsts wept together for their loss.

Flew's chance to study in Germany completed the laying of his foundations. It was vital to his future development both as scholar and ecumenist. It made him proficient in German – essential to the 'compleat' theologian. Did not someone once say that Newman's greatest disadvantage was that he did not know German? Years afterwards in Cambridge, he was able to help the young C. F. D. Moule to become a theologian by lending him German books, which were in Flew's library alone among the Cambridge scholars. Earlier, in an Oxford vacation, he had cycled through the Rhineland with Roderick Macleod, waving his hand and shouting 'Schönes mädchen' to every little girl he saw! Now Bonn and Marburg brought him up to date with continental Bible studies, embryonic form criticism to supplement the source-criticism of the Oxford schools.

His principal teachers were Wilhelm Herrmann, disciple of the great systematic theologian, Albrecht Ritschl, and Adolf Jülicher, celebrated for his work on the parables of Jesus. More than twenty years earlier, Herrmann had written his *chef d'oeuvre, The Communion of the Christian with God*, a massive affirmation of the historic Jesus as the mediator of our whole relationship to God, characterised by a Ritschlian antipathy to mysticism. Flew never escaped from this influence, though he was to observe Herrmann's scanty treatment of the idea of the Church. Jülicher, who cut back the tendency to allegorise the parables among serious scholars for the next fifty years and insisted that in each of the original stories of Jesus there was but one main point, equipped Flew for later courses at Cambridge.

Flew seems to have missed Bultmann, his senior by two years, who had studied at Marburg and was to return in 1912. Much of his later New Testament teaching would be in opposition to Bultmann's historical scepticism. His critical standpoint was much more that of the older men.

But it was on one evening at Bonn that perhaps the greatest decision of his life was made. He was with Roderick Macleod, who was deep almost to somnolence in volumes of Mommsen, but Flew was thinking of his home, the Wesleyan tradition, the life of the manse, the sermons he had heard and the Jesus of the gospels. It was then that he decided that, whatever opportunities he might have to pursue a career of scholarship, all would be subordinate to the following of one whom he was to describe, in Tyrrell's phrase, as 'that strange man on the cross'.

We may assume that all through his life there had been within him a scholar and a preacher. It is not now easy for anyone younger than middle-age to recall the atmosphere of the Wesleyan home, with its chapel-going twice every Sunday and the sermon as the numinous climax of worship, received with dedicated attention as though the preacher had come straight from God. The sermon would be discussed in the family in the course of the following week rather as intellectuals now carry around the Sunday *Observer* until Tuesday or Wednesday, and an impressionable young boy, gazing upwards to the rostrum, could feel that the greatest glory of his life would be himself to stand there and proclaim the word of God in Christ. Many of the sermons Flew heard would be those of his own loved father and it is easy to see that not all the enticements of *academe* could take him finally from the chapel and from the service of those who had taught him to revere preaching and to listen for the call to it himself. The pulpit would always be a kindred point with the study and he would speak of himself as a 'scholar-*evangelist*'.

2

The Young Minister

THE TRADITIONAL procedures of the Wesleyan Methodist Church demanded that each candidate for the ministry be first a local preacher. Flew was accepted as such in his Oxford days. Then there was a ladder of ascent, from a vote in the March Quarterly Meeting of the circuit to which the man belonged, to written papers, a trial sermon, and an oral examination in his District Synod and, if he had so far been successful, a further sermon, an interview before the Candidates' Committee of the Connexion and a final vote in the annual ministerial session of Conference. Accepted candidates were placed on trial for seven years, two or three of which were usually spent at one of the 'theological institutions', the rest 'on probation' in circuits. Assuming that they survived all this, they were then 'received into full Connexion' by a standing vote of Conference and ordained by the imposition of the hands of the President of the Conference and senior ministers, one being the candidate's own choice. Only then was he allowed to marry.

For University graduates, the process was curtailed somewhat. By 1910, Flew was a Bachelor of Arts at Oxford, with successes in two schools behind him and on the eve of a first in Theology with prospect of further honours still. Since the 'theological institutions' were intended for the most part to give men training in elementary theology, it would have been pointless to expect Flew to take the normal course. And so it was decided to use him at once as a teacher, to send him to the 'Theological Institution – Handsworth Branch' as 'assistant tutor' with responsibility for Theology and Classics. This would enable him to continue his Oxford studies; and his Handsworth years coruscate with University prizes. In 1911 he won the Senior Hall Houghton Greek Testament Prize; in 1912, the Senior Hall Houghton Septuagint Prize and the Prize awarded by the Examiners for the Denyer and Johnson Scholarship and in 1913 the Ellerton Essay Prize. *Proxime accessit* for the last was Geoffrey Francis Fisher, future Archbishop of Canterbury. The two had not met then, but the early academic rivalry did much to foster their personal friendship in the years of Anglican-Free Church conversations three decades on. It was not to his denomination's future disadvantage that the Methodist should outdo the Anglican.

At this time, non-Anglicans were still excluded from higher divinity degrees in theology at Oxford. T. B. Strong, Dean of Christ Church and later Bishop, was anxious to break the Anglican monopoly. But, one day in April 1913, the country parsons emerged from their parishes to make the Sheldonian black with their presence and Strong was shouted down. Flew was there as a Master of Arts. It was poetic justice that seventeen years and a world war later he should be awarded the first Nonconformist doctorate of divinity by thesis at Oxford. Meanwhile, Henry Scott Holland had become Regius Professor of Divinity early in 1911, in succession to the aged and rather insignificant William Ince. Asquith had been expected to appoint W. R. Inge, who instead was preferred to the Deanery of St Paul's, but his choice of the ebullient 'Scotty', a public character with a brilliant style and a social conscience, was unerringly right and Flew was one of

the beneficiaries. Scott Holland was able in 1915 to
secure his election to the Senior Denyer and Johnson
Travelling Scholarship.

The Wesleyan tutors at Handsworth to whom Flew
was assistant were headed by J. G. Tasker, known as
'the Doctor' and a formidable pundit in his day. The
others were Frederic Platt, W. W. Holdsworth (a
former Indian missionary) and W. F. Lofthouse. Both
Platt and Lofthouse lived to be over ninety. Platt was a
liberal and enlightened teacher, whose students remembered him always with affection; Lofthouse was the
most renowned and academically versatile of the four.
He was of an earlier generation than Flew at Oxford and
was to precede him as a Methodist leader in the ecumenical movement and to review his books with critical
penetration not unbarbed. The two were fascinatingly
different in temperament and intellect. There was in
Lofthouse, with all his graces, a streak of the unpredictable and, at times, the unintelligible (though his
octogenarian essay on Charles Wesley in the first volume
of *A History of the Methodist Church in Great Britain* (1966)
belies all criticism). He was more rigorous than Flew
and could be scathing. Flew thought him, in 1910,
rather unrealistic in his treatment of the men and was
instrumental in the discontinuance of a 'golden book' of
good deeds and achievements which Lofthouse had
inaugurated. He remained somewhat in awe of him.

At first, Flew was disconcerted by Handsworth, so
different from Oxford. He was heard to bemoan the
lack of 'intellectual distinction'. This was hurtful to
men several of whom had left school at the age of
thirteen and who had no knowledge of the charmed
world of Christ's Hospital, Merton, Marburg and Bonn.
When this was pointed out to him by the students
themselves, his contrition knew no bounds and the
memory lingers still. Some thought his penitence
excessive, but he would have doubtless applied to it his

own rejoinder to one of his Handsworth students years later on the occasion, famous in the oral tradition of Wesleyan Methodists, when F. L. Wiseman sought the forgiveness of Conference for some intemperate words the day before. The Handsworth man commented to Flew that Wiseman had gone far beyond what so venial an offence required, but Flew protested, his eyes shining, 'No! No! Never check the penitent as he makes confession. It is good for him to humble himself and lay bare his soul.'

Handsworth gave Flew the friendship of the Brash family. William Bardsley Brash was a young Wesleyan minister in the city of Birmingham and his father, John Denholm Brash, was living with him in retirement after a stroke. Here was another father-son relationship as intensely devoted as that between Josiah and Newton Flew. As a schoolboy, Bardsley Brash had often put his head beneath the blankets and sobbed because he thought that death would come and take his father away. The father lingered for rather less than two years after Flew's arrival at Handsworth and, when he died, Flew was one of those who persuaded the son to break the accepted canons of the time and write his father's life. It was felt that normally a son was ill-qualified to write about his father and that no biography should appear too closely in the wake of death. Flew not only encouraged Brash to proceed at once but also read the proofs of *Love and Life*, which was published in November 1913 and was in its fifth edition within five months.

The memoir describes a Wesleyan minister whose watchword was *love*. 'I was born in the Tropics – in Edinburgh – in the Tropics of love.' Denholm Brash was steeped in Wesley's hymns, his hymn-book, like Lancelot Andrewes' manuscript of *Preces Privatae*, pencil-scored and tear-stained, yet he was debating the selection of the English Test Team (the Australians were here!) a few days before his death. 'He would speak about Christ and cricket in the same breath, and about cricket averages and the missionary problem.' He was also interested in football, athletics and golf.

Twenty years later, Flew was to cite John Denholm Brash in *The Idea of Perfection in Christian Theology*:

'That gay saint was once accused of saintliness. "No," he cried out in his dramatic way, "I'm a Hound of Hell." There was no pose about this remark; it was the cry of the contrite heart of the holy man. He meant it, but he withdrew it. His daughter in bringing up his breakfast said with such a happy mirth: "Here's your breakfast hell-hound!" and he smiled "After all, perhaps I am not a hound of hell." Such humility may preserve both penitence and the sense of walking in the light.'

As well as the Brashes, Handsworth brought Flew into contact with James Alexander Findlay, who also ministered in Birmingham at that time. He was an able classicist, something of a spiritual genius, and future New Testament tutor at Didsbury College, Manchester, one of a remarkable family whose father, G. G. Findlay of Headingley, was a Biblical scholar of some renown in his day.

Before Flew left Handsworth, his vocation to the ministry was tested by the offer of an attractive academic post in Canada. His friend Blewett had died and his name was put forward to succeed him by W. D. Ross, later Sir David, and Provost of Oriel. He consulted his closest friends, Methodists and others, including Codd, W. J. Rose, Brash, Beaugié and 'my dear Doctor' (Tasker). But, tempted as he was, he declined.

The post is one of the best in Canada, it is one that a rising young Canadian professor himself covets, but sees no chance of attaining, it is obviously one of strategic importance, and one out of which a youngster might carve a great career. You are in the centre of Canadian life, in the heart of a country of tremendous possibilities, and you assist in the building up of a magnificent nation. Your supporters are millionaires of scholarship and insight – how strange it sounds but it is true! And so on ad lib. And yet inspite of all this I propose to write to Ross on Monday, a week after I have received this tempting exciting offer, to say that I am called in another direction and that I want to be a preacher of the gospel, and not a lecturer to defend it. That is to say, I shall do this unless a telegram comes to me before 9 oclock in the evening from you to tell me to take time for further consultation and deliberation. I have put the case as strongly as I can in favour of this post, not to impress anybody with what I'm giving up, but to impress myself with the fact that God is leading me elsewhere. It is that strange wonderful sense of vocation that has come to me before, and forced me into the ministry. I'm terribly commercial I fear, and certainly not saint enough to despise three thousand dollars a year. And the road of scholarship, with the white light of generations of learning down it – it's horribly attractive. But I can't help feeling that "that strange man on the cross" has other things in store for me.

He intended mentioning Alec Findlay's name to Ross, as a most suitable man, but demurred on the grounds that 'Alec has very little philosophy – practically none. I hae me doots about his management of an unruly classroom.'

In September 1913, Flew was sent to be Wesleyan minister at Winchmore Hill, in the Finsbury Park circuit, which was one of the Methodist societies in North London. He found it a delectable and health-giving suburb with fields and lanes towards Enfield, and lilac and laburnum trees heavy with blossom in the spring.

Flew entered upon his ministry with great eagerness. This *was* his vocation and he found a Methodist society ready to respond to his leadership and give to him, in his own rather florid phrase, 'abundant entrance' to their hearts. He was as full of ideas for Church administration as he was of scholarship. He longed to share everything with his people and he found complete fulfilment in the varied tasks of preaching, teaching, visiting and organisation. He had the gift of imparting his own enthusiasm to others, so that he was no solitary prophet but the captain of a team. Nor did he lack patience or expect his plans to be accepted all at once. There was no brash, immature, arrogant expectation that all his ideas would be implemented by the first Christmas. But his ministry was knit together by one unwavering purpose and inexhaustable theme. It was said of him 'He came preaching the Cross of Christ – as the beacon that illuminates the darkness of the world, the joy and goal of all true disciples, as it is the point of their union together, the criterion of all culture, the foundation of all reform'.

He never forgot the commission to 'do the work of an evangelist'. Forty years later he told in the third person how

'One spring morning as he was out for his half hour's walk before breakfast, he saw a horse grazing and a gypsy tent, and at the bend of the lane a gypsy not much older than himself. He stopped. The two fell into talk. The gypsy, it seemed had dodged all the national laws which make education compulsory. He could not read or write but he could add up fast enough! He had never heard the name of Jesus Christ! He knew that there was a Bank Holiday coming, but he did not know that the reason was that Someone was put to death, and rose again. So for the first time in his life, the young minister was given the ineffable privilege of telling the old, old story to a grown-up human being who had not heard the name of Jesus, and who only vaguely remembered that his mother had spoken sometimes of 'One Above'. But he listened eagerly. The story was told. The parson paused. The gypsy said slowly, almost to himself: 'I never knew that before. It seems to make the "One Above" quite near to you like!'

At Winchmore Hill itself, the membership doubled under Flew's five-year ministry and he was always urging the Finsbury Park circuit to the task of evangelism.

The circuit gave him leave of absence for July and August 1915 and April, May and much of June 1916 in order that he might take up his travelling scholarship. It is an interesting sidelight on the Great War that he was able to travel on the Continent and to stay in Paris *en route* to neutral Switzerland and allied Rome.

His first visit was to Fribourg and the Catholic university. He broke his journey in Paris after an adventurous crossing of the submarine-infested Channel. He was given hospitality and help in his sight-seeing by the Wesleyan minister and his family, the Allens of the Rue Roquepine. He noted that 'tout le monde' was in black. He was taken to the *Opera Comique* for a performance which included *Le Jongleur de Notre Dame*, the well-known story of the juggler, who with no worthier gift to offer, sang and danced before the altar of the monastery Church, so that the statue of the Virgin came alive and blessed him. He applied the tale to himself: 'That's just what I am doing now – giving my little bit of theology to the glory of the Lord. Yea verily and the next time I make people laugh in my children's talks I shall say to myself I too am juggling and dancing before the Master like simple Jean!'

The *pièce de résistance* was, however, a patriotic tableau.

The marvellous actress who had sung the part of Jean came back transformed into a figure of *La belle France*, wrapped in the *drapeau*, the tricolor – and *ciel*, she sang the Marseillaise. Never so long as I live shall I forget that song. I have never heard anything like it. All the passion and longing of France were put into that song of Mlle Martle Chenal. I blush to confess it but *God Save the King* is poor beside it. We have nothing comparable. But Oh! the emotion, the passion, the heart! Every fibre in my poor body tingled and I would

cross the channel and laugh at submarines once again to
hear her sing that song! It is one of the great things of Paris
today. Everybody waits twenty minutes while she changes –
just to hear her for ten! Everybody stands up, everybody
cheers. And I knew as I listened that France was morally
alive. And England? I wonder.

Flew bought a good deal of theology in Paris and
then continued his journey via Neuchâtel to Fribourg,
which at first seemed slightly alien, since many of the
pensions were occupied by hostile German Swiss and
there was hardly a Protestant service in the place! He
began to feel homesick for Winchmore Hill and hungry
for a prayer meeting. He also developed a cold and
toothache. But, after some searching, he secured
comfortable accommodation *chez* Mlle Bussard and
began to feel at home among Catholics. He discovered a
compatriot, Father Freeley, with whom he got on well,
and an Irishman, Father Professor Rowan of the
Albertinium.

He entered the last, the Dominican seminary founded
by Leo XIII, in the main square of Fribourg, with some
trepidation:

Imagine the Methodist knocking at the doors of a seminary
of Rome. A domestic opens, clad in the habit of a nun. With
hardly a sound, she signs to the Methodist to follow her, and
noiselessly conducts him to the room of le père Madonnet.
What are those paintings on the first floor? One of them is
a mediaeval scroll of the Blessed Thomas Aquinas, Angelicus
Doctor, and the other if I mistake not is one of his teacher
the holy Albertus Magnus himself. The Methodist has a
feeling of awe which affects even a Puritan who gazes at the
works of Rome. A white clad figure glides noiselessly across
the corridor. His beads are at his waist. We pass a few doors
and the next moment I find myself face to face with the
renowned Professor le père Madonnet himself; I present my
letters, and stammer out my few sentences of bad French. He
receives me graciously and while he reads the letters I have

time to look at him. He is stout but obviously learned and
intellectual. He is clad in the white habit of the Dominican
the material of which is made of a sort of coarse creamy
flannel. There is a flowing skirt somewhat like our Christ's
Hospital costume, but not opened as that was. Then there is
a sort of cape or mantle for the upper part of the body. And
he too seems to have a chain of beads at his waist. We talk a
little. He has met Rashdall. Was surprised to learn that
nothing much in English was written on my subject. Like
me considers Harnack's treatment superficial. I remarked
that Harnack had obviously no sympathy with the school-
men. 'Because he has not studied them' came the answer
quickly.

Flew found the University library astonishingly poor,
but marvelled at the comprehensiveness of the private
collections of the Dominican professors, which included
liberal theology and the volumes of the International
Critical Commentary.

Catholicism was casting the spell which remained to
the end. But there was no danger of his conversion.
Rather, through his love of Roman spirituality, he was
made more aware of the Catholic character of Methodism,
which he pointed out forcefully in his talks with a
Pembroke, Oxford, man named Fox, who had just
turned from 'ritualism' to popery and was in Fribourg.
Fox had been cast off by his family and must have found
Flew's understanding of his convictions a help.

The 6th July, 1915, was the five-hundredth anniversary
of the burning of John Hus, the Czech martyr, and so
Flew, free of lectures in his 'unprotestant' city, decided
to counter the lures of Catholicism by attending the
commemoration in Geneva. He discovered that ironically
Cardinal Brogny, the President of the Council of
Constance, which condemned Hus, is buried in the
Cathedral of the Reformation city. He managed to
obtain a front seat for the meeting, at which the principal
speaker was M. Ernest Denis of the Sorbonne. The

analogy between Hus's struggles and the Austrian
repression of those days and the current war against
the German powers was irresistible for M. Denis, and the
meeting seems to have been less an assertion of Protestantism than propaganda for the allied cause, not altogether
unlike the tableau at the *Opera Comique*. Afterwards
Flew 'with the effrontery I never learnt at home – was
it from Billy Rose or Brash, or the result of original
sin?' – introduced himself to M. Denis and complimented
him on his address.

September 1915 saw him back in North London.
Not all the fascination of Switzerland had diminished
his curiosity about what had happened at the Wesleyan
Conference or competed for interest with the draft of the
'stations' of the ministers for 1915–16, which he devoured
the moment it arrived in Fribourg and a pox on the
early fathers! His studies and travels had given him
plenty of material for lectures and addresses and many
ideas for sermons. He asked his parents' advice on a
Sunday School Anniversary talk – 'Red, White and
Blue'.

1   (Red) Sacrifice
2   (White) Purity
3   (Blue) Temperance.

'Is this a hackneyed idea? . . . I can draw most of the
illustrations from this holiday or from the war. What
does the Mater think?' He had planned to visit Italy,
but the British Consul strongly advised him not to cross
the frontier.

The next April he was in Rome, having attended some
Italian classes in the winter. He went via Dijon with its
relics of Clairvaux. He attended Palm Sunday Mass at
the cathedral and was by now much more at home with
the Roman liturgy than at Fribourg the previous summer.
'Everybody carried *un rameau* . . . and there was a
glorious procession at the end with candles and the
choir boys singing and the bass answering and the

bishop blessing us. Oh it was a fine show, and everybody
calls me M. le Curé and I'm the spectacle at which
everybody looks in the streets. It's really very jolly to be
called M. le Curé for you can imagine yourself quite
other than you are and I give the blessing gravely and
generously to all sorts of children.' But he hurried from
Mass to the Protestant service and was just in time for a
beautiful sermon on 'Palm Sunday – the Feast of Contrasts'. The pastor described it as a feast of suffering and
joy, inconstancy and fidelity, and a feast of enthusiasm
which yet calls us to participation in the work of our
Lord. 'And just here we had the warm individual note
which Romanism can so rarely win in its public services.
He made me feel that the Lord had need of me till I
almost cried out amazed.'

And so to Rome via Milan and Florence. Flew was so
moved by Florence that he could hardly tear himself
away and forwent the Good Friday ceremonies in
Rome. At first Rome rather repelled him. The stucco
reminded him of Berlin, the architecture seemed
inferior to Chartres, 'a display of grandeur rather than
an aspiration of faith', with St Peter's, enormous and
self-satisfied, lacking the wistful hints of an unattainable
infinite he found in the Florentine pictures, and he was
reminded of the proverb 'Rome seen, faith lost'. The
exhibition of relics, the holy thorn, the veil of Mary, the
wood of the true cross and the like, and the crowds
making their way up the *Santa Scala* on their knees
provoked the thought that a faith which can survive
such superstition must be enormously tough. But the
'real Rome' had captured him after a week. It could not
fail with one with his sense of history and romantic
imagination.

Does Father remember Browning's poem of the Bishop –
orders his tomb at St Praxed's? Isn't there something about
St Praxed's being the Church for peace and the bishop

glorying in the thought that for centuries he will see God made and eaten all day long? Well I'm looking out on to St Praxed's. St Maria Maggiore dominates our Piazza – the most beautiful Church in Rome. Quite near – I pass it every day – is the Church of St Pudentrania, sister of Prassed or Praxed and daughter of Pudens. This is the most ancient of the Roman Churches, supposed to be built on the site of the house where Paul lodged with Pudens, whose family were his first converts. Then if I want to be a pagan Maecenas had a villa here, two minutes away, where Horace is buried. Cicero's father lived on the Esquiline and every morning young Tully went to the Forum to listen to the orators.

He spent a good deal of time with evangelical Protestants and with the Wesleyan mission, whose representative, William Burgess, hinted that Flew might succeed him. Flew thought Burgess's successor would have an impossible task. 'He is very wealthy, most acute in business, speaks Italian like a native, and defies the Mission House.' But he admired his vigorous anti-pacificism.

There was the English colony to be met, notably Mrs Arthur Strong, sister-in-law of the Dean of Christ Church, and a learned high Anglican, Dr Bannister. There were week-ends at Assisi and Naples. There were the colleges, especially the Collegio Angelico, and the libraries. Above all there were the Roman Catholic scholars, notably Garrigou-Lagrange, Duchesne, whose works had recently been put on the index, and Cardinal Gasquet, the Benedictine, who gave him an introduction to the monastery at Monte Cassino.

The Italian visit reached its climax on that great hill, which became so tragic a victim of the second world war. Flew went to see the library and the rare unpublished manuscripts of the middle ages, especially 'of one Erasmus (*not* the Renascence humanist but the teacher of St Thomas Aquinas)'.

'The motto of the Benedictine order is *Pax* and truly
if peace is ever to be found it should be here.' But even
in that conflict Monte Cassino could not wholly escape.
More than a dozen monks had been taken for the forces
and the news of Jutland was coming through during
Flew's short stay. Yet his mind dwelt chiefly on the
incredible calm, the Turner-like sunset after a great
storm, the song of the nightingales, the view towards
Aquino whence the young Thomas had come for his education, and, above all, those seemingly eternal rites which
had been handed down from the days of Benedict himself.

Compline was most impressive. We all sat in the carved
choir stalls of the great church. Everything was dark but for
the few candles burning constantly night and day round the
tomb of St Benedict beneath the high altar and one dim
light over the reader's head. First there was an exhortation
read in Italian with a list of sins, asking forgiveness if we had
committed any of these – and then we had the Latin part –
we chanted the psalms and then responded to countless
prayers. About 20 or 30 saints' names were read and we
responded (*I* stood quiet here) *ora pro nobis*. The Virgin was
hailed with many titles and after each one we said *Ora pro
nobis*. But the whole atmosphere of the service was strangely
humbling and devout.

Happily fulfilled as he was during these years, he was
not unaware of the crisis for Christianity marked by the
outbreak of war in 1914 and from which the Churches
would not emerge in his lifetime or since. All the most
sensitive Christian leaders of this time, though like Flew
and his father they might strongly support the allied
cause and have no truck with pacifists, had a sense of
malaise and of great depression. Flew would quote the
Anglican, Neville Talbot, 'We were all overtaken in a
state of great poverty towards God.'
There were many reasons for this: the collapse into
carnage of an order which had seemed secure and which,

whatever its injustices, had provided a framework of civilisation in which arts and sciences might flourish and life for increasing numbers of people have great opportunities and noble purpose; an order which was the heir to the glories of the past and notably to the beneficial and sacrificial witness of Christians throughout nineteen hundred years. But behind the political disintegration and the slaughter, was the intellectual collapse. The philosophy of enlightenment had awakened men from dogmatic slumber and had made them restless for freedom. Nothing could be taken for granted. Man's certainties were seen as a prison house which meant security for some but slavery for many and which could not wholly withstand examination by the new tools of historical and scientific method. In 1914 Christians were still frightened by the theory of evolution and the higher criticism.

Flew himself seems already to have reached the position which he held for the rest of his life that the Jesus of the first three gospels emerges unscathed from the severest critical scrutiny. His was the faith of Browning's *Epilogue*:

> That one Face, far from vanish, rather grows,
> Or decomposes but to recompose,
> Become my universe that feels and knows.

Of this Jesus, the most understanding interpreter, apart from the evangelists themselves, was St Paul, and the Methodist tradition so glitteringly enshrined in the hymns of Charles Wesley was in the direct line of the historic Jesus. The hymns in fact supplied the clue to what was lacking in 1914 – a religion based not in acceptance at one remove of certain propositions which could survive scientific examination, but a living experience of God-in-Christ here and now.

Flew became associated with many other ministers of his own generation and a little older, who felt the same need. Meetings held during the war developed in 1920 into the 'Fellowship of the Kingdom', which still exists and claims to follow both a quest and a crusade. He was also concerned with the founding of the School of Fellowship, a movement which included lay people and which like F.K. had as its focal point an annual Conference at Swanwick.

The leader in all this was a Wesleyan minister twenty years older than Flew, a man of remarkable qualities and a touch of genius, William Russell Maltby. He was the Warden of the Wesley Deaconess Institute at Ilkley. Maltby, a rare artist in expression, was famed for his *obiter dicta*: 'Can Christians dance? Some can and some can't.' 'Draw deep from the well of Biblical criticism, but do not give your congregation too much rope to chew.' He was also a Christian humanist who felt that much Victorian Methodism had been far too narrow in its repudiation of whole areas of human life. In December 1916 he wrote an article for the *Methodist Recorder* from which Flew later quotes a long extract to conclude his chapter on Methodism in *The Idea of Perfection in Christian Theology*.

Our theological coat was cut for the figure of Total Depravity, but when tried on, it was found not to fit any kind of human nature. Accordingly we let out a seam in the back as far as it would go, and the margin thus gained, with the stitches still showing, we call prevenient grace. Still the coat does not fit, for it is not by any afterthought that we can do justice to that boundless patience and holiness of God, which love goodness everywhere, labour for it and delight in it everywhere. We have often thought of God as though it were 'all or nothing' with Him. But it is not true. In his mysterious humility He tends the last smouldering lamp in every rebellious heart. . . . It is He who defends the last strip of territory against the invasion of passion, when all the rest is gone, and raises mysterious defences about beleaguered virtues whose doom seemed sure. When He is denied or

unrecognised in His own person, He still lingers about
a man, dimly apprehended as a sense of duty, or as some
indestructible principle, some notion of what is 'not cricket',
some code of thieves, or He returns upon us in some New
Thought, some shadowy Infinite, some impersonal Life-
Force, some half-crazy system like Christian Science,
worshipping its fragment of the truth – and so men entertain
Him unawares. These vast tracts of unbaptized human life
we make over to poets, and novelists and dramatists, who
explore them with inexhaustible interest and sympathy. Yet
this interest and sympathy comes from God, Who loves this
human life of ours, not only as a moralist approving where it is
good, and disapproving where it is bad, but as a poet or
artist loves it, because he cannot help loving a thing so
strange, piteous and enthralling as the story of every human
soul must be.

Maltby had not the younger man's erudition but they
were both products of a Wesleyan Methodism which was
eager to transcend the cultural barriers of the Victorian
shopkeeper, yet was deeply disturbed by some of the
signs of the times, the growing disenchantment with the
Churches and the triviality of much Church life. The
only reaction of some preachers to the ferment of the
times was to denounce strong drink and Sabbath
breaking and to dragoon people to the penitent form to
confess sins they did not understand or might not have
committed and accept a Saviour who was a temporary
emotional excitement rather than a real presence. The
life of prayer, for instance, was never explained. Many
church members on the other hand, were mere conformists, void of spiritual understanding different from
the non-churchgoing multitudes only in what they did
not do. Flew condemned some of the methods of his
Finsbury Park colleagues in a letter to his mother on
14th October, 1915:

The Lord forgive me for relying too much on meetings. But I
am greatly disappointed. Eighty people turned up tonight

for our ministerial convention. Seven ministers on the platform, or I'm a Turk by Abdul the ——. And De M (DeMouilpied) speaks like an angel bless his saintly heart. And Windsor (sic) Yeo speaks not without sense on entire sanctification. But he ends up by asking all who want to claim the blessing straight away to come out and line up in front, takes the meeting out of the Super's hands, lines up himself, dragoons two or three hoary saints out of their seats, including Mrs Rogers, who has got it, who lives in Beulah land (witness that five quid!) two or three trembling girls, and has a high old time procuring the second blessing for these lined up sinners. God forgive me but I do not like this way and fall into profanity when I think about it. Were Peter and John and the rest lined up, in front on the day of Pentecost. Was our founder (whom Waights affectionately alludes to as old Jack) lined up in Aldersgate Street? And must you, venerable sinner whom I love be lined up to get a blessing for your wicked old heart which I love every inch of it sins and all, if they are there? I trow not. But lining up spoilt our meeting and I groaned in the spirit. I rejoice to say that although Middleton lined up, grace was given to the rest of us to stand our ground, and abide (sins and all) on the platform, including old De Mouilp who has more holiness in his little finger than Yeo, Middleton, the Pentecosters of Clapham, Miss Parsons, Emily Fisher, Miss Stephens, Miss Powell, Cliff College, Keswick and all the second Blessingites in Creation have in the massed girth of their aggregated bodies of sin. Moreover the effect on at least one sinner is to make him execute a Satanic dance round his room, pharisaically thanking God that he is not as these entirely sanctified people are, glad that he is still feeling a double dyed sinner and still smiting his breast from afar off. Must I really line up in front if I want to see the Lord? Ah no, verily but it is hard for those of us who love him in sincerity and passion to see misguided fanatics come along torture sensitive hearts, spoil meetings aflame with desire and try to force every experience onto the Procrustean bed of their narrow holiness. When will these fellows learn something of the awe, the tenderness the delicacy the mysterious issues which belong to the ministry of souls?

Forgive me! But I must unburden myself – to another wicked sinner who understands me, bless her lovely old heart. Then again there was Tuesday at Wood Green – a meeting packed, a glorious opportunity not badly used till the end. Brown spoke a little more than usual, Middleton started at 7 mins to 9, and went on (God forgive him) till 20 minutes past 9 – too long, but what he said was good, bar the first 10 mins which could have been left out. Goldhawk was chafing at being cooped up to 5 minutes (which certainly was not enough) – but instead of taking it like a sportsman, making a five minute appeal on a lofty level, he fools away perfectly, has the people in roars of laughter, and some of us sat in terror and heaviness of heart as another holy occasion is spilt like water. How long, o Lord, how long? And aren't we ministers the real culprits in this sickness and impotence of Thy Church?

Maltby and Flew became literary partners in the *Manuals* of *Fellowship* which they edited jointly from 1917–1930. Maltby himself was directly responsible for six of the twenty-four titles. Flew's sole contribution in his own name was *The Forgiveness of Sins*, first published in 1917.

Already he had written *The Teaching of the Apostles*, which appeared in 1914. *The Forgiveness of Sins*, with which he had wrestled during his stay in Italy in 1916, is a mere pamphlet. Yet some have thought it a miniature masterpiece, the quintessence of the gospel in thirty lucid pages. Granted that it owes something to Maltby's editorship – Flew wanted his name on the title-page and some of the questions for discussion have his indubitable stamp – it is none the less a remarkably mature treatment for a man of thirty. It is profound in its understanding of human nature and relationships and in its unerring sense of what the Christian faith is all about.

It opens with the testimony of Christians to the *wonder* of forgiveness and notes that 'it does not please God to give us all a profound sense of sin at the beginning

of our Christian life'. Then it outlines the *problem* from
human analogies, the difficulty of at once pardoning the
sinner without condoning the offence and transgressing
those principles of human life which it is death to deny.
Forgiveness 'demands conditions which affect both the
persons, the person who is forgiven and the person who
forgives. In the first case, the conditions may be summed
up in the one word "repentance"; in the second by the
word "sacrifice"'. But the former conditions adds to the
immensity of the problem for one of the worst results of
sin is that it atrophies the capacity for repentance. There
is also the fact that sin is not simply what we do but
what we are, that it becomes a part of our very nature
and that its effects are irreversible. 'In most cases any
adequate reparation even to our fellow men is impossible;
the act is done and its consequences are beyond recall.'
Similarly, the person who forgives genuinely can do so
only at tremendous cost. He must identify himself with
the sinner, '*go after the sheep* until he find it' and this is
bitter pain and the costliest self-sacrifice.

All these observations from human experience bring
us to the Cross. There

> the problem of repentance is not *solved in Christ*, but *left with
> Christ*. . . . It proves to be true that there is no power on earth
> to awaken penitence in the human heart like the power of
> the Cross. Since the day when that Holy One ascended it and
> stretched his arms on its cruel branches and lowered his
> head and died, men have found there a power of God which
> shows them to themselves, and reveals to them the sinfulness
> of their sin, which strangely delivers them from themselves
> and makes them glad to enter the 'fellowship of His sufferings'
> lending their human hands to help His great task of redeeming
> the world.

The last section of the manual is headed 'The Acceptance of Forgiveness at the Cross'. The Cross saves us as

we accept it, not as we seek to construct theories of atonement. About much we must be agnostic.

> We cannot reach the mystery
> The length, the breadth, the height.

But if we take the forgiveness which God offers through the Cross, then we shall be freed from remorse and sinful habit and from 'all dismal preoccupation with ourselves'. We shall enter into the family life of the children of God.

One would wish, perhaps, in view of later discussions and controversies, that a little more had been said specifically in the last pages about the sacrifice of the Cross. The idea is there and in a form which translates into the language of human experience some of the recondite and ritualistic terminology of evangelical or catholic conservatism. But a few additional sentences might have made this even more valuable. The manual had a long run in Methodism; outside, Edward Woods, Bishop of Croydon and Lichfield, read it each Holy Week. Here is profound theology set free from all jargon and all abstraction. It is not beyond the humblest Christian who has really lived, while a scholar would find it wholly satisfying. The impression is of a young man who has read all the literature, and studied all the arguments, but who is able to go direct to the main issues because of his sheer humanity.

Some pages survive of a diary which Flew kept in December 1917. They concern meetings of ministerial groups. The first consisted of men who were roughly Flew's contemporaries, the embryonic Fellowship of the Kingdom.

The Group met for the promised conversation on the actual state of our own religious experience. Seven men were there.

Boyling and Lewis could not come, and Whitham had forgotten. Ream and Boyns were also absent.

Bernard Harris opened by confession of his finding and losing. Christ was real to him for some weeks, but again he had lost the sense of the Presence. Mayes had come almost in despair. Chapman found something last February owing to the reading of Burroughs which he had never lost. I spoke of the state of my life since August. At the end Mayes asked us to pray for his old Father who is in a state of great darkness, almost in despair.

If we are a typical set of young preachers, if the occasion was not unfortunate, then there must be hundreds who are hungry for the rich experience of Christ. But when we are frank enough to unveil our own hearts we certainly do not seem victorious. But it is something gained that we can be so open. It is seldom that men can thus deliberately tell the exact truth to one another of the present state of their religious life.

The second was a much more senior sub-committee on doctrine which met at the house of the eminent Wesleyan historian Dr H. B. Workman, authority on monasticism and the Principal of Westminster College. As well as some lesser luminaries, the company included John Scott Lidgett and W. T. Davison, the Principal of Richmond College, Surrey. Maltby was there as Workman had wired for him. It is obvious that the meeting was concerned with the doctrinal divisions of the Church and the 'fundamentalist-modernist' issue and the heresy hunts of an organisation known as the Wesley Bible Union.

I went to Westminster to Dr Workman's house for the meeting of the Sub-Committee on Doctrine. Near Campbell's church I met Lidgett looking worried and hunted, as usual, with sheaves of papers in his pockets. He was disturbed by Chapman's Memorandum. We found all in the room except Morton who came late. Maltby . . . had travelled up in the night with some drunken soldiers. Davison was put in the chair, and W.R.M. prayed with strange intimacy and power. The first thing considered was the opening protest of my memo; all agreed to it, and G.A.B. and H.C.M. did not defend the November issue of the W.B.U. Journal. The subject was not pursued. It was agreed that not a word should be said of our discussions even to a member of the larger committee. We discussed our powers and the terms of reference. It was the turn of H.B.W. to be censured by J.S.L. and W.T.D. for not having taken exact note of the larger committee resolution. Davison had three questions ready, one of which we discussed. Inspiration was the main topic. Before we settled down to this W.R.M. and I tried to emphasise the fellowship between men of divergent views (e.g. as in the hymn book, in our knowledge of Christ) as vastly more important than our divergencies. He suggested that if we could only find some way of procedure which let the vast uniting power have full play, the impulse to unity and fellowship would be irresistible and divergencies seem irrelevant. But this view made little impression.

On Inspiration, we talked at large. H.C.M. considered the authorship of Ecclesiastes 'crucial'. G.A.B. held the historical truth of the early chapters of Genesis to be fundamental. The Standards held a system. If anyone subtracted one doctrine, the system was undermined and destroyed. Men who did not hold the view of Inspiration implied in the Standards were out of harmony with them. Eventually we agreed to the subjects to be discussed at a two day meeting of the larger committee in April. I urged that we should meet again in sub-committee to seek the *modus vivendi*. We ought not merely to state the problem but to try to solve it.

H.C.M. and G.A.B. are without humour. When the rest of us laughed, they protested that it was no laughing matter! *Sal facit theologum* – as well as the heart. Two amusing things happened, at which the Committee did not laugh. Davison was impatient and Lidgett provoking – he would make speeches himself and interrupt others on minor matters. After one speech Davison more than usually restless said with tired self-restraint, 'I think that is enough on that subject'. Whereat Lidgett sat down near W.T.D. so that the latter could not see him, looked at me, smiled broadly and tipped me a prodigious wink with the eye near the other doctor of divinity! So our theologians love one another!

Lidgett was no help to us. His mind was alert and powerful but not relevant. He went off at phrases. He was more anxious to expound his own views than to grapple with the practical problem. And thus he delayed us, again and again. When I said that there were many in the ministry who viewed the early narratives of Genesis as singularly profound myths analogous to but greater than the myths of Plato, he tried to argue such a view down and convict it of inadequacy instead of facing the real problem, which is – what is to be done when there are a large number of men who hold such views? Are they within the Standards or outside? So when H.B.W., W.R.M. and I got away to lunch, H.B.W. gave me the 3/6 and I asked him if he had paid J.S.L. No, he said wrathfully, he isn't worth the 3/6! W.R.M. and I agreed on the lack of leadership once more. There isn't one man who sees – even partially and dimly – a way through.

H. B. Workman became one of Flew's benefactors early in his London ministry, and introduced him to the London Society for the Study of Religion. He read his first paper there on Tuesday 5th March, 1918. It was on 'The Early Methodist Preachers'. The typescript has been mutilated – one suspects by the author excising some of his best gobbets for use on other occasions. His main sources are the thirty-six autobiographies published in the seven volumes entitled *Wesley's Veterans*, the *Journals* of John and Charles Wesley and Wesley's *Life of Fletcher*. He explains his purpose as 'to examine the spiritual background of these autobiographies; to penetrate to the secret of a popular religious movement which for rapidity of expansion and pervasiveness of influence is comparable to early Christianity itself; and to enquire into its limitations and narrowness with an eye on the needs of today and the immediate future of religion among the people'.

In the last aim there is once more the sense that the Methodism of Wesley had not the complete Christian answer for the twentieth century and that, in spite of its incalculable powers as a folk movement, it had certain congenital inadequacies. In the spirit of Maltby and his circle, Flew condemns that aspect of legitimate and noble Methodist asceticism, which turned aside 'from the spacious regions of man's earthly life'. But his explanation of the cause of it must be attributed to other encounters and experiences:

To the influence of this rigid view of the world and the narrowed conception of God's working implied in it must be ascribed the evangelical horror of papacy. It was almost a mental impossibility for the best of the Methodists to think of God as working in the Church of Rome. Romanism was emphatically on the dark side of the line. It is enough for some to cite the traditional abhorrence of Englishmen for the Italian Bishop, as though there were something in the English climate or the English blood which made all Englishmen spue his name out of their mouths. 'There are two things that the Englishman hates with a perfect hatred', said Gladstone, 'an abstract proposition and the Pope'. Both Wesley and Butler in the days of their unpopularity were accused of being papists, for as Bagehot wittily observes 'whenever an Englishman hears of anything in religion that he does not understand he straightway sets it down to the Pope'. But ultimately this intolerance of the saints of evangelicalism is due to deeper cause than mere national prejudice or their historical recollections of the reign of Bloody Mary. They had not seen a vision of God affirming the world as good, as delighting in the colour and gaiety and many-sidedness of human life, ceaselessly operative as in Nature so among men and their systems and their creeds, striving against all evil and yet inspiring and strengthening all impulses after the pure and true and beautiful. This was the ultimate reason for the discrimination and the absence of sympathy in their horror of Rome.

There speaks the traveller to Fribourg, Rome and Monte Cassino; but there also the member of the London Society for the Study of Religion in which he had met Claude Goldsmid Montefiore, the Liberal Jew, and, above all, Baron Friedrich von Hügel, the Liberal Roman Catholic, who had founded the Society in 1904.

My dearest Mother,

The Baron has replied by return that he will be delighted to come on Friday. I offered to call at Kensington and pilot him out. So he has gladly accepted this and I'm to call there at 2–30. He hopes to stay 1 hour or 1½ hours – so that he can be back at 5–30. He wonders whether he is to bring his dog "Puckie". I'm risking it and saying "yes" because to see the Baron with Puckie is an unforgettable experience! And inconvenience caused at no 37 will be more than compensated by the sight of the Baron with the dog!!

Von Hügel, now 66 years old and increasingly afflicted by the deafness which had resulted from typhus in his young manhood, had emerged from the Modernist controversy of the first decade of the century, with his standing in the Church unassailed and none of his writings on the Index. Some feel that he lapsed into undue caution after the Papal condemnation of the movement and that his part in it subsequently embarrassed him. It has even been suggested that he escaped censure only because of his influential friends in the Curia. But his embarrassment might have been less through lack of courage than through a difference of emphasis, indeed of principle, which is germane to some of the controversies of the later twentieth century. Von Hügel both by temperament and training was a metaphysician; God for him was the ultimate explanation of the scheme of things. He believed that there was a cosmic order, which derived from the Transcendent Divine Original. Thus he could not, like most of the

Modernists, and so many later 'radicals' who have combined scepticism with a Barthian repudiation of 'natural theology', regard philosophy as incapable of constructing a system to interpret ultimate reality. Putting this in religious terms, for the Baron was above all *homo religiosus*, he had a tremendous capacity for adoration and in spite of his recognition of the difficulties of belief, the relativities of history which affected even the Gospel records, and the imperfections of the Church, he never lost his awareness of the Transcendent God, who, in his infinite condescension, did stoop to reveal himself through institutions and what the jargon of the cliché-ridden nineteen-seventies calls 'structures'. Indeed he saw three abiding elements of religion – the mystical (witness his *magnum opus* on St Catherine of Genoa), the intellectual, and the institutional.

It was von Hügel's genuine Catholicism as well as his great kindness which appealed to Flew. Here was a convinced Roman, an avowed apologist for his own Church (sometimes defending the indefensible by a Christian sophistry as in his advocacy of *limbo*), who looked for the marks of the Lord Jesus beyond its frontiers, in Methodism, for instance, but also in other religions; and supremely in the hearts of humble men and women, like the horse-bus drivers of Hampstead, who were not always outwardly religious. For him, as Flew would quote for the rest of his life, 'Grace was not the cuckoo, which drove all other birds out of the nest'. Christianity was 'Asceticism without Rigorism and Love without Sentimentality' and his religion could somehow comprehend everything from green lizards to the complex forces of history and the cry of dereliction on the Cross.

Mrs Flew, a staunch Protestant, seems to have expressed some fears that the Baron was out to make her son a Romanist, but these were dispelled at the Ealing tea-party. Both the senior Flews felt an immediate

affinity with the Catholic layman. Von Hügel recognised
Flew's abilities and recommended him to C. C. J. Webb
for 'junior work' in a letter of August 15th, 1919.[1]

Throughout the Winchmore Hill period, Flew's
parents were in London, first at Clapham, then at
Ealing and he went home frequently and sometimes met
his parents and sister in town. The letters reveal anxiety
over an operation undergone by his mother and contain
much help and counsel for his sister in her examinations.
For his mother's birthday in the September after his
return from Italy, he writes bidding her and her 'sinful
daughter' meet him at '7–15 of the clock precisely'
outside the Queen's Hall, Langham Place, in order 'to be
transported on a magic stairway to a realm beyond
time. What is the magic stairway? – it is Jacob's ladder,
the *Santa Scala*, builded of beautiful sound. And who is
the magician, the builder, the architect of the Holy
Stairs? It is Wagner, of the land of enemy aliens – but
we wage no war with the Dead.' So off they went,
presumably on Monday, the traditional Wagner night, to
the 'Proms'. And Flew does not, like some, find in
Wagner the sinister and brutal crescendos of German
militarism, but rather entrance to an eternal world and
a vision in Siegfried's journey to the Rhine of the
dawning of a Divine Kingdom.

But by 1918, he was beginning to feel that both his
duty and his development required that he experience
the war at closer quarters than the care of a congregation,
though it suffered the alarms of casualty lists and
zeppelin raids, and two crossings of a submarine-infested
Channel allowed. He obtained permission and offered
himself as a chaplain. This brought a 'perfectly spiffing'
letter from von Hügel.

March 1918 was one of the crises of the conflict in
France, but it marked the last great German offensive,

[1] See von Hügel, *Selected Letters*, p. 284.

and before Flew could be embodied in the Forces, it was clear that the war might be over by Christmas. At the May Synod of the London North District, Flew intervened little in the discussion, contrary to his wont, and was depressed by the proceedings, which were 'dull, mechanical, full of routine; void of colour'; but he spoke to William Goudie of the Missionary Society about the possibilities of an Indian tour should he be sent to the Middle East and chaplaincy work run out. This, to his great excitement, was welcomed.

High summer saw his departure, not without tears, from Winchmore Hill, where his prayer meetings had often brought fifty people and his own class two dozen. He was commissioned in the Royal Newfoundland Regiment and told to be prepared to embark for Mesopotamia 'on or after the 1st January, 1919'. This gave him time to vote in the December election and he did so for the Labour candidate. He was indeed invited to return to Winchmore Hill to speak with Tudor Rhys at almost the last meeting before the polling day, Thursday, 12th December. This was a signal tribute to his oratorical powers and personal standing, but he did not feel that it would be fair to his former Church to make his first return appearance on a political platform. But he wrote a letter for publication in support of the Labour candidate, thus aligning himself, as he was quick to point out to his possibly critical parents, with Dr Clifford, J. E. Rattenbury and – most propitious name of all – 'Billy Temple'.

He set sail gaily to conquer fresh worlds. Dramatic as ever, he quoted the lines:

Yonder the wide horizon lies and there by night and day
The old ships come to home again, the young ships sail away
And come I may, but go I must, and if men ask you why
You may put the blame on the sea and the stars and the
   white road and the sky.

But he had another lodestar, not of the mystic East. There had come to teach at Winchmore Hill Collegiate School, Miss Winifred Garrard, daughter of a Luton hat manufacturer. She had almost gone to Loughborough, but was deterred by what sounded like the vicar's threat that a Miss Peasgood, whose name conjured up an unattractive vision, would help her to find rooms. Winchmore Hill won her heart on a spring day and so it was destined that she, a Wesleyan Methodist, would, soon after her arrival, be summoned from her classroom to meet the young minister. They talked for a while and he went away having discovered that she loved poetry. From then the friendship blossomed. They walked home together from a lecture at the Old Southgate Church on *A Tale of Two Cities*. Miss Garrard joined the minister's class; and although, after he had left Winchmore Hill, they met but a few times before his embarkation, her name shared pride of place with his parents' on his oriental letter list.

3

From Mesopotamia
to Muswell Hill

THE DESTINATION was Basra, where Flew, as Senior
Chaplain, would have his headquarters. The war was
over, but Mesopotamia was not necessarily at peace.
Were all the scattered villages and nomadic tribes
aware of the armistice? Was there much difference
among these turbulent, feuding peoples between peace
and war?

Flew had responsibilities in Basra and down the line.
As well as British troops there were Sikhs and Burmese
and a Chinese labour corps. He was greeted as he left
the ship by the duty officer, a former Hendon boy, who,
warned to expect 'Mr Flew' was on the look-out for
Josiah, whom he remembered as a Superintendent
Minister of the Finchley and Hendon Circuit. The sight
of the 'dapper little Padre' amazed him.

Temperatures of 120 degrees in the shade did not dim
Flew's bright eyes or abate his energies. He was for ever
active, for ever observant, interested in the whole
kaleidoscope. The multifarious curiosities of the scholar,
the antiquarian, avid for the sight of excavations (he
arrived at Ur on the day that H. K. Hall uncovered the
remains of the palace of Ur-nina, built 1,300 years *before*
Abraham), and the lover of people were merged in the

zeal of the evangelist. Devotion to Jesus Christ unified all he did and was the inspiration of his manifold interests, whether of his eagerness to tread in the steps of Abraham, to find out all he could about the varied religions concentrated in the vicinity of Basra, to gain a smattering of the Babel of tongues, or to comfort the homesick and the feverish of many nations.

He showed great courage and often volunteered to enter Arab towns and villages in advance of the British troops, using his linguistic skill and force of personality to pacify the inhabitants, so that on many occasions, no shot was fired. It used to be said that a man with a smiling face and a few hundred words of Arabic could go anywhere in Mesopotamia in safety. Flew had both.

In Basra itself he held a Bible class for men on the roof of his house. 'What will you have to drink?' was his first question as they arrived, though the drink was always boiled water, lime juice or coffee. He went on to teach in the style of the *Manuals of Fellowship* and the memory of the meetings has not dimmed in the minds of those present who survive.

He cared much for the Chinese. He envied their skill in occupying the leisure hours which so oppressed the Tommies, and admired one of them who would tell largish audiences of his compatriots nightly stories from Chinese history. But he admitted the extent of Chinese gambling and was about to start a campaign against the opium ration with which the British were enticing the Celestials, many of whom had broken their addiction, when suddenly it was stopped.

The Chinese Christians' work had apparently begun because two of the Chinese themselves asked their commanding officer for permission to preach the gospel in a regimental hut when off duty. The Reverend H. R. Hindley, who was one of Flew's fellow-chaplains, commented thus in his diary:

. . . they said they did not expect payment. In saying this they may have had in mind British soldiers who had been actors, musicians, or entertainers in civilian life but did not blush to send a hat round after a Regimental concert in which they had taken part. When the Chinese leader was brought before the commanding officer to present their request, the following conversation took place:—

C.O.: So you want to be a preacher?

John Chinaman: Yes, sir; me want stay YMCA; preach Jesus.

C.O.: But who is going to pay you?

John Chinaman: My God, *He* pay me.

C.O. (rather embarrassed): All right; we'll see what we can do.

These Chinese know their New Testament very well. Flew told them that they would not be able to stay at the YMCA until the building was ready, so they must sleep rough for a few days. So their leader quickly replied, 'That all right! Paul, he say, in prison, he happy. Jesus, He say (putting his head on his hand as if to sleep) bird, nest got it; but He no place to lay His head.' So these Chinese Christians are evidently made of the right stuff. Flew tells me that they get a regular evening congregation each Sunday in the Regimental hut of between 40 & 50 of their fellow-countrymen from the Labour Corps.

The Chinese Christians seemed to have come from New Testament times. There was Loo Tai Van, ex-murderer and ex-polygamist, who on his return from hospital was still in a fever and tormented by a vision of two devils who seemed to be eager for his soul. Flew felt that he should go back to hospital, but he was reluctant because of the taunts of the heathen, 'Where's your Jesus Christ? Why doesn't he heal you? He angry with you!' Flew could but point him to One of whom it was claimed that he had conquered the devils.

Three Chinese presented themselves for Baptism. They had learned a Chinese catechism by heart and expected Flew to ask them questions to which they

could give the stock answers. Instead he asked them to
tell him which word or action of Jesus they liked best.
At first they were bewildered, but then, after a silence,
one chose the golden rule and another the healing of the
blind man (which, Flew does not say). The third said,
tremblingly, that he liked everything, but then plumped,
with sudden inspiration, for the healing of the deaf mute.

It all took a long time owing to difficulties of interpretation.
But we eked it out with pidgin English famously. And
finally all doubt was removed from my mind when the
dullest (number three) who only knew Matthew's Gospel
and had never heard of the two robbers crucified with Jesus,
answered my question 'What for Jesus die?' by smiling and
saying in Chinese – 'Because he loved me and loved everybody'. Good for you, I thought, that's enough for any one of
us poor sinners to float into eternity with – 'This my hope
and all my plea' – and I guess that even Apollos baptized
some Corinthians on the strength of less knowledge of Jesus
than these Chinese possess.
    So I propose to baptize them publicly at my evening
service on Sunday September 21st. I am making out a
special baptismal service. The one for adults in our book
would be incomprehensible to them. Sung Sing Tsar is
translating my questions into Chinese and I hope to have
copies of the form of service cyclostyled before then, some in
Chinese and the rest in English. Meanwhile Sung Sing Tsar
and the three candidates are reading selected parts of the
gospels together every night.

At Sheighal on Sunday, 25th January, 1920, he
preached to the Burmese. The O.C., Major Liddell,
accompanied him, and the two sat on chairs while
thirty or so Burmese squatted on the floor of a specially
erected tent and fervently sang Sankey hymns, which
they knew much better than did Flew and the Major.
Flew preached 'in simple English about the Good
Shepherd and acted a good deal of it'. The next day, he

discovered that 'if the Burmese sing and smile like heaven, they drive their Ford vans like h-ll'.

He was on the way to possibly the most intriguing expedition of his life. He was determined to visit the Devil Worshippers of Yezidi and their shrine at Sheikh Adi.

This religion seems to be an amalgam of most of the oriental faiths, not excluding a touch of the Christianity of the *Apocalypse*. Every man must one day be judged before Allah, who will expect him to have been faithful to his own religion. The present age is a 10,000 year reign of Satan of which 6,000 years are over. After another 4,000 years comes Melek Isa (Jesus) to overthrow Satan, who will repent in hell and the tears of his weeping will put out the flames. Meanwhile it is but wisely realistic to pay court to the terrible power who at present rules the world.

Flew had to surmount a good many obstacles on the part of the political and, especially, the military officers. 'It's all mountain country you know, Padre, and very difficult riding.' 'You may not be able to get horses, all the horses will be in the field ploughing.' 'It is rather dangerous out there, Padre. Who's going to punish the murderers if the Kurds swoop down and kill you as they did Scott last year?' 'You may be cut off by snow and kept up there a week.' 'You'll have to get official sanction for the cars from Brigade and the staff captain is a devil!'

There was real point in some of these objections, not least in the hint that Flew would have to overcome the devils of the plain before he met the worshippers in the mountains! And he nearly was marooned by snow! But he persisted and was given imposing credentials, notably a letter to the Amir or Mira of the Devil Worshippers, which stated that he was a priest of high degree and a truly great man. The Arab secretary translated this to mean 'First degree' and Flew was saluted as a Bishop throughout his stay in the country of the devil!

In his negotiations with the military authorities, he overheard the secret scandal of the Nineveh stones, which for centuries were taken as legitimate materials for the building or improving of local houses. The British government officially stopped the quarrying, but two chaplains, one Methodist and one Church of England, prowling round the ruins one day, discovered that the Army had given contractors permission to build a bridge by extracting stone from the palace of Sennacherib.

Flew himself visited Nineveh a couple of days before his journey to the Devil Worshippers. It rained and, not unusually, his photographs miscarried.

But even the site of the supposed tomb of Jonah was as nothing to the call of the mountains and their strange inhabitants. Flew set off from Nineveh in a Ford van. Besides the driver and himself, the passengers were his servant and another Wesleyan chaplain, F. W. Beal, who was to remain with the party until the roads became impassable for motor transport and the van had to turn back. This happened just outside a Chaldaean Christian village called Tell Ushkof.

It seemed as though Flew would have to proceed on foot. But some donkeys were grazing near by and Flew, with his ready charm and Arabic vocabulary, commandeered two or three for himself and his kit. But just as the donkeys were loaded, the van driver spotted a mare on the brow of a hill. He persuaded a reluctant owner to part with it temporarily, and so Flew mounted, and with his retinue of donkeys and armed servant, waved good-bye to his cheering friends with the words, so one of them testified, 'The Lord is good to his own!'

The Quri, the religious chief of Tell Ushkof, the Priest, Hormuzd, was waiting to do him honour. He treated him as a son, led him into the audience chamber, seated him on a settee or divan, while he himself sat on the floor in the corner and smoked his five foot long pipe, its bowl resting on a tray on the ground. Notables of the neighbourhood came in to see the stranger and other priests surrounded the Quri. 'There was no need to talk; the one necessity was to smoke and look profound.'

Occasionally, the placid surface was stirred to animation. Once I asked the Quri, in Arabic, of course, whether he had ever seen the cinema at Mosul. Every old face lit up. 'No,' said the Quri, 'but I have heard of it. Wallah (i.e. Mon Dieu) it is wonderful.' 'Wallah' said one of the chief guests, 'it is wonderful. It is like this (and he made a rapid St Vitus-dance like motion with his hands). I saw the cinema once at Mosul. Wallah!' And the rest gazed at him in envy. Here we were 20 miles from Mosul and only one of the notables had ever been to the movies and he only once! *In sha Allah*', said the Quri, 'if the Lord will, I shall get on my horse some day and see the pictures before I die.' And a smile of anticipation came over his wrinkled old face.

After a meal, and provided with three ponies, one for himself, one for his servant and one for the baggage, Flew left the last vestiges of Christian civilisation and entered the country of the devil. The servant, Mahmud, carried a rifle. Flew himself was unarmed, on the principle 'that a revolver is only a temptation to a Kurd to kill you for the sake of possessing it'. Mahmud knew the dialect of Kurdish which the Yezidis speak and had in fact lived among them for a few years.

On the road we had some conversation on the words to avoid. You must never say SHEITÂN (Satan) or even the first syllable of the dreaded name. You must not say keitan (thread); nor shatt (the common Arabic word for *river*); nor must you use the words for malediction.

Mahmud and I satisfied each other of our orthodoxy on this point. It is as well. For the old Yezidi rule is that if any of the faithful hears the word SHEITÂN spoken, he is bound either to kill the speaker or to kill himself. Neither Mahmud nor I wished to be in at the death!

There was an amusing sequel to our conversation a couple of days later. We reached a spot amid the snows where the vast plain opened out before us, ringed with mountains, misty and immeasurable, and lo in the distance flashing in the morning sunlight was the River, the Tigris itself. Mahmud was nervous lest I be betrayed into an exclamation – (Shuf – Esh Shatt – see the River) and a Yezidi horseman was with us. So Mahmud himself cried: Shuf Sahib el mai kabir yem el Mosul! (See Sahib, the great water near Mosul!). I took him up at once and sagely answered, with an air of profound comprehension – Ah, it is the Dijla is it? (i.e. the Tigris). And Mahmud grinned. He knew that we were safe.

The journey up the mountain track was perilous; a slip would have meant a fall into a ravine fifty feet or more beneath. But the ponies were well chosen and safe, and after five hours they discerned the tower of the Mira's castle at Ba'adri. They rode into a filthy court-yard, stabled their horses and Flew presented his letter, which was read while he waited in a dark, smoke-filled room in which his smarting eyes could discern the dim shapes of men. But before long, the Mira's uncle appeared and besought him to enter the audience chamber. There he was hailed as a Bishop and put on the couch of honour. When Seyyid Beg, the Mira, entered, the letter was read once more and the Mira, in true Arab fashion, assured him that 'my house will be your house'. Flew reciprocated, wondering what his parents would think should the chief of the Devil Worshippers ever arrive in Ealing. Then came coffee, tea, and a meal served in a manner not calculated to aid the digestion of the squeamish. The Arab loaves, or chupatties, rather like pancakes, hung over the rim of the tray on which they were served, and touched the floor; the chicken was torn up by the fingers of the host and pieces passed round. To moisten the rice, chicken and plums, sour milk was drunk from a ladle shared by all the eaters.

The next day Flew rode to the shrine of Sheikh Adi,
the Mecca of the Devil Worshippers, – 160,000 of them –
where there was a festival. The shrine is in a deep valley,
surrounded by precipitous hills and mostly hidden from
the sun. Sheikh Adi may well have been an historical
person, a tenth-century prophet. Some traditions regard
him as almost Divine; at the last day he will bear all the
Yezidis in a tray on his head safely into heaven. There
is also a legend of his violent death as a result of a trick.
He went on pilgrimage to Mecca and while he was gone,
Melek Taus, the Peacock King, impersonated him
among his disciples and, after teaching them, ascended
visibly into heaven. When the real Sheikh Adi returned,
he was slain as an impostor. Melek Taus reappeared,
acknowledged his deception and instituted the cult of
Sheikh Adi.

There are four orders of Yezidi priesthood. Chief is the
Pir, a person of great sanctity and austerity; then comes
the Sheikh, the resident priest or ruler; then the Qa wwal,
an itinerant speaker, expected to sing and dance at
festivals; finally the Faqir, a servitor or deacon, who
in return for a tribute paid to the Mira, pockets the
offerings of the pilgrims to the shrine.

Flew made his way into the court of the temple and
cringed a little before the sinister symbol of the snake
carved in relief on the door of the shrine, and blacked to
heighten its effect. The approaching pilgrims were
accompanied by a flute-player and two drummers,
playing a dirge to Melek Taus. The image of the peacock
is kept in one of the big chests, like the ark in the shrine
of St Alban. It is believed that no Christian eye has seen
it, or the similar images at Bari, though some years
before Flew's visit, Dr Stanley was secretly allowed to
photograph the latter.

Flew was led through the shrine in his stockinged feet.
Beyond the lamps and the tomb of the saint, he noticed
a small door. When he asked what was on the other side

of it, the Faqir hurriedly answered 'Nothing! Nothing!',
but Flew had every reason to believe that it opened on to
a steep stone staircase descending to the bowels of the
rock. Wigram the author of *The Cradle of Mankind* had
penetrated this in 1907, when the Yezidis were enduring
Muslim persecution and the shrine was in charge of a
Mullah, who himself believed that the abyss was the
home of the foul fiend. But Wigram, though guided only
by matches, saw enough to convince him that here was
the source of the sacred spring which feeds the temple
tanks. Devil-worship had derived from the yet more
ancient cult of fountain-worship.

The pilgrims allowed Flew to photograph them. They
did not join in any service of public worship or use any
formulae of prayer. They simply prostrated themselves
and kissed the threshold of the shrine and left the
praying to the priests.

Back in Ba'adri, there occurred a remarkable episode:

It was after our evening meal. I had wielded the wooden
spoon manfully especially as there were almonds and other
nuts hidden amid the rice and I had eaten wings of chicken
and Hussein Beg had torn morsels off the breast for me with
his own fingers (Allah reward him according to his works).
After I had sighed the sigh of contentment and had tucked
up my feet under me and was sitting solemn on the couch,
the Kurdish minstrel sang. It was a passionate ditty, they
told me, of the man serenading the woman, now half-
moaning, now rising furiously – and all in one monotonous
cadence so unlike anything ever heard at the Queen's Hall.
When it was over and I had congratulated the singer, I
announced that I would sing an English love song! 'All were
silent and fixed their gazing eyes'. One needs to quote Virgil to
give the true effect. Then from my high couch I thus began:
    Drink to me only with thine eyes . . .
and so on to 'I would not change for thine'. The sensation
was so profound and the effect so immediate that I could not
proceed to the second verse. The Scribe, whose religion was

Chaldaean (Christian), decided to sing himself so he wailed a Chaldaean hymn (applause). All looked to me to repeat my triumph. So as the atmosphere was now more religious I sang

How sweet the name of Jesus sounds . . .

to the new tune of T. Tertius Noble, remembering where Rosalie and I first heard it and striving vainly to fit in the religion of Swanwick with my present company. No, even Swanwick revellers in their wildest revels never imagined that the hymn would be sung in the Palace of the Devil's Own.

The next day he was told by some of the officials of the fear for his life, in which the reigning Mira, Seyyid Beg, went all his days. At least four assassins were lurking somewhere to kill him. The Mira's scribe, Shewass, who had read Flew's letter on his arrival, begged him, as a Bishop, to send Christian priests as missionaries and overthrow the superstition of Devil Worship once and for all.

And so Flew and Mahmud departed amid the ostentatious general grief, which is Arab courtesy, and returned, via the Chaldaeans and their form of the Orthodox liturgy, to Mosul and Basra.

On 11th August, 1920, Capt. Flew, R.N., Royal Army Chaplains' Department (Wesleyan) embarked on the Army transport ship *Varela* for 'Demobilisation India'. He was to teach at the United Theological College at Bangalore. Already he had received the gratitude of the eminent Wesleyan missionary, Charles W. Posnett of Medak, for his work among Telegu-speaking Christians in Mesopotamia and it was expected that, in vacations from Bangalore, he would travel extensively in the sub-continent.

At the College he taught a variety of pupils from many Churches, some of whom, such as the future Metropoli-tan Juhanon of the ancient Syrian Church, were destined for positions of leadership. He also caught up

with academic news and gossip and first heard – from
visiting Professor Westman of Uppsala – the name of
Friedrich Heiler and of his famous book on *Prayer*.
Heiler had succeeded Flew's old Professor Herrmann at
Marburg and was an ex-Roman Catholic.

In his wanderings, he observed almost every form of
Indian religion. He spent much time with Wesleyan
missionaries and was the first guest of the young Leslie
Weatherheads at Madras after their marriage. He was
welcomed in every compound and talked more than he
listened. Naturally loquacious, he could not help himself, for the missionaries wanted to know about everything he could describe, from Swanwick Schools of Fellowship to Devil Worshippers. He claimed to have poured
out four million words one week in Madras alone!

He was anxious as ever to do his own missionary work
when and where he could. At Tanjore, where the shrine
of Karttikeja, the son of Shriva and the God of War,
impressed him with its exquisite workmanship and
noteworthy architectural restraint, he met a Brahmin
with his little son paying tribute to the small image of a
god. Flew asked for the details, and, after they had been
plentifully supplied, enquired further if the Brahmin,
who had compared worship of the minor deities of
Hinduism to the Catholic veneration of saints, had read
the Gospels. The Brahmin said that he had, at the High
School. Flew marvelled that, having seen the beauty of
the life of Jesus, the Brahmin could turn away to worship
anyone else.

He thought that this thrust the Hindu on to the
defensive. It provoked a voluble apologia for his own
religion, the nobility of its philosophy, the saintliness of
its saints. Flew granted all this and cited, with admiration, the mystic, Kabir, whom the Brahmin had not
read, but, none the less, pleaded with him to look again
at the first three Gospels. The Brahmin retorted that the
lives of Christians were no better than those of Hindus

and that Christ would disown ninety-nine per cent of his followers. Flew conceded that one hundred per cent of Christians were unworthy of their Lord; but Jesus would not disown them if they were penitent. Again he begged him to study the Gospels, for his son's sake as well as his own. 'Come now, could you wish anything better for this little boy whom you love than that he should grow up reverencing Jesus Christ?'

The Brahmin made no direct reply and the conversation changed to other things. In parting, the Brahmin bowed and said, 'Not for a long time, sir, have I enjoyed a conversation such as we have had here today.' One is left wondering to what extent Flew's accommodating yet resolute testimony to the Jesus of the synoptic gospels had made impact and what would be the reaction to it of a Brahmin of the years since the Raj departed.

A story Flew heard about Gandhi, 'whose name, for good or evil is on everyman's lips', filled him with admiration and Christian confidence, but might also have made him a little less sure that the Christianity of the Churches would prevail by out and out conquest. A Punjab missionary was so impressed with the visiting Gandhi's knowledge of the New Testament that he invited him to lead the Christian Bible Class during his stay. Gandhi consented, and each week taught the Christians about Christ. No minister could have outdone him either in his Scriptural understanding or his devotion. And he confessed privately 'All my inspiration for my life work I draw from Jesus Christ'.

To Bangalore came E. Stanley Jones, then about Flew's own age, the missionary of the American Methodist Episcopal Church, who was to write *The Christ of the Indian Road*. He was particularly an evangelist to educated Hindus and drew audiences of hundreds of non-Christians to his lectures on the claims of Christ. He always gave up a great deal of the time to answering questions and debated with his hearers, who became most animated, such philosophic problems as the transmigration of souls and corporate personality, 'free will, fixed fate, foreknowledge absolute'. They also wanted to know about the reliability of the Gospel records and the contrast between Christ and Socrates.

Flew had not been too well disposed towards an allegorising devotional address which Jones had given to the Bangalore staff. In 1947, after the opening rally of the London Christian Commando Campaign, he was still sufficiently Jülicher's pupil to deplore, at the expense of Bishop Christopher Chavasse of Rochester, this method of interpreting Scripture. But although he thought that Jones's lecture material was an amalgam of new ideas and old illustrations, he admitted that he preached passionately and that it *was* the Gospel. Flew could feel, in the large audience, the resistance against the speaker, which gradually Jones overcame, so that, as he told the story of Christ's death, many had to leave the hall to avoid being too much influenced against their Hindu convictions, while, at the end of the final lecture, a Hindu leapt on a chair and exhorted the dispersing crowd not to take any decisive step (i.e. acceptance of Christianity) in a hurry. Jones had spoken that night on *Bhakti*, the mysticism of the Indian mediaeval poets, including Kabir, who figured in Flew's conversation with the Brahmin. Jones applied Bhakti to Christ and showed what personal communion with Jesus meant to the Christian. One of the sad incidents of these remarkable occasions was the manifest opposition of the more conservative Indian Christians, who distributed tracts against Jones because he did not hold the substitutionary theory of the Atonement. Flew felt that the Viceroy's responsibilities and powers were mere trifles compared with Jones's and quoted the Wesley hymn:

> On all the kings of earth,
> With pity we look down.

He saw something of the less reassuring side of Indian life and the Christian mission. At Mannargudi there was a lovely little Church built to replace one burned down ten years earlier by the mob in revenge for the conversion of Paul Rangaramanujam and Krishnaswamy. The college at Bangalore had its nationalists and agitators, though he felt that a sermon he preached on 'Jesus only: Jesus everywhere', coupling Mark 9:8 and Colossians 3:11, transcended the divisions, at least for an hour! But the response of students to disciplinary action, taken sometimes against outbursts of brutal and injurious bad temper and violence, are an odd foreshadowing of what has become familiar in the strange years since Flew himself has been beyond the reach of student power and unrest.

His much garlanded departure from Bangalore was almost marred by a violent speech from an Indian YMCA representative, who had attended Flew's New Testament lectures and sermons most admiringly, but who chose the *tomasha*, or farewell festivities, to read an anti-missionary manuscript of the 'Tell England' type. The majority of the students seem to have been distressed by the outburst and accompanied Flew to the railway station and insisted on doing the low caste, almost untouchable, coolie work of carrying his many bags.

He had been a popular teacher, preacher and guest. He visited Medak, where Posnett's great Gothic church, now the cathedral, was being built and wondered if it were not too costly a scheme, but then reflected on the vast numbers of men, women and children employed in the work and felt as though he had been present at Chartres when that masterpiece of the middle ages was being reared. He was impressed by the teaching methods of the Wesleyan Women's Auxiliaries. They reminded him of Tolstoy's way of composing his short stories by asking the village people to tell them for him. The ladies would recount a parable or incident in the life of Jesus to a group of Indian Bible women. The women would then re-tell it in their own language with vivid local colouring. The best of the results would then be turned into Telugu lyrics.

It was in India, above all, that Flew became convinced of 'the pressing need for Christian Reunion'. Some supplementary notes to one of his long letters home retail certain unhappy incidents vouched for by Garfield Williams, later Dean of Manchester:

A group of Mohammedans, nearly 5,000 in number, desires to embrace Christianity. Majority live in area where Nonconformist missionary society is in control. Minority including most of the leaders of the group live in district where Anglican missionaries are working. This group of Moslems, united in Mohammed is thus unless something unforeseen happens to be divided in Christ.

A young Indian was converted and became a communicant member of a certain church. For some years he lived in a city where the representatives of that church were working. He was employed by the railway and in the ordinary course of things was transferred to a far-distant place on the same line. Unfortunately at this new place missionaries of different denominations were working. If he had to ally himself with Christian folk at all he had to take part in the Church life of the members of the new denomination and attend their services; there was no alternative. His pastor fearing that he might come to ally himself permanently with this other denomination warned him of its teaching and its practices with the result that when he got to his new home he lived as much apart as possible from the little community of Christians there and in particular, kept away from their services and the sacraments.

Alone, among the appallingly secularising influences of heathendom, he fell into sin.

He was last seen as a denizen of an Indian bazaar where he was living with some Indian woman whom he had picked up. He had not merely reverted to type. He was a clean living Hindu boy when he came to Christ and was made a member of His body. His last state had become worse than his first. Who of the twain, the pastor or the boy, is more responsible for that disaster?

If the pastor, what share of the blame is due to the Church who made him what he was?

A group of Indian Christians met to discuss the future of their native land.

3 RCs. Some Anglican laymen. 1 Anglican priest, rest nonconformists.

Started with prayer. 3 RCs did not join but came in after. Next day Sunday. All except RCs went to a nonconformist chapel close at hand for service. Then communion service. All stayed except Anglican priest. He told the story. He *had* to separate himself from his Xtn fellow countrymen at the Table of the Lord. He left them he said out of loyalty to a Western Church, but it hurt and he knew it was wrong. United by national ties these men were divided in Christ. Yet they all knew that Christ was the one hope of a safe and fruitful national life.

The chief point is this. The RCs felt this keenly – *Not a man among those Xtns felt that they were divided by Christ. They were certain that they were divided not by Jesus who is univeral but by a Church which is Western.* Are they right or wrong?

In the College at Bangalore, he had discovered that the Indians took all too readily to Western schisms and denominations. The converts of the London Missionary Society were far more Congregational than their tutors; the Methodists far more bigoted than Flew.

One detects that after eighteen months absence, Flew was restive for home. He had accepted an invitation to the Clapham Circuit and the High Street Church, where his father had been minister a decade or so previously. He was due to begin there on 1st September, 1921. The work included the Chaplaincy of Queenswood, then in its final post-war period at Clapham Park before its move to Hatfield, Hertfordshire, in 1925. In his last months in India, he was gathering material for his talks to the girls and was excited to find that one of the Women's Auxiliaries at Medak, Miss Edge, graduate of Newnham College, Cambridge, was an old Queenswoodian. He wondered how a bachelor minister would fare with Miss Trew, the redoubtable Headmistress, and her pupils. But his speculations were never to be put to the test.

Throughout his time abroad, he had maintained a regular correspondence with Winifred Garrard. She addressed him as 'Padre', he her as 'My dear Dauphinesse', because she loved the story of the Dauphinesse who had kissed the sleeping poet Alain Chartier, 'for the beautiful words his lips had spoken'.

He had intended a leisurely journey home with some sight of Egypt and Athens. But he was drawn by a magnet more powerful than the Sphinx or the Acropolis and contented himself with a brief tour of Palestine. He had contemplated proposing to Miss Garrard by cable, but repudiated that as insufficiently romantic. He asked her to meet his boat at Dover.

Afterwards, he used to say that he had made up his mind to propose to the first woman he saw on the landing stage. As it happened there were two women in sight, but Miss Garrard was conspicuous in a mauve mackintosh. Within half an hour he had proposed, been accepted and was engaged.

The wedding took place ten weeks later, a little after his sister's. The week before he had been at the School of Fellowship at Swanwick, from whence his fiancée received mysterious telegrams supposedly from the King of the Devil Worshippers – 'Expect me on Saturday. (Sgd Sheitan)!'

The marriage was solemnised at Chapel Street Wesleyan Church, Luton, by the Reverend Dr Josiah Flew, J. Henry Cartwright and Harold Chapman. The honeymoon occupied several of the weeks between late July and September and, beginning in a country cottage near Penshurst in Kent, moved on to Paris, Lugano, Como and Engelberg. It was the start of a long and joyous companionship, which was characterised by many travels abroad. Newton Flew was never happy to be separated from his 'lady' as he so often called her. In all their years together they found a remarkable sufficiency in each other and the fulfilment and compatibility of natures both alike romantic. Browning was a source of inspiration and, in 1934, it was to him that Flew inevitably turned in dedicating his first big book, *The Idea of Perfection*,

To W.F.
Take them, Love, the book and me together:
Where the heart lies, let the brain lie also.

His own experience of marriage confirmed his suspicions of a too ruthless dichotomy between *agape* and *eros*. He was never in favour of John Wesley's translation of Antoinette Bourignon

Empty my heart of earthly love
And for Thyself prepare the place.

A student who had been observed walking in the college court with a beautiful girl and on the next day chose that hymn for prayers was rebuked quite sternly.

Flew was glad to resume his Circuit ministry in London. He retained his membership of the London Society for the Study of Religion and he worked for his Oxford B.D which he gained in 1925. But although he most properly continued his work of scholarship, deepened by his many travels and his studies in the spirituality of Eastern religions, he used all his gifts and energies in the service of the people of Clapham. Open-air speaking went hand in hand with a teaching ministry. For the

Jubilee of High Street Wesleyan Church in March-April 1923 he announced a course of popular lectures on the world's religions, which, be it remembered, he had not merely read about but seen for himself. The following Christmas he complains of having preached badly, through tiredness. But by then there was a baby in the house. His only son, Antony Garrard Newton Flew, was born on February 18th, 1923.

In 1924, after the customary Wesleyan three year period, he moved to Muswell Hill. The Wesleyan Church in Colney Hatch Lane, built in what to the taste of the later twentieth century seems a somewhat over-elaborate redbrick Gothic, with a choir screen, was approaching the apotheosis of its strength in what was then one of the most affluent London suburbs. It was, like many of its kind in those days, a Church which used the Order for Morning Prayer each Sunday. It boasted a large congregation and many young people. Flew had a force of personality and a variety of gifts which endeared him to all ages and styles. By then he seems to have taken to the pince-nez with the black cords which were associated with him in public for the rest of his life. These were something of a 'gimmick', though he would have scorned the word or the idea; but they added to the mystique of his authoritative but gracious and fundamentally gentle *persona*. Young men might be amused at first, but they stayed to listen, and children loved him as they had done everywhere. They begged him to repeat his stories – 'the camel who came into the tent' was an especial favourite – and felt that he was their friend, who would never slight or ignore them. One Harvest Festival at Clapham, the children's gifts had been received and dedicated at a special service in the afternoon. They had been placed on a table which was discreetly removed before the evening worship. Flew noticed that it was gone and refused to begin the service until it had been replaced. On a Sunday morning at

Muswell Hill, a little girl had mislaid her penny when
the collection plate was brought round, but she found it
just as the children were leaving in the hymn before the
sermon. Without demur she broke from the line of
departing boys and girls and walked straight up the
pulpit steps to give it to her friend, Mr Flew!

His was no conventional ministry, not even for a
'scholar-evangelist'. He pioneered what were then new
methods both of teaching and devotion, methods, which
though they were redolent of 'Fellowship Swanwick',
began slowly to penetrate the Methodist Societies as a
whole only after the second world war.

In January 1925, he sent out a leaflet to the members
of the Muswell Hill Church headed 'An Experiment'. It
invited them to 'a novel kind of Conference' to be held
on the last day of the month. The theme was to be 'The
New Testament Experience of God in Christ'. With the
leaflet was enclosed a study paper for preparatory
consideration. The Conference itself consisted of two
periods of group discussion, on 'The Nature of the
Experience' and 'The Power and the Message', and a
reporting and summary in plenary session. The pattern
has become all too familiar; but in those days it was new
and fruitful. The subject shows Flew as part of the
continuing movement to recover Methodist experiential
Christianity based on a deeper theology and a Scriptural
understanding which took the higher criticism in its
stride. From 1921–3 he was editing a short-lived 'journal
of fellowship' called *Experience*.

For Flew, scholarship was to be shared with the people
of the Churches. He had a class in elementary New
Testament Greek after his Sunday evening service. His
sermons were simple and became simpler, so that
sometimes in later years people expressed disappointment
that so eminent an academic gave so little sign of
his learning. But in his circuit ministry, he did not
believe that new knowledge of the things of Christ

was to be kept hidden in his own heart and mind. He owed much to the work of the Anglican Catholic Modernist, Archdeacon Lilley, and, especially, to his book *Prayer in Christian Theology*. He made this the basis of much teaching at Muswell Hill.

He was anxious also to deepen the devotion of public prayer. Sometimes in Divine Worship the prayers would take the form of meditations on Jesus and the Gospels. On Good Friday, he would lead worship from the back of the Church and base the whole service on one of the Passion Hymns of Wesley with appropriate scriptures and prayers. On Sunday evening, 18th April, 1926, he announced as his subject 'How do you begin?' i.e. to pray. A special issue of the Church messenger, *The Quest*, gave an introduction of limpid clarity. 'Prayer is not primarily nor mainly petition for ourselves; it is the ascent of the mind to God.' You begin by getting quiet. 'As George Tyrrell used to say; "God does not like fidgets". Or as old William Penn put it; "Stand still in thy mind". This does not mean that the activity of the mind is suspended. . . . Each of us must discover the way that suits him best. But no one can live the true life of the spirit without some reference to Jesus . . .' And so there follows this meditation:

O Love that wilt not let me go

Let us contemplate Jesus in His temptations;
   how He rejected all the lower ways of winning men to
   God's Kingdom and chose the way of humble love; even
   though that way should lead Him to suffering and a Cross.
Let us contemplate Jesus as He re-affirmed His choice;
   in all His daily deeds of kindness;
   in His refusal to condemn, or to call down fire from heaven
   or to take the easy and the popular way; in His prayer on
   the Mountain, when, meditating on His inevitable Death,
   He was transfigured as with the glory of God, and went
   down to continue His work to the end.

Let us contemplate Jesus in His daily bearing of the Cross;
long years before He was nailed to the wood on Calvary.

Let us contemplate Jesus in His compassion for the multitude,
seeing them as sheep not having a shepherd;
in His eagerness to heal them, Himself taking their
infirmities and bearing their diseases;
in His yearning to speak the words of forgiveness, and to
loose them from the habit of their sins.
'Thy sins be forgiven thee; go in peace.'

Let us seek to understand His suffering when men rejected
His message and disappointed His hopes.
'Upon this many of His disciples went back and walked
no more with Him.'

Let us seek to enter into His mind when He saw that His
very message of love had stung the leaders of the people
into a blind pasion of hate and fear.
'How often would I have gathered thy children together,
even as a hen gathereth her chickens under her wings,
and ye would not.'

Let us contemplate Jesus as He bore all the desertions and
denials of men at the last; the accusations of His enemies;
the flight of His friends; the betrayal of Judas; the mock-
ings of Herod and the soldiers; the murderous clamour of
the crowd; the scourging and the crucifixion.

Let us now seek a deeper meaning in His prayer in Gethsemane, as He faced the bitter thought of all the accumulated
failures of the human beings whom He loved.
'Father, if it be possible, let this cup pass.'

Let us adore the triumph of the Love that endured and
would not let us go.
'Father, forgive them, for they know not what they do.'

The knowledgeable will recognise there the influence
of Maltby, just as the preceding paragraphs epitomise
all that Flew had learned from Catholic and Eastern
sources and his wide reading in *theologia spiritualis*. But
all is Christocentric. 'If that meditation led the praying
soul to adore God, to wonder at the love revealed in
Jesus, the soul would be brought to the innermost shrine,

where Intercession for others and Petition for the best gifts are as natural as the breathing of the air of heaven. And there is a sure place, too, for Thanksgiving and Confession.'

During 1925, Baron von Hügel died, and, even more devastatingly, on Palm Sunday, Josiah Flew. Since 1917, the latter had been a member of the 'legal hundred' of the Wesleyan Conference. This constituted the official assembly, though, since 1877, there had been District representation and an equal number of ministers and laymen present. But every decision had to be ratified by this august body. Josiah Flew had retired rather early to Harrow and was still within a month of his sixty-sixth birthday when the end came. It was said of him that he had 'the power and skill of great love'.

It was obvious, that effective as Flew's circuit ministry was, his scholarship and varied experience qualified him more than most men for the work of ministerial training. He was therefore nominated in 1927 to become tutor in English and the English Bible at Didsbury College, Manchester, in 1928. Meanwhile it was decided to appoint an additional tutor to the small post-graduate college, Wesley House, Cambridge, which had begun in 1921. Flew's old friend W. Bardsley Brash was nominated for this, which was to take place immediately after the Conference of 1927.

Brash had the confidence of the Principal of Wesley House, Dr H. Maldwyn Hughes. He had twice been minister in Oxford and chaplain to the Wesleyan students, and had obtained the Bachelor of Letters degree. But some in the representative session of the Conference preferred F. Bertram Clogg, the New Testament Tutor at Richmond College, who was a Cambridge man. Brash however defeated him by 253 votes to 168.

The matter now had to go down to the pastoral session to be confirmed. Normally this would have been a matter of course, but the ministers were uneasy. Was not Flew the man for Wesley House? And so as well as Clogg, R. Newton Flew was nominated against Brash. He won by 302 votes to 141 for Clogg and but 101 for Brash. It was a rare exercise of pastoral prerogative, but a wise and obvious one. Brash had his consolation in being designated for the English and English Bible Chair at Didsbury for which Flew had been intended, and, himself the most magnanimous of men, recognised the justice of the reversal and remained Flew's close friend for the rest of his life. He became Principal of Didsbury College in 1939 and guided its move from Manchester to Bristol six years later.

Flew's departure from Muswell Hill was therefore sudden and sorrowful, for the Circuit ministry exercised all his powers and the life of a College tutor was lonelier and gave fewer opportunities for regular preaching and the education of the laity. But the way was now open for the great work of his life.

4

Cambridge and Ministerial Training

IT COULD be argued that the decisive event in the Church history of the past hundred years was the abolition in 1871 of religious tests at the Universities of Oxford and Cambridge. The great English Protestant communions all had their roots in the older universities, and non-Anglicans could feel that they were being allowed to return home. It was not long before they were planning to establish houses dedicated to what Milton had regarded as the supreme academic task – the training of ministers. Mansfield College, Oxford, was opened in 1889.

Not all nonconformists rejoiced at the prospect. Some feared that in returning to these pleasant pastures they were going home to die, and that their distinctive traditions would soon be lost. But there were many laymen who were convinced that a surer and speedier way to desuetude was to remain in self-conscious isolation from the centres of theological scholarship and debate. These men coveted for the ministers of the future what they themselves had mostly been denied – full entry into the inheritance of the Christian academic tradition.

One such was Michael Gutteridge, a prosperous Wesleyan business man and local preacher, who at the Cardiff Conference of 1911, moved that consideration be

given to the establishment of a hostel for graduate ministerial candidates at Cambridge. The existence of the Leys
School, founded in 1872, had done much to give
Methodism scholarly status in the university town, and
this is one of the reasons why Cambridge was preferred
to the Wesleys' Oxford. Gutteridge ended his speech with
the offer of £5,000 towards the cost of the new institution.
This was the first of his multifarious benefactions during
the next quarter-century. He began a Trust Fund, to
which the generosity of others could be directed.

Next in honour to Gutteridge is William Greenhalgh
of Southport, who was advised by his minister, Henry
Maldwyn Hughes, to bequeath £20,000 to the scheme
with the stipulation that a few non-graduates be
admitted. It was Hughes who was designated the first
Principal in 1920.

To find a site in Cambridge was not easy. At length,
arrangements were made for students to live at Cheshunt
College and to rent no. 2 Brookside as Principal's lodgings
and lecture rooms. The first students, who included
three future Presidents of the Methodist Conference,
arrived for the Michaelmas term of 1921.

In the autumn of 1922, Jesus College agreed to sell
some stables, a row of shops and several houses to make
room for buildings in Jesus Lane, just over the road from
the Anglican seminary, Westcott House. The site is a
very good one, in the centre of Cambridge and less than
five minutes walk – up the lane, across Sidney Street and
through All Saints Passage – to the Divinity School.
Plans were prepared by Sir Aston Webb, who became
President of the Royal Academy in 1923, and, when
Flew arrived in 1927, the House was still lacking a
Chapel and a Principal's lodge. These were erected by
1930, though the full scheme has not yet been completed.
The Chapel, the gift of another Methodist layman,
Edmund S. Lamplough, in memory of his brother,
Williamson, was somewhat controversial, with the apse

designs and wall frescoes by Harold Speed. For a Methodist place of worship it was highly decorated. The apse depicted the Being of God, 'the perfect round', with the human Jesus, very different from the conception of an Epstein or a Sutherland, in the centre, his arms outstretched in mercy towards a family caught in the coils of the old serpent. Rays of light from the golden orb merged in the four canvas murals which showed 'the sunshine of God's presence' in the life of the shepherd, fisher, ploughman and family. The style was not in keeping with what came to be the theological fashions of the second World War and its aftermath, nor with the art forms which have predominated since. Flew, however, approved and would point out that each design was inspired by a Scriptural image for the minister of the Word, while the Christ in the posture of his Passion and Ascension repeats a theme prominent in Christian art from early days.

Maldwyn Hughes, whom Flew joined, had already begun to make Wesley House a Cambridge institution, and, with the ever-remembered help of his wife, a family. His health was always fragile and when the Wesleyan Conference called him to its Chair, it did so in 1932, the year of the Methodist union, so that he held office for a matter of weeks only and was spared the arduous itineraries which custom exacted from those who served the full term. Hughes was known affectionately among his students as 'Boss'. He did not display any flamboyant scholarship, but his quiet wisdom and humility immortalised him in the lives and ministries of those he taught. It was he who chose the inscription over the Chapel porch – 'Learn of me for I am meek and lowly of heart'.

Wesley House was fortunate in the benefactors of its first decade. In addition to Gutteridge, Greenhalgh and Lamplough, there was the Reverend Dr John H. Ritson, the constant friend and adviser of Michael Gutteridge,

who by happy coincidence was President of the Wesleyan
Conference when the Jesus Lane buildings were formally
opened in 1925 and who remained a Governor until his
death in 1953. He admired Flew greatly and encouraged
him much in his early Cambridge years as the hopes for
the academic successes of the House were more than
fulfilled. Mr and Mrs John Finch endowed the Finch
Travelling Scholarship, which enables a Wesley House
man of sufficient distinction to spend a year of study
abroad. Flew's own experience made him particularly
well qualified to exploit this.

What follows will desert strict chronology for the sake
of a fully-rounded portrait of Flew at Cambridge in his
heyday, but it will be as well to bear in mind that his
active work at Wesley House and in the university between 1927 and 1955, falls into three periods:

(1) The years until the outbreak of the war in 1939.
This was the time when his own scholarship flowered.
In 1930 he received the Oxford Doctorate of Divinity,
the first nonconformist to do so by examination; in 1934,
the thesis was published as *The Idea of Perfection in
Christian Theology*; in 1938 came his Fernley-Hartley
lecture *Jesus and His Church*. Meanwhile, in 1937, he had
attended both the Oxford Conference on Church, Community and State and the Edinburgh Conference on
Faith and Order, and succeeded Hughes as Principal of
Wesley House.

(2) The twilight period of the war. During these years,
Wesley House was threatened by enemy action, by
danger of military or governmental requisitioning and
by the fact that, after 1939, the Methodist Conference
accepted no ministerial candidates and, from 1940, its
theological colleges were progressively closed down. By
the end of hostilities, Wesley House alone remained.
It had survived ostensibly because its smallness and
location at Cambridge, where departments of several
other universities were evacuated, made it the obvious

place to accommodate men from the other colleges who were completing London external B.D. courses and certain overseas students, who were doing London degrees or Cambridge diplomas. But in 1944–5 Joseph William de Graft Johnson from the Gold Coast (now Ghana) was, as Flew put it, 'the one black thread on which Wesley House hung'.

(3) The years of Church statesmanship and ecumenical eminence, during which Flew was Moderator of the Free Church Federal Council (1945–6), President of the Methodist Conference (1946–7), Chairman of the World Council of Churches Commission on the Church, and much engaged in inter-Church discussions in England.

The University

Cambridge must have been at its loveliest in the years before war restricted the spaciousness of its living, increase of student population necessitated vast new buildings, and the internal combustion engine polluted the country freshness with roar and stench, and bull-dozed some of the grassy plots into car parks. Flew's prior loyalty to Oxford never made him disparage his adopted home. In his retirement, he would describe the 'Backs' as 'the most beautiful mile in England, and therefore in the world'. For more than a quarter of a century he was a familiar Cambridge figure, bespectacled and beaming on his bicycle.

He soon made his mark. On 24th October, 1929 he was appointed to the Faculty of Divinity and on 12th November, 1931 was elected to the Board. From 1932 he was an examiner in the Tripos, except in the years 1945–8, when his ecclesiastical commitments made it impossible. He also on several occasions examined for University prizes and higher degrees both at Cambridge and elsewhere. In 1945, he was one of the examiners of Geoffrey Nuttall's thesis on *The Holy Spirit in Puritan Faith and Experience*, which made Nuttall the second

nonconformist to obtain the Oxford D.D. by examination, while he also read Constantin Hopf's work on
Martin Bucer. To equip himself for the latter task, he
read the whole of Bucer's works, to the amazement of his
colleague, Claude Jenkins, the Regius Professor of
Ecclesiastical History at Oxford.

At a Faculty meeting on 6th November, 1930 he made
an intervention, characteristic as a sign of his perpetual
concern for the less-favoured student. The minute runs as
follows:

> Mr Flew called the attention of the meeting to the fact that
> the passages for comment set in Paper 4 of Section B of
> the Theological Tripos Part 1 were given in the original
> languages whereas similar passages set in Paper 5 of Section
> A and Paper 6 of Section B were usually given in English. He
> considered that the Latin passages presented difficulty to
> certain candidates. It was agreed to ask the Faculty Board
> to consider the matter.

Flew yielded to no man in the belief that the classical
tongues were the basis of all sound learning, and he later
fought for the retention of Latin as a requirement for
Cambridge entrance. In 1935, he was pleading the claims
of an advanced linguistic study at the Faculty Board. But
he knew already, and future experience was to confirm
his judgement in some signal instances, that a potentially
able theologian might not be from a school where
advanced Latin was taught, or might have graduated in
one of the sciences and thus have been preoccupied for
some years with studies far from classical. He did not
wish such men to be penalised.

His lecture courses came regularly to be recognised on
the official university list. In 1932–3, he dealt with 'The
Authenticity of the Sayings of Jesus', in 1933–4 with 'The
Authenticity and Interpretation of the Parables', in 1934–5
and 1937–8 with 'The Teaching of Jesus', in 1935–6 with
'The Sayings of Jesus and Recent Criticism', in 1936–7 with

'The Idea of the Ecclesia in Early Christianity'. In 1939–40, he had to substitute for J. M. Creed, the Ely Professor of Divinity who had died, and take over the course on 'The Person of Christ in the New Testament'.

He was also appointed to a committee, of which the other members were Professor Creed, Dr Telfer, Sir Edwyn Hoskyns and Mr Hugh Burnaby, to report on the teaching of Greek in the Faculty. But the most important Faculty work in which he had a large share was the reform of the Theological Tripos.

Honours examinations at Cambridge are known as Triposes after the three-legged stool or tripod on which the mediaeval candidate sat for his *viva voce* or public disputation. By the mid-1930's there was some discontent with the syllabus and scope of the Theological Tripos, dominated as it was by the ancient languages and early Church history to 451. As far as candidates for Part 1 were concerned, the Protestant Reformation might never have taken place. A motion in the Board for the re-organisation of the Tripos was proposed by Dr H. Watson in 1935 and found no seconder, but early in 1939 Professor Creed was himself speaking in favour of change. In 1943, Flew was made a member of the committee set up to consider revision and by 1950 the reforms had been implemented. It was his advocacy of the present papers 1–3 of Part II (The Religion of Israel, the New Testament in Greek and English, and the Theology and Ethics of the New Testament) as the fundamental study, which made agreement possible. The process of change was unhurried to say the least, but those were times when the academic world, anxious to maintain its stability in the world crisis, would not be stampeded. And 'student power' was unknown.

Professor Creed's untimely death in 1939 was a personal grief to Flew. Ten years later, he was saying that he still missed him. Near contemporaries and not dissimilar in style, the two found themselves early *en rapport.* A link was supplied by the fact that Creed had married a daughter of Canon Lilley the liberal Anglican Catholic and friend of von Hügel's, whose book, *Prayer in Christian Theology*, Flew so much admired. The Preface to Flew's *Jesus and His Church* (1938) acknowledges the help of Creed's 'exact and profound scholarship' together with that of the Methodist, Vincent Taylor. Creed himself wrote the Macmillan commentary on St Luke (1930), a volume which was severely criticised, partly by erstwhile liberals who had become cautious with the years, such as Hensley Henson, Bishop of Durham, who was frightened of its apparent historical scepticism, and partly by scholars who differed from its condemnation of the 'proto-Luke hypothesis' – the suggestion, canvassed, for instance by B. H. Streeter and Vincent Taylor, that a first draft document lies behind the third gospel. In spite of a certain austerity and dryness which made only the most prophetic and discerning scholars such as Hoskyns and R. H. Lightfoot receive it with enthusiasm, the volume has been the standard English commentary on the Gospel for forty years. The 'scepticism' seems mild and commonplace now, while New Testament criticism has shifted decisively from source-criticism to form-criticism and documentary hypotheses are less in fashion.

Creed was also a fine historian of religious thought and edited, with his successor, J. S. Boys-Smith, a selection of eighteenth century writings. In 1936, he was Hulsean lecturer at Cambridge and the resultant volume was *The Divinity of Jesus Christ: a study in the history of Christian Doctrine since Kant*. It was re-issued in Collins' Fontana series in 1963, with an introduction by D. M. MacKinnon, Norris-Hulse Professor of Divinity at Cambridge. With Donald Baillie's *God was in Christ* (1948) and W. R. Matthews' *The Problem of Christ in The Twentieth Century* (1950), it ranks among the outstanding British Christological studies of the past half-century.

But it was in a friendship which transcended the divisions between Anglicans and Methodists that Flew knew and loved Creed. He wrote a brief tribute for the *Methodist Recorder*, ending with the couplet from Wesley's great hymn on Christian unity:

> Names and sects and parties fall
> Thou, O Christ, art all in all.

Another with whom Flew was closely associated in his first decade at Cambridge was Edwyn Clement Hoskyns, baronet, and priest of the Church of England, Fellow and Dean of the Chapel at Corpus Christi College. He died, also before time, in 1937, leaving to the expert care of a pupil and colleague, Noel Davey, the publication of his great commentary on *The Fourth Gospel* (1940). Hoskyns and Davey had already collaborated in *The Riddle of the New Testament* (1931) and Flew made invaluable suggestions for the extension and improvement of the bibliography in the second edition.

Hoskyns probably transformed Anglican New Testament scholarship. He was a man to whom theology was all, an Anglo-Catholic who was the first English translator of Barth's *Romans* and a friend of Gerhard Kittel, the editor of *Theologisches Wörtebuch zum Neuen Testament* who used the phrase 'the scandal of particularity' to express the fact that when God became man it had to be of a particular time and place i.e. a first century Jew. Hoskyns believed that the two most important lecture courses in Theology at Cambridge were those on 'The Religion of the Old Testament' and on 'The Theology and Ethics of the New Testament'. (Flew's advocacy of these in the reformed Tripos was, in some sense, his memorial.) In contrast to the prevailing scholarship of the Faculty, which was erudite and meticulous beyond question, but well content to be neither inspiring nor inspired, Hoskyns talked of Christ and the forgiveness of sins in accents which still ring in the ears of his students. He was mistrusted by many of his colleagues, who were mildly (or even subconsciously) contemptuous because he had not read the Theological Tripos himself. After a mere second in History, he had departed for Germany and studied under Harnack.

'Can we rescue a word, and discover a universe? Can we study a language, and awake to the Truth? Can we bury ourselves in a lexicon and arise in the presence of God?' These were questions, which to the prevailing caution and reserve of the Faculty seemed almost indecent. Sometimes, it must be admitted, such ardent religious desires led Hoskyns astray, as in his emphasis on the word *trogein* for 'to eat' in John 6. Hoskyns claimed that this meant, literally, 'to munch' and such an interpretation makes the words about eating the flesh of the Son of Man all the more awesomely 'scandalous'. But, in fact, by the time of the New Testament, 'trogein' had become one of the common words for 'to eat', as it is in modern Greek, so that Hoskyns' contention collapses.

Hoskyns' lectures were said to be sermons (and his sermons lectures) but a year of him at the onset of his fatal illness made at least one Wesley House man (C. K. Barrett) a dedicated New Testament student for life. He was passionately against 'the tyranny of liberalism' in both theology and politics and *non persona grata* to many in the University – pacifists and others – at the time of the rise of Hitler. At first, he had hoped good of the Nazi revolution. This was due to his close friendship with Kittel, whose book on the Jews, he encouraged Fabers to consider translating. But this was *before* it was published in Germany. When it appeared, in 1934, Hoskyns was so shocked by its contents that he immediately saw the Nazi regime for what it was, renounced his interest in the book and drew away from his friend.

The liberal, so Hoskyns averred, tends to decide all questions by what he thinks is true in contemporary life. Hoskyns believed that liberalism resulted in an unholy compound of emotional blackmail, moral laxity and religious reductionism, while as Kenneth Pickthorn, the University Member of Parliament put it, he 'was incapable of assuming that what he wanted for the times was what the Lord always intended'.

Flew called him a saint, which made Lady Hoskyns incredulous at first, but posterity has confirmed his judgement. In January 1939, he reviewed Hoskyns' posthumously published *Cambridge Sermons* for the last issue of T. S. Eliot's critical quarterly, *The Criterion*, the only time that a Methodist minister can have figured in such pages. He notes that Hoskyns' lectures on 'The Theology and Ethics of the New Testament', had been attended enthusiastically, not only by his fellow Anglo-Catholics, but by members of Wesley House. 'His teaching fell on the minds of his hearers with something of the force of a revelation. Again and again he spoke as if he were wearing not a mere academic gown but the mantle of a prophet.'

Flew singles out three main features of Hoskyns' emphasis: (1) He exulted in the strangeness of the Gospel. The fact that the Christian message comes in a tongue which is to us ancient and alien is no handicap. It enables us the better to wrestle with that which is not of this world and defies the normal processes of reason, in short to acknowledge that God is 'wholly Other'. (2) For him the principle of revelation was supreme for theology and preaching. (3) He was overwhelmed by the utter reality, unchangeableness and givenness of God and his consequent activity in human life, especially in the transformation of sinful man. 'The paradox was that this passionate assertion of the sinfulness of man made Hoskyns more of a lover of mankind. His rejection of humanism made him not less but more human. He had the perennial secret of those who know that the ultimate attitude of man is adoration.'

Flew understood Hoskyns, the Methodist felt at one with the Anglo-Catholic, the total abstainer from the home of 'decent poverty' with the 'ascetic gourmet'. They had one indulgence in common, which later medical science condemned. They both loved a pipe of tobacco, though Hoskyns was possibly the heavier smoker.

Hoskyns left five children, none of whom was adult at his death. Flew remained in touch with Lady Hoskyns and the family. On 15th March, 1942 we find him the sole guest at Catharine Mary Hoskyns' seventh birthday party and on another occasion teaching her the rhyme, 'Betty Botter bought some butter'.

No greater contrast to Sir Edwyn Hoskyns could be imagined than the man who was elected Regius Professor of Divinity in 1932, Charles Earle Raven. It cannot be pretended that the years of Raven's tenure which ended in 1950, were favourable to the friends and pupils of Hoskyns. Raven, too, was a saint and a prophet, a charismatic man, with a handsome presence and an irresistible winsomeness, who inspired and won the love of disciples. But, for him, New Testament Theology, though climactic, was part of a much wider whole. The world was animated by the Creator Spirit and Christ was no Divine invader but the consummation of the creative process. The eighth of Romans was Raven's chapter and the contemporary with whom he most suggests comparison is the Jesuit Teilhard de Chardin. A biologist as well as a theologian, he was dedicated to the reconciliation of science and Christianity, to a new Christ - centred cosmology. The Barthian attack on natural theology in the interests of a theology of revelation and its renewed sense of the gravity of sin, borne out it would seem by the events leading up to Hitler's war, appeared to Raven as a 'great blight'. Whether our generation with its increasing reluctance on the part of scientists to construct a world view and the repudiation of metaphysics by those theologians most concerned with the secular and this world is, in spite of the cult of Teilhard, any more congenial to Charles Raven's heroic efforts may be doubted. Some would feel that Raven's lack of experience of the tougher physical sciences was a disqualification and that direct knowledge of their fields would have made him, like many physicists, more sympathetic to the Barthian approach. He was a pacifist, forbidden to broadcast during the war, and also on Hitler's list for liquidation, should England be conquered.

As Regius Professor, Raven, who had no patience with narrow denominationalism, was a good friend to Wesley House and gratified by the glory which its outstanding students brought to the Faculty. He also valued Flew's gifts as an ecumenical theologian. 'You know how much we lean upon you' he wrote, when inviting him to a theological consultation in the autumn of 1937. From that date, Flew was party to many ecumenical discussions on the nature of revelation, the Sacraments and other 'Faith and Order' matters, held in Raven's rooms. For Wesley House's sake and because his own sympathies could honour both Hoskyns and Raven, he was neutral in the battles between the personalities, which the symbolic figure of Hoskyns and the neo-orthodox revival provoked. But, on balance, and without his being a Barthian, or ever doubting that the first three gospels present a Jesus who is more than the creation of the Church's faith, Flew found Hoskyns' resolute insistence on the givenness of the Gospel nearer to his own predilections and piety than Raven's evolutionary creed. Who would expect otherwise, knowing his fidelity to Methodism and to von Hügel! Yet when it was suggested that Flew might take C. H. Dodd's course on 'The Doctrine of the Holy Spirit in the New Testament', during Dodd's illness in 1941–2, he was troubled for fear of hurting Raven, who was also well-qualified to be lecturer on the subject, though it was feared, more from a 'modern' than a New Testament perspective.

Another Anglican whom Flew always regarded with deep respect was Dr William Telfer, successively Dean of Clare College, Ely Professor of Divinity after Boys-Smith's brief occupancy, and Master of Selwyn College. Telfer wrote comparatively little until his retirement, apart from learned articles, though in a few words of his condensed but authoritative treatment of *The Forgiveness of Sins*, published in 1959, he shows a deep understanding of Wesley, which may well have derived in part from Flew's *The Idea of Perfection in Christian Theology* listed in the bibliography. Telfer's lectures were packed tight with patristic learning. He had the habit of reeling off Greek and Latin phrases at tremendous rate and then pausing to write on the blackboard some fairly simple word, not beyond most of his hearers. Flew admired his austere integrity and valued his moral judgements, which he, at times, sought out in the case of student and domestic staff misdemeanours. Telfer was a High Churchman, who was too learned and too rigorous to accept the more superficial Anglo-Catholic accounts of the origins of episcopacy.

There was also F. S. Marsh, Lady Margaret Professor of Divinity, from 1935 to 1951, a profound but self-effacing Old Testament scholar, who published hardly anything, but whose personal influence extended far beyond his public fame. Hoskyns puzzled him rather and he was a severe examiner in high table and combination room discussion of any too theologically attractive interpretations of New Testament words with Hebrew roots. Behind the objectivity of the academic was the warmth of a holy and humble man of heart, who had taught at Kelham and lived austerely at Selwyn in a constant fight against ill-health, and whose devotion Flew loved.

The Free Churchman to whom Flew owed the most was the Presbyterian, Charles Anderson Scott, New Testament Professor at Westminster College, but already on the verge of retirement when Flew arrived at Wesley House. He was born on 31st May, 1859, the day before Josiah Flew, and Newton Flew looked to him as a father and took to him all his problems. Anderson Scott was the first nonconformist to be given the Cambridge D.D., the first to be elected to the Faculty Board, the first to be appointed Hulsean lecturer, the first to be made President of the University Theological Society. Flew succeeded him on the Faculty Board.

Scott's most important book, *Christianity According to St Paul*, was published a few months before Flew's appointment to Cambridge. Flew much admired the masterly arrangement of the material, which enables the complex themes to be handled with effortless ease. The author comprehends the whole of St Paul's theology under the term 'Salvation' and expounds it thus:

> As a fact of the Past
> Its Appropriation, Faith
> As a Progressive Experience
> Its Consummation in the Future
> Its Author and Perfecter, Christ.

If Flew's devotion to Paul needed confirmation, Scott supplied it. Many years earlier, when a minister in Kensington, Scott had written *Evangelical Doctrine – Bible Truth*, a refutation of the claims of the more exorbitant Anglo-Catholics, cast in the form of letters. All the quotations were drawn as far as possible from Anglican sources, to condemn his opponents out of the mouth of their own communion and to rebut any charge that Protestant scholars are not acquainted with Anglican divinity. Flew may have been more sympathetic to Anglo-Catholics than the Scott of 1901 – he certainly was when he met a Hoskyns – but it is probably true that throughout his work for Christian unity it was the extremer Anglicans of this temper whom he found hardest to bear. Rome, in his day, had a logical and definable system for which he had great respect, though in his earlier Cambridge years he had little sympathy with those who 'went over', and a spirituality with which he had strong affinities. But he always felt that there was an intolerable weakness in the position of the more unyielding Anglo-Catholics, poised as they were, in Scott's phrase 'between the Scylla of Erastianism and the Charybdis of a Papacy'.

Anderson Scott died in July 1941. Flew's last talk with him was on 10th July, just before he departed for the Methodist Conference at Leeds. Afterwards he helped to carry him up to bed. When Flew returned from Conference, his old friend was unconscious, in his penultimate, morphia-induced sleep. The memorial service meant that Flew was unable to attend the consecration in Westminster Abbey of Edward Wynn of Pembroke College as Bishop of Ely. Flew was one of the four specified persons to whom Scott had instructed his daughter to write letters after his death, thanking them for their friendship.

Another Free Churchman, who influenced Flew greatly, was the Baptist layman Terrot Reaveley Glover, Fellow of St John's College and Public Orator. Glover's books, *The Jesus of History*, *The Conflict of Religions in the Early Roman Empire*, *The Disciple* and many others, with their background of classical scholarship, their limpid English style and their understanding of how ordinary people questioned and felt, were as famous in their day as those of William Barclay since. Flew told how one Monday morning, walking back from the station bus to Wesley House he met Glover. 'What have you been doing?' asked the other. 'Preaching your books' said Flew.

Glover was disappointed that even higher academic rewards had not come his way and at times revealed a certain bitterness. Flew used to tell how Glover's own minister, Maclaren Cooke, once rebuked him for an uncharitable remark by telling him that it was unworthy of the man who had written *The Jesus of History*. Glover was contrite at once.

Flew loved the *Book of Common Prayer*. He used to like to think that Cranmer had turned over its rolling periods as he paced the grounds of Jesus College on which Wesley House now stood. He told the young Chaplain of Sidney Sussex College, Kenneth Riches, later a colleague in the ecumenical movement and Bishop of Lincoln, that he never went away without carrying a New Testament, a Methodist Hymn Book, and a *Book of Common Prayer*. He sometimes preached on a collect. His love was deepened by his association with the Congregationalist layman, Bernard Lord Manning, historian and Fellow of Jesus College. He too was destined to die when his powers were at their ripest. Flew had listened to his papers at the University Methodist Society on the hymns of Wesley and Watts. He wrote to his mother about an address, which Manning had given at Wesley House in the last months of his life. It was on the Burial Service (and afterwards printed in *More Sermons of a Layman*). 'It may sound lugubrious on paper but no subject is lugubrious in Bernard Manning's brilliant hands. I certainly saw the essential fitness of the Anglican Burial Service (which was ours up to our last revision a year or two ago) more than I had ever seen it before. And I am beginning to regret the omission of the reverent and awful prayer:

Suffer us not at our last hour for any pains of death to fall from Thee.'

Manning had shown that a true Christian liturgy of the Burial Service should include (1) A clear statement of the ugly and devastating fact of death (no nonsense about 'Welcome sister death'); (2) The statement of the ground of Christian hope i.e. the resurrection of Christ. (3) The message of comfort.

There were younger men too, Anglicans and nonconformists, among Flew's Cambridge friends. Canon
Charles Smyth of Corpus, the historian, writer of the
appreciation which introduces Hoskyns' *Cambridge
Sermons* and, later, biographer of Archbishop Garbett,
was a scholar for whom Flew had unstinted admiration.
He honoured his devotion to the Prayer Book and his
understanding of its true liturgical shape, so often missed
by students of 'comparative liturgiology'. Flew tells of a
long walk the two of them took in 1941, because Smyth
'wanted to pick my brains about the evangelical movement; I fear I learnt far more from him than he did from
me'. In 1946, in Flew's absence as President of the
Conference, though doubtless with his warm approval if
not on his specific instructions, Charles Smyth was
remembered in Wesley House Chapel on his institution
to the Rectory of St Margaret's, Westminster, and
installation as a Canon of Westminster Abbey, as was
George Armitage Chase, former Master of Selwyn
College, who was being consecrated Bishop of Ripon the
same day.

There was J. S. Whale, the Congregationalist President
of Cheshunt College until 1944, partner with Bernard
Manning and, at that time also, Nathaniel Micklem, of
Mansfield College Oxford, in a revival of 'orthodox
dissent'. Flew was always as elated by his friends'
triumphs as by his own and he was thrilled to recount
the success of Whale's open lectures on *Christian
Doctrine* in the Michaelmas term of 1940, when the course,
thronged with students, had to be transferred to ever
larger rooms. Whale consulted Flew about a small
textual problem in publication. He had quoted Charles
Wesley's lines:

> O for a thousand tongues to sing
> My *great* Redeemer's praise.

The perspicacious proof-reader of the Cambridge University Press queried this and suggested it should read

My *dear* Redeemer's praise.

as in the *English Hymnal*. Whale's attitude was 'I am not going to have these Anglicans telling me what the hymn should be. We and you, Congregationalists and Methodists, always sing "great" '. Flew pointed out that Charles Wesley had written 'dear', but in the 1779 Hymn Book, John altered it to 'great' probably because as with *Jesu, Lover of my soul*, he had thought this language too familiar to use of our Lord. But Flew thought that Whale was, on the whole, right to prefer the adjective which Wesley's people took to their hearts. And 'great' it is in all the many editions of Whale's notable book.

Flew found donnish conversation and humour immensely congenial. He liked the story of the dream of the sometime Master of St John's, which satirised the ready wit of H. Montagu Butler, his contemporary as Master of Trinity. 'I dreamt that it was the Last Judgement and I saw all the people who had ever lived being dealt with most efficiently and expeditiously by Omnipotence. When it was all over I saw a familiar figure rise to propose a vote of thanks to Deity for the admirable way in which the proceedings had been conducted. "I am sure that you will agree, sir" said the speaker, who was none other than our dear and eloquent friend the Master of Trinity, "that it is fitting that I should thus voice the universal feeling of admiration, since you are Trinity and therefore may be said to belong in a special way to my College".'

He also enjoyed a true story told to him by Mrs Venn, wife of the then President of Queens', College about her father, Sir William Ridgeway, a famous classicist. Ridgeway always tied his own dress ties – and often not very well. Once he was dining in Gonville and Caius College and enjoying leek soup. He was very near sighted and found great difficulty with one of his leeks. After at length despatching it, he sighed and remarked, 'I've not had so much difficulty with a leek before.' 'No wonder,' said his neighbour, grimly, 'You've just swallowed your dress tie!'

Flew had an academic disappointment in 1935. The Norrisian and Hulsean Chairs of Divinity had been combined into one, which was not to be limited to a clergyman or layman of the Church of England. Anderson Scott persuaded Flew to apply and supported him strongly; but Dr C. H. Dodd, then Rylands Professor of Biblical Criticism and Exegesis at Manchester, was elected. The failure probably sealed Flew's career and turned him from pure scholarship to the ways of inter-Church negotiations and ecclesiastical statesmanship.

Wesley House

Flew became Principal of Wesley House in 1937. In March, Maldwyn Hughes returned home ill from a Committee in London, and in the course of the Easter vacation told Flew that he must retire with effect from the forthcoming Methodist Conference. Flew was thus the first – apart from Mrs Hughes – to know of the decision, and, when the matter had been brought before a specially convened meeting of the Board of Governors, on 26th April, Hughes took the lead in nominating his colleague as the new Principal and holder of the Michael Gutteridge Chair of Systematic Theology. As J. H. Ritson and W. T. A. Barber, former Headmaster of the Leys School, said privately, any other choice would have been unthinkable, while, outside Cambridge, W. F. Lofthouse had told Flew some little time previously that he was convinced that the hour had come for him to be given command.

The elevation meant the Flews' second move in twelve months. From 1927 to 1936 they had lived at 31 Jesus Lane, one of the two fine Georgian houses at the college gates. Then a more spacious house, 46 Lensfield Road, was purchased, where they spent but the inside of a year, and so it was back, books and all to Jesus Lane, and the lodge in the college court, next to the chapel. And this in the summer of the great Oxford and Edinburgh ecumenical Conferences! Flew's library was so vast that a special room on the second floor of the lodge had to be set aside for him apart from the study and to this he banished 'all works of English Lit., all vols of sermons, even my very fine library of mystics and spiritual writers'. The theologians, the 'commentators on Holy Writ, the serried ranks of the Fathers of the early period' were arranged in the study – 'an awesome room'. He was helped in this arrangement by the five days he spent in A. S. Peake's library at Manchester, after the latter's death in 1929, when he bought 800 books, mostly for Wesley House, whose library early became his concern.

Flew's new colleague was W. F. Flemington, a Jesus College, Oxford man, who had gained a First in advanced New Testament studies while at Wesley House before Flew's time, and who himself was destined for a distinguished teaching career in Cambridge as Tutor and Principal of the College. He gained his B.D. with a much-lauded study of *The New Testament Doctrine of Baptism*, published in 1948.

Flew's great quality as Tutor and Principal was his humanity, though this does not mean that he was not a strict disciplinarian, who expected hard work. His waiting classes ceased any noise or tomfoolery the moment he was seen to emerge from the Lodge on the way to the lecture room. He began, on his arrival in Cambridge, to concentrate the training of his men on basic essentials. He regarded private study as of greater value than too catholic an attendance at lecture-courses.

He discouraged the dissipation of scholastic energies down the more alluring and primrose paths marked 'contemporary' and 'relevant'. The foundations of a minister's scholarship must be solidly laid on the knowledge of the New Testament, which meant the study of Greek and the principles of exegesis. Because the New Testament could be understood neither apart from the Old nor without some awareness of the sub-apostolic and patristic ages, it was necessary to extend the study backwards and forwards beyond the first century A.D. But however brilliant the degree in history, philosophy or classics with which a man came to Wesley House, Flew always insisted that he knuckle under to the Tripos, and, then, should his achievements warrant it, extend his horizons. He felt it was a mistake to pursue other branches of Theology until these foundations were laid, while he was always suspicious of the new sciences, such as psychology, and to some extent of philosophy too. His old students will easily imagine what he would have thought of the modern lust for sociology.

Some would argue that this gave Wesley House men rather a narrow training and that they were better qualified to bear witness to what was the Gospel than to argue in its defence. Flew would have been unrepentant and retorted that the Christian cause more often goes by default because it is not known than because of any lack of sophisticated techniques of debate. He also knew very well that if a man is able to achieve real competence in a comparatively limited area, he will master wider fields more easily when the time comes. He liked men who were 'not afraid of the big book' and besought them to eschew primers of potted information for passing examinations in the interests of definitive tomes.

He had some very able pupils who have become renowned scholars and whose gifts he fostered and opportunities he created. But he rarely failed to understand his less academically gifted men. Sometimes a third class man's achievement of a 'second' gave him more satisfaction than a dazzling 'first'. He encouraged sportsmanship and was particularly proud of Irvonwy Morgan's rugger. He was interested in the men's 'ladies' as he always called them, and coveted his own married happiness for others. 'Think of me as a father' he would say and although one did not thereupon call him 'Daddy', one could always open one's heart to him in confidence of understanding and of wise pastoral counsel. To break the news of bereavement or tragedy to his men cost him dear, but he was able to do so with unerring sensitiveness.

He worried about illnesses and troubles and identified himself with them. He became expert in diagnosing appendicitis and sometimes seemed almost 'let down' by the invalid if he were proved incorrect! He was never so sure of himself as to be detached or to meet likely disaster with Stoic apathy or Ignatian indifference (qualities, not perhaps, so unChristian as he thought, though entirely foreign to his nature). Sometimes this manifested itself in irritation, but if ever he spoke harshly to a sufferer or a college official, his penitence was as quick and overwhelming as in his Handsworth days. 'Can you find a fine phrase to forgive an old man?' he said one afternoon to one of his later College Chairmen, whose defence of a suspected malingerer had briefly annoyed him earlier in the day.

There was one pre-war House man, whose background and previous academic career had been very different from most of his contemporaries. One night, in conversation with Flew in the library, somewhat resentful of his fellows' greater prowess and of what seemed to him to be the worship of the 'first class', he lost control of his feelings and, through angry tears, spoke bitter words. Flew completely understood and guided that man's future studies with particular care, helping him long after he went down from Cambridge. He received his reward when the man published an especially fine B.D. thesis.

Years later, another student had preached what he himself has called 'the most dreadful sermon in Wesley House Chapel, cheap, pretentious and superficial'. Flew led him into the drawing room of the lodge and asked him to kneel down by the sofa and pray for humility and sincerity. But then he himself took a quotation from the sermon and used it – with due acknowledgement to his pupil – in a book he was writing at the time.

With few exceptions, Flew knew what was in his men and was usually able to suggest just the right subjects for them to study when they left. His memorial is found in the continuing scholarship of his pupils, who throughout the five continents have taught and written and preached and, in varying degrees, made themselves experts in almost every branch of Christian theology. He had some men of genius and many of outstanding academic ability; but they would all testify to the help and encouragement he gave.

He was able to prune men's excesses and discipline their extravagances and keep them on the path of sober scholarship. Gordon Rupp once wrote in an undergraduate essay of the 'bewhiskered agnostics' of the Victorian age. Flew wrote in the margin 'why the hirsute appendages?' The present writer once adorned an essay on Arianism with references to A. N. Whitehead, Reinhold Niebuhr, and several other luminaries of the twentieth century. He was told to bid them a regretful farewell; and then came the deserved rebuke which damned the piece as serious history and which has haunted the memory in warning ever since – 'you have made the controversy a modern one'.

In the years immediately before and at the beginning of the war, Flew did not always find his pacifist students easy. He himself, no more in the second war than in the first, could subscribe to the pacifist position, which he felt ignored the issues and was sometimes adhered to with a certain arrogance. He found the much older students, pacifist and non-pacifist, who had lived through the war and returned after a variety of harsh experiences, more mature and tolerant. Some overseas students did not always understand him and his particularly English humour, but the late Peter Dagadu, future leader of the World Church, who died far too young, was a whole-hearted admirer and ever afterwards wrote in the highest terms of Flew's integrity and winsomeness.

Flew never forgot that he was training evangelists as well as scholars. He was gratified when the men's lights burned late over their books, though he did not encourage over-work; he was even more deeply thankful when he knew that the lights meant that the men were sitting long after the dispersal of a Methodist Society group to wrestle with some individual's problem and bring him to a decision for Christ.

Flew was at his best in the weekly sermon class. It is the custom at Wesley House on Wednesday nights between tea and hall, for the college to repair to the Chapel, where one of the members preaches a sermon, which then is criticised in the large lecture room. One student is deputed to assess the sermon as to 'matter' and another as to 'manner'. There is an open discussion and the tutors and Principal sum up.

Flew conducted this in a masterly way. He could always go straight to the strength or weakness of a sermon, discern its artistry (if any), give evidence of its powers, sometimes to the astonishment of the preacher, but probe its infelicities of illustration, its inconsequential arguments, its bad exegesis and false doctrine, and above all, its faults of construction. Flew was a great believer in the conventional shape of a sermon – introduction, three points and conclusion. This disciplined the material and attended to clarity, a virtue in preachers to be greatly prized. Flew could often demolish a sermon and then build it up again from the same materials into a thing of power. Though, like Wesley, he desired plain truth for plain people, he did not despise oratory properly used and did not wish for preaching to be so perspicuous that it lacked 'the element of surprise', the wonder of the gospel. The 'offer' of the gospel must always precede its 'demand'.

Towards the end of his time, Flew set down for his old friend Professor W. J. Rose the sum of his teaching about the work of the minister. He pointed to a five-fold division of the minister's time:

(1) *Preaching the Gospel.* I should make it clear that teaching is an essential part of this, so as to avoid the error that preaching is confined to the official act of entering the pulpit twice on Sunday and delivering a discourse carefully prepared. This heading also includes the time for the study required for making sermons and preparing teaching lessons.

(2) *Leadership in Worship, Public and Private.* This would include the administration of the sacraments and the specific task of teaching little groups how to pray. I make this to include the time spent by all of us, even prior to the days of Leslie Weatherhead's fame, in the task of dealing with individual souls. Indeed, the prior activities of preaching and teaching all should lead up to this function of the Minister, which you have described rightly as 'Priestly'. But I find that this word has to be explained carefully as a task to which all believers are called! This is the meaning of the doctrine which is universally held in the church, both by 'Catholics' Roman and Eastern, and by Protestants, the priesthood of all believers.

(3) *Pastoral Visitation.* This means the actual visitation of the homes of the people, and the modern task of getting at the men in their factories and places of business.

(4) *Administration.* This includes conduct of meetings; knowledge of Methodist law essential for the same; how to ensure a large attendance at an overseas mission

meeting; how to conduct special 'campaigns', youth work building schemes and the like. Special stress has to be laid nowadays on the right ordering of a Minister's personal finances.

(5) *Service of the Community.* This subject within *British* Methodism is comparatively new. It means that the local Minister, whose duty is primarily of course, to his own local church, has to take into account the welfare of the community in which he lives. This leads him through the primary work of the denomination to which he belongs i.e. Evangelisation to interest in overseas missions, to what is called nowadays the Ecumenical movement, to the study of social questions and international affairs, and to some form of service in the local community.

I think that you find every part of a Minister's work can be subsumed under these five headings. But mere enumeration of them shows the miracles which we are expecting of the young and untried men, when we send them out at the age of 24, 25, or 26, to take charge of a local church or parish. The work under No. 4 and No. 5 has increased enormously during the last forty years. The meaning of No.2 has deepened immeasurably. The difficulty of No. 1 is greater than ever it was.

One thing I would emphasise first of all about the vocation to be a minister. Traditionally, Methodism demands 'a call to preach'. But this verb 'to preach' has become narrowed in practice. Preaching now means for the populace the standing up on Sunday morning, or Sunday afternoon or evening to deliver a discourse. The pamphlet *Catholicity* is a clear indication of the unthinking popular view on this point. But preaching is larger than this. It includes the word of a Mother to her son or the word of a wise Sunday School teacher to the laddie under his care 'Don't you think it's time you gave your heart to God?' Again, the most important thing of all is to realise that the main task of the Minister is not exhausted by these five categories. The main call of the minister is 'to care' for people. 'Caring is the principal thing; caring matters most.'

In addition to Maldwyn Hughes and W. F. Flemington, Flew had as colleague for most of his time at the House, a remarkable clergyman of the Church of England who taught voice production. His name was C. M. Rice, which, prompted by a suggestion of Dr Hughes, he had come to pronounce 'Reece'. Of Irish descent, he had been chaplain of King's College and thereafter had held a succession of country livings. Venerable and bearded, he continued to pay fortnightly visits in full term until his death as a septuagenarian in 1950. He was a great character, a liberal education in himself, who, well aware that his subject was regarded as something of a light relief to men dominated by the Tripos, managed to convey the basic common-sense of good speaking in his junior combination room classes, while setting an example of superb practice when he took prayers in Chapel. His various gimmicks were recalled all over the world. 'The swelling aaah', resounded in the Himalayas, the low larynx was exercised in the depths of Africa, his vowel lines 'Ned's best friend went west'; 'Ann hands back bad jam'; 'just shunt up one truck' remained to correct false quantities in rural circuits and city missions.

The other and very contrasted assistant of Flew's was Morgan, porter of the House in all for twenty-eight years. He was a man of tremendous competence and shrewdness, who sometimes had to sustain the domestic side of the House when other staff were unreliable or hard to find. There was a great alarm, when in August 1941 he received his call-up papers, but Flew managed to retain him by discovering that the medical examination to which he was summoned was to take place within a week of his forty-first birthday, which age was beyond that of military service. Whether Morgan would have passed his medical examination may be doubted for he was never robust and died in the long vacation of 1953. The Flews were summoned home from Switzerland where they had just arrived on holiday. Flew's panegyric made moving use of John 14 – 'I go to prepare a place for you'. Morgan's life had been devoted to getting people's rooms ready, seeing them in and out of college. Now he had gone to the place prepared for him in the many mansions of the Father's house.

In earlier years, much help was given to Wesley House in the teaching of Church history by a Methodist don Mr (now Sir) Herbert Butterfield, later Regius Professor of Modern History and Master of Peterhouse. Flew officiated at his very quiet wedding, which he arranged at his old church at Muswell Hill.

It was there, by coincidence, that the funeral of Dr Hughes took place in 1940. Flew, in the congregation, could not but recall the Easter Sunday of 1925 when he had had to preach from that pulpit immediately after his father's death. He did not feel that the funeral tributes quite captured the significance of Hughes or showed proper understanding of his achievement, but this was repaired by the memorial service which Flew arranged for the Michaelmas term in the House Chapel in the presence of the Vice-Chancellor. Harold Roberts, who had returned to be Hughes' assistant Tutor between 1924 and 1926, gave an address fitting alike in eloquence, understanding and simplicity, and Flew concluded the Service with the House Bidding Prayer which was his own composition.

All his years at Wesley House, quite apart from his exceptional itineraries in the interest of World Methodism and the Ecumenical Movement and as Free Church Moderator and Methodist President, Flew was preaching constantly. His free weekends were few. Most modern members of Theological Faculties would look askance at his diary for summer and autumn of 1937.

In addition to the great ecumenical conferences, he is preaching in Edinburgh and Glasgow and is off to Letchworth within days of his hectic removal to the Lodge. At the beginning of October he is being thanked by the minister for what must have been an intensive weekend at Mill Hill in North West London.

The war, which added to his anxieties for the College property and its future as well as for his son, whose winning of an Exhibition at St John's College, Oxford, coincided with his reaching military age, both narrowed and widened his preaching activities. There were Brains Trusts and courses for the troops as well as A.R.P. work and Ph.D. theses read in shelters. He left Cambridge less, and preached in more College chapels, and parish churches. There was a memorable sermon at Queens' followed by his receiving Communion – 'We have no middle walls of partition here', wrote the young Dean, Henry St John Hart. In the same term there was the Girton commemoration sermon. In October 1941 he was preaching at a Sunday evening service for undergraduates at St Mary's Oxford in a series on the 'Evidence of things not seen'. His subject was 'the Fact of Christ'. The preachment was part of a week-end which included a talk to the John Wesley Society of which he was by now a permanent vice-president and Sunday morning service at Wesley Memorial Church.

Most important of all, on 25th April, 1942, he became the first Methodist since John Wesley at Oxford on 24th August, 1744, to preach a University Sermon. Cambridge opened its pulpit to Free Churchmen that year. W. A. L. Elmslie, Principal of Westminster College, was the first (wearing Flew's Cambridge B.D. hood), J. S. Whale the second and R. N. Flew the third.

Flew revelled in the Methodist system whereby one could preach to hundreds in a town or suburban or university church one week and a handful of villagers the next. He would ask to be planned in the small societies of the Cambridge circuit, whereas for obvious reasons, it was felt that the Principal of Wesley House should be kept to the town. He would cycle miles against the wind to a small congregation in the Fens and would feel proud of the physical achievement, as though his days on the track and the football pitch were not so far distant.

In several Augusts before and in the early years of the war, he preached at the Central Hall, Tollcross Edinburgh, for Eric Baker, one of the first generation of Wesley House men. In August 1940 he took the pulpit of Wellington Church, Glasgow, one of the leading Church of Scotland preaching places in the city. His family teased him about this because they said that for the first time people made more comments on his sermons than on his children's addresses which usually seemed to steal the limelight. One old lady in Oldham told him that he would have made an ideal teacher of infants!

Flew also became a broadcaster. In 1932 he once deputised on the air for his successor at Muswell Hill, Colin A. Roberts, who was unwell. In March 1942 he delivered a sermon from the BBC studio then at Bedford. This gives a very good illustration of his preaching method. The text is St Luke 15:20 'He arose and came to his Father'. The subject of the sermon was *Going Home*. Flew began by recalling the S.O.S. messages temporarily in abeyance during the war, which used to be given on the wireless. They always prompted the speculation as to what sad story lay behind them and raised the question as to why it should be so difficult to go home. So Flew came to the parable of the lost son, and expounded it, characteristically, under three headings. 1. Going home to be judged; 2. Going home to be forgiven; 3. Going home to live.

The sermon which survives in manuscript, is probably a perfect example of Flew's style and of the great power of his preaching at its best. First to phone him after the broadcast was Margaret Flemington, his colleague's small daughter. He received many letters of appreciation, notably one from John Scott Lidgett as well as from many invalids and elderly people deprived by the black-out of attendance at worship.

In 1942, he received a further academic honour in the award of the Honorary Doctorate of Divinity of the University of Aberdeen. Lord Vansittart was also an Honorary graduand at this ceremony, and it was feared that there might be demonstrations against him because of his severe attitude to Germany as 'the butcher bird' of Europe. Nothing materialised, but the danger added to the excitement of the occasion and Flew was very interested to have speech with Vansittart, who claimed that it was untrue that the Nazis had used his polemical pamphlet, *Black Record*, for their own propaganda.

He befriended refugees from Nazi oppression, notably Franz Hildebrandt, Bonhoeffer's close friend, and allowed the Cambridge Lutherans to hold services in Wesley House Chapel. Later he supported their request for a resident pastor. He gave his blessing to the formation of the Council of Christians and Jews and was proud that an old 'House man', W. W. Simpson, should be 'permitted to serve' as its General Secretary. The Welsh, too, worshipped on Sunday afternoons in the House Chapel and were always glad, when on returning from the University sermon, Dr and Mrs Flew joined them for tea.

Throughout the years at Cambridge, Flew depended completely on the security of his home and the understanding of his wife. His letters to his mother are full of astonishment at the way in which Mrs Flew managed to eke out the rations during war time and still give the appearance of plenty when entertaining distinguished visitors or catering for the regular tea and coffee parties for the men. Parents and 'ladies' were always welcomed at the Lodge and it was from the happiness of his own marriage that Flew was able, not only to work as hard as he did in so many varied ways, but also to show those large human sympathies for which he will ever be remembered by those who knew and loved him.

Wesley House Bidding Prayer*

Let us pray for the One Holy Catholic Church of our Lord Jesus Christ, that is for the whole company of Christian people throughout the world, that it would please Almighty God to purge it from worldliness and respect of persons, from faint-heartedness and indifference to the needs of mankind; that God may indue his Church with desire of holiness and Christian virtues, unite it in one bond of faith and love, and uphold it in weakness and affliction by the power of his Spirit. Let us pray that God's everlasting gospel may be proclaimed throughout the world in word and deed, that all may turn to Christ, the Giver of life and health and peace, and that the kingdoms of this world may become the kingdom of our God and of his Christ.

Let us pray especially for the people called Methodists, in gratitude remembering those, living and departed, who broke to us the bread of life, and manifested the might of God in their lives. More particularly let us praise God for his servants John and Charles Wesley, and for the preachers raised up by God after them to the revival of his work and the renewal of his Church, asking that the Spirit who dwelt richly in them may also empower us, in our time, to spread scriptural holiness throughout the world.

Let us pray for all ministers of God's holy Word and Sacraments, that the Word of grace and truth may always be proclaimed and the sheep of Christ's flock gathered in and fed.

Let us pray for all theological colleges, for those who teach in them and those who learn, that there may never be lacking those called of God, who in word and life are true ministers of

---

* This was composed by R. Newton Flew, though it is reproduced in the form used at the time of writing, with Flew himself commemorated. As well as some of the great phrases of classic Methodism, it echoes the Liturgies of St John Chrysostom and St James.

his saving grace in Christ; and particularly let us pray for this college, that we may be a community for the worship of God and the spread of his gospel, a family of God where his truth is honoured and his will obeyed and the burdens of each are borne by all. Let us pray for the past students of this College, that God may increase their faith, strengthen their hope, and replenish their love, that they may know his presence and saving power in every difficulty and discouragement, and that by his grace they may acquit themselves as good soldiers of Jesus Christ.

Let us pray for all men, that God may establish peace and justice among the nations and within our own nation, and may help all those in affliction through callousness, prejudice or apathy, destitution, sickness, sorrow or anxiety.

Finally, let us praise God for all those who rest after their labours, and particularly as in private duty bound for Michael Gutteridge, Founder of this College, for Edmund Lamplough, who gave us this Chapel, for William Greenhalgh, John Finch, John Newton Davies, and other Benefactors, as also for Henry Maldwyn Hughes and Robert Newton Flew, sometime Principals of this House, and let us pray that God may direct the end of our lives to be Christian and well pleasing in his sight, taking us to himself when he will and as he will, only without shame and sin.

Our Father.

5
The Theologian

FLEW's theological position did not vary much with the
years. His work does not bear the marks of those
'agonising re-appraisals', which are evident in the
careers of some who have entered the world of theology
since 1945. Nor can one imagine him, like one of his
much younger contemporaries on the Cambridge faculty,
stepping out one night into a fogbound court and
acknowledging a precise resemblance to his theological
state. Flew would not have made that kind of joke.

For this there are several reasons. Some of the changes
of heart and mind experienced by more recent theologians are due to the ecumenical movement and to the
discovery that Christians outside their own obedience
not only hold the Catholic faith (or *mutatis mutandis* the
great Protestant doctrines) but evidence the fruits of true
Christianity in their lives. Indeed there is often the
surprised recognition that members of other communions
may both correct the errors of one's own while appre-
ciating profoundly its distinctive truths. But Flew's ecumenical education began with the type of Methodism
he inherited – the 'Catholic spirit' and 'scriptural holiness' of John Wesley and the *Christian Library* – and was
in its main lessons complete by the time he had left Rome
in 1916. He did not have to wait until middle-age for
some ecumenical assembly, or colleagueship with those

of different persuasions, to open his eyes to the virtues of non-Methodists or the glories of 'the great Church', and then revise his theology to accommodate the grace beyond sectarian boundaries.

Also, he knew German, and from his visits to Bonn and Marburg in 1909 was able to come to terms, to his own satisfaction, with all that the Germans could do. Nothing Bultmann wrote would shake his confidence that the first three gospels and Paul between them interpret the authentic mind of the historical Jesus. This was the subject of his last Cambridge utterance, the Hulsean sermon on 29th April, 1956. His text was I Corinthians 2:16 b: 'We have the mind of Christ'. He dismissed as 'sheer fantasy' the claim of the form critics that the lyrical sayings of Jesus were the creations of the early Christian communities. They were taught by Jesus to his disciples in rhythmic form and thus easily memorised and passed on during the thirty or forty years of 'oral tradition' before the Gospel of St Mark.

But, chiefly, Flew's theological position became fixed because his theological work was always an extension of his ministry. Because of his pastoral concern, his theology had to be definite, though not rigid; because he was a preacher, it had to issue in 'plain truth for plain people'. Though he could not share all Barth's presuppositions, he would have adopted, subject to his own definition of both terms, the Barthian concept of *Church* dogmatics.

Many in later years would regard this as a serious limitation and we are now in the age of the professional theologian, who may sit very loose to his clericalism, if indeed, he is in orders or even a church member at all. The Church has declined more than the study of theology and while there is a dearth of candidates for ordination, there are more men and women reading theology in University degree courses than ever, though often as a part of wider 'religious' and other studies. Their teachers understand theology as an approach to truth, which is greater than any system of the Christian past, and must not be blinkered by traditional axioms. For instance:

> We cannot say in advance that Christianity, as man's faithful response to Jesus of Nazareth, may not continue to change as the human situation changes, nor can we set any limits to the extent of the change it can undergo without ceasing to be Christianity.[1]

By the time of Flew's death, there were several University theologians who, like A. R. Vidler, were wishing that Christian origins could be taught away from the sound of church bells by those 'less apparently tarred with a bias'.[2]

Flew's theological method was that of a preacher. Sometimes a sermonic illustration with a touch of poetry will adorn a page of exposition:

> There is a place near Chamonix in the high Alps where in June the Alpine flowers bloom in profusion – saffron, purple, crimson. The marvel of this garden is not the perpetual wonder that flowers bloom at all, but that such beauty may be seen in those perilous distances at that height, amid the awful purity of the snow. So, too, the doctrine that God is love is not unknown in other religions, but set against the austere background of perfect purity and transcendent power it becomes a marvel of marvels beyond all telling wonderful.[3]

But the signal characteristic of the preacher's craft applied to theology is in Flew's invariable technique of organising his material under points. The crux of *Jesus*

---

[1] John Hick, 'The Reconstruction of Christian Belief for Today and Tomorrow': I, *Theology* Vol. LXXIII, No. 602, p. 340.
[2] Cf. A. R. Vidler, *Objections to Christian Belief* (Constable 1963), pp. 70ff.
[3] R. N. Flew, *The Idea of Perfection in Christian Theology* (Oxford 1934), p. 14.

and His Church is a fivefold argument. In *The Idea of
Perfection* there are 'eight main elements in the ideal which
Jesus held out to mankind'; twelve effects of the Gospel
in the experience of St Paul, three critical observations
on the Augustinian teaching about contemplation and so
on in every chapter, with many subdivisions too. This
leads to clarity and ease of learning, and although the
literary graces, which are considerable, may be somewhat sacrificed, the complex mass of material – sources,
commentaries, hypotheses – is reduced to order and the
argument marches with the relentless discipline of a
trained platoon, though in Flew's case a light rather than
a heavy brigade.

No scholar can organise his material without some
such method, and, if the reader is to make notes of a
book, which is not already so arranged for him, he can
best do so by dividing the chapters into sections and
sub-sections. The method has its parallel in *theologia
spiritualis*, for it is essentially that of meditation. *The
Spiritual Exercises of St Ignatius Loyola* are regimented as a
military text-book and teach systematic examination of
the soul and the gospel under several series of precisely
enumerated rules. But the Ignatian exercises, like a
Methodist sermon, were an instrument of conversion.
Their purpose was not debate or discovery but decision.
They were to lead to change of heart, to certainty and
to resolution.

The danger of such a method for the theologian is
twofold. He may have insufficient regard for the re-
calcitrance of his material and subdue it too easily.
To continue the military metaphor, he may win a
head-on engagement without much difficulty, while
failing to overcome the guerrillas in the jungle. Not all
the evidence may yield to his organisation. Also, he may
resort to torture, though in Flew's case, with a velvet
glove! He may impose a pattern on his material and
may force the evidence into his scheme.

The method of more recent theology would seem to be dialectical, based on a more ruthless questioning and with the antithesis of scepticism answering every thesis of faith. New Testament scholars have in fact been heard to lament the lack of documentation of those heresies, or alternative expressions of Christianity, which are refuted in, say, the letter to the Colossians. What became orthodox has an unfair advantage with us, so it is claimed.

Again, to pursue the analogy with *theologia spiritualis*, there are many who feel that contemplation rather than meditation is the truer norm of prayer for our time. Contemplation is openness to reality without the attempt to discipline it into orthodoxy or resolution. It may at times seem lazy, reluctant to gird up its mental loins, to quote one of Flew's favourite phrases, to persevere to decision. At its worst it may merge into a pseudo-mystical vagueness and become a spiritual drug; on the other hand it may cast out fear and escape from the burdensome paradigms of spiritual grammar to the music of new worlds of discovery of Divine truth in Christ.

Autre temps, autres moeurs. We shall have to note occasions when Flew's method may have led him astray, but, we cannot fail to acknowledge the achievement, which presented such wealth of scholarship with lucidity. 'Dr Flew has not only read his authors ancient and modern;' wrote W. F. Lofthouse of *The Idea of Perfection* 'he appears to have read all that the Germans have said about them. But his pages, so far from being over-weighted with their learning, read lightly and easily – often almost trippingly.' [4]

Circumstances and responsibilities caused a shift of emphasis in Flew's theological work. Until 1934, his main interest was in spirituality and the attempt to

[4] W. F. Lofthouse, *Journal of Theological Studies*, October 1934.

relate the Methodist understanding of Christian perfection to Catholic Christianity and post-Wesleyan developments. Afterwards, he was compelled to concentrate on
the doctrine of the Church, which had been much
neglected by Protestant theologians of the nineteenth and
early twentieth centuries, but which was being thrust to
the fore, not simply by the encounter of Protestant and
Catholics in the ecumenical movement, but by the
recovered awareness of the solidarity of all mankind and
the anguished questions about the nature of the Christian
community posed by the German Church struggle.

In 1933, N. P. Williams, then Lady Margaret
Professor of Divinity at Oxford, and Prebendary Charles
Harris of Hereford, edited a volume of essays called
Northern Catholicism in commemoration of the centenary
of the Oxford Movement. The symposium was published
by S.P.C.K. for the Literature Committee of the English
Church Union and treated of every aspect of the Trac-
tarian revival and its evolution, including some account of
parallel developments in other churches, some of them
outside the Anglican communion, such as German
Lutheranism, the Dutch Reformed Church, and the
Church of Scotland. It is rather strange that there is no
separate chapter on the Swedish Lutherans. An appendix
outlines the history of the Old Catholic Church, an afterthought dictated by the euphoria which the recent establishment of full inter-communion between this body and
the Church of England had inspired in the editors.

Flew contributed the final chapter on 'Methodism and
the Catholic Tradition'. Characteristically, he discovers
three main Catholic notes of Methodism – the passion
for holiness, the communion of saints and doctrinal
orthodoxy. The first establishes immediate kinship with
the original Tractarians. The volumes of Newman's
Parochial and Plain Sermons start with a sermon on
'Holiness without which no man shall see the Lord'.
Flew is soon among the Wesley hymns ('Our hymnbook

is our liturgy. It is our liturgy in both public worship and private prayer'). Chiefly from these, he illustrates his contention that, according to the Methodists, holiness is offered to all, is centred in the Cross, is essential for the success of evangelism and is founded on the great Christian tradition, which transcends all ecclesiastical divisions. He quotes John Wesley's Preface to the *Christian Library*: 'The same spirit works the same work of grace in men upright in heart of whatever denomination' and he points out with some relish, that in those fifty volumes, 'St Ignatius and St Polycarp, Fénelon and Don Juan d'Avila, the Puritans and the Cambridge Platonists – all yield their fruits to be tasted by the humble Methodists, and in his biographical series Wesley deliberately includes the lives of devout men of the Church of Rome'.

Under 'the communion of saints', Flew, naturally, refers to the Class-meetings, and then the Holy Communion. He draws on Principal T. H. Barratt's pioneer article in *The London Quarterly* of July 1923, which opened many Anglican and some Methodist eyes to the fact that the Wesleyan revival was highly sacramental, with frequent, crowded Communion Services, at a time when eucharistic devotion in the generality of parishes was somewhat cold. The article has been much used ever since and the facts are now well-known.

Flew then turns to the fact that 'the early Methodists regarded the Lord's Supper as a converting ordinance' because 'the consciousness of personal relationship with God was passed on in the fellowship and often at this Sacrament'. He uses one of his own favourite aphorisms: 'The bread of life is the gift of God, but it is broken from hand to hand'. He quotes Newman in support, though using a different metaphor 'Each (apostle) receives and transmits the sacred flame, trimming it in rivalry of his predecessor, and fully purposed to send it on as bright as it has reached him; and thus the self-same fire once kindled on Moriah, though seeming at intervals to fail, has at last reached us in safety, and will in like manner as we trust be carried forward even to the end'. But for Flew the succession is not historic so much as evangelical. 'This nexus of Christian personalities, all learning the secret of God's personal dealings with us, and passing it on again to others, *is* the Church. With their eyes fixed on these spiritual facts, the sons of the evangelical tradition do not see what additional certitude could be added to their rich spiritual inheritance by the acceptance of the doctrine usually known as the apostolical succession.'

Doctrine takes Flew back again to the hymns and 'their full-orbed orthodoxy', passionate witnesses to the 'givenness' of the Christian religion. He mentions William Burt Pope, Methodism's one great systematic theologian, and John Scott Lidgett's Inaugural Address to the Uniting Conference of 1932 on the Nicene Creed. He touches on the new emphasis which the Methodists brought to the doctrine of the Holy Spirit, and then concludes his essay with a kind of coda on Discipline, a theme congenial to the Tractarians. His final hope is for complete Methodist dedication to the cause of Reunion.

Norman Sykes the Anglican historian, then at London, but destined to be Dixie Professor at Cambridge, sensitive as ever to the piety within the eighteenth-century Church of England, felt that the implications even of so eirenical an essay as this, might be a little unfair to *ecclesia Anglicana* if they were interpreted to mean that the Church wantonly broke with societies of holy men and women, whose devotion shamed its privileged complacency. In the *Church Quarterly Review*, he pointed out that it was impossible for the Church of England to contain an organisation set up outside its discipline and in disregard of its rules. But Flew disclaims any mandate to discuss or justify the separation and his chapter stands as an early essay in ecumenism directed

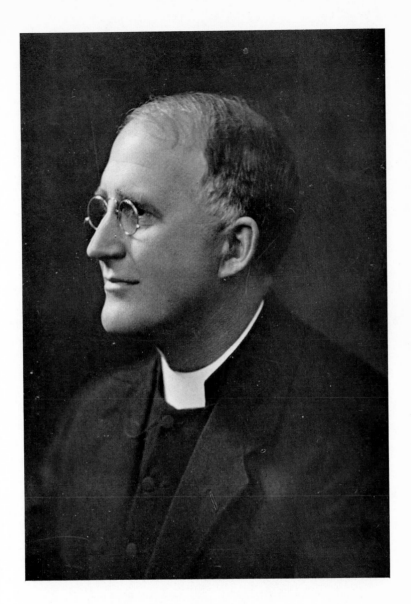

ROBERT NEWTON FLEW
Tutor of Wesley House

RNF at Lund 1952, proposing that Archbishop Brilioth (right), *should preside*

towards those higher Anglicans, who were to occupy so much of his life in future negotiations.

Christian Perfection

Flew's greatest book is *The Idea of Perfection in Christian Theology*. His Fernley-Hartley Lecture, *Jesus and His Church*, sold far more copies in his lifetime and was in demand for almost a quarter of a century, but it is significant that the Oxford University Press brought out the second edition of *The Idea of Perfection*, after thirty-four years, in 1968. Churchmanship is at the mercy of changing fashions; spirituality is of perennial interest and worth.

The book raises the questions: 'What is the Christian ideal for the present life? And is it the will of God that by His grace we should attain it?' [5] The author examines and criticises the treatment of Perfection in the writings of twenty-one different periods of Christian history, with especial attention to developments within Protestantism.

He begins with the teaching of Jesus for which he confines himself to the first three gospels. He has to face two problems. The lesser for his theme is implicit rather than explicit in his exposition – to what extent do the gospels preserve the *ipsissima verba* of Jesus? He turns this neatly by pointing out that 'the more doubt we may have that the saying derives from Jesus Himself, the more certain we may be that the saying proves the existence of a conviction in the community'.[6] Thus the idea of perfection remains for our investigation.

The more serious difficulty is that of the apocalyptic language attributed to Jesus. If he believed that the final crisis of the existing order was imminent, how could he proclaim an ideal which seems to demand growth and progress in time? If his perfectionism was related to a

[5] *The Idea of Perfection*, p. xi.
[6] *Ibid.*, p. 3.

conviction that the end of all things was at hand must it not be fantastically irrelevant to continuing life in unborn civilisations, which he could not contemplate? On the contrary, Flew maintains that apocalyptic is an especially good medium for the prophet of perfection, for it expresses, in a phrase of von Hügel's, 'the junction between the simultaneity of God and the successiveness of man'.

> It teaches that the ultimate ideal of man is the pure gift of God; that, in the present age, forgiveness, communion with God, a life of love among men, a life lived on the level of a miracle – all flow from the infinite love of the Father. It proclaims that Perfection is never merely individual and that the ideal for the race must be a society knit together by communion with God. The ideal is inextricably bound with the Person of Jesus and the thought of His Cross. And finally it teaches that since this world is God's world, the history of man upon this planet will end worthily of Him Who made the world and guided its destiny.[7]

Jesus's idea of perfection is, simply, the Kingdom of God. St Paul does not use the term, but Flew finds in his letters the identical eight elements, which he distinguishes in the synoptic gospel of the Kingdom:

(1) The final victory of God is the victory of love with a supernatural quality in it miraculous as the raising of Jesus from the dead.
(2) The love shed abroad in human hearts is God's gift.
(3) It is communion with God.
(4) It points forward to a perfected society.
(5) It admits of infinite progress, and yet it is a life that can be lived in Corinth or Thessalonica in the first century because it is God's will and God's gift.

[7] *Ibid.*, p. 40.

(6) It accepts all the goodness that there is in human nature and is glad in it; and it is not blind to the life and work of the present world.

(7) Love is a life founded on the personality of Jesus Himself; indeed the love wherewith one Christian loves another can be called the love of Christ Himself.

(8) Love is linked with the Cross.[8]

All other writings both in the New Testament and in subsequent Church history are tested by this eight-fold norm. *Hebrews* is compared by Flew to a mediaeval Cathedral with three different styles of architecture. Its ground-plan of the human life and death of Jesus is cruciform, but then we may trace the idea of priesthood, taken over from Judaism and transformed by Alexandrian exegesis, while 'crowning and dominating the whole is the Platonic doctrine of the two worlds'.[9] Many of the points discovered in Jesus and Paul are repeated in *Hebrews*, but the book has its own stern and rigorist view of the seeming impossibility of a second repentance:

> For if we sin wilfully after that we have received the knowledge of the truth, there remaineth no more sacrifice for sins but a certain fearful expectation of judgement (*Hebrews* 10:26).

Flew softens this with the help of Moffatt. The 'dead works, from which there is no second repentance' are those 'occupations, interests and pleasures', which remove a man completely from Christian life and faith. There is a distinction in *Hebrews* between mortal and venial sins, though as the Christian becomes mature, he should increasingly put away the latter. The author is very much a perfectionist, though there is a tension in his thought between the 'now' of Platonic reality into

[8] *Ibid.*, p. 72.
[9] *Ibid.*, p. 75.

which through Christ we have already entered, and the full consummation of the parousia, the imminence of which should encourage believers to yet more urgent endeavours of love and good works as they see the Day drawing near.

The Johannine writings are relegated to the end of Flew's consideration of the New Testament. In contrast to his great contemporary, William Temple, Flew's Christianity was Pauline rather than Johannine, and it is by no means certain that he would have endorsed the verdict of his own pupil, C. K. Barrett, that the fourth evangelist was 'perhaps the greatest theologian in all the history of the Church'.[10] Not that he fails to recognise John's stupendous achievement. But although it is in the fourth gospel and the epistles of John that there is stated the doctrine that God is love and that there is possible a new birth into an eternal life of communion with him in which sin is overcome, Flew remarks the absence of any emphasis on growth in the spiritual life.[11] He also discerns the shadow of a Stoic *apatheia* over the Johannine Jesus, whose tears are more a 'refutation of Docetism than the sob of a wounded heart', and a certain 'detached, intellectualist, abstractive tendency' which may have unfortunate consequences in the future development of the Christian ideal.[12]

In the sub-apostolic and patristic period the purity of the synoptic teaching is alloyed by alien ideas and by a lack of immediate inspiration. 'Somehow the sense of God has grown dim, the consciousness of present communion is not so joyful and convincing; an excellent and worthy moralism is usurping the place of that splendid awareness of the perpetual activity of Christ which still makes the New Testament the most interesting and the

[10] C. K. Barrett, *The Gospel According to St John* (SPCK 1955), p. 114.
[11] *The Idea of Perfection*, p. 116.
[12] *Ibid.*, p. 117.

most influential book in the world.'[13] Yet there is still
the claim that Christ casts out sin and makes perfection
possible. But this is so often conceived of as primarily
deliverance from bodily corruption and the lusts of the
flesh. Clement of Alexandria is perhaps the most attractive of the Fathers, and in so many ways is a kindred spirit
of St Paul. 'There are few of the Christian writers of that
age, or indeed of any age, who see with such clearness as
Clement that the gift of communion with God brings with
it not only a reinforcement of heavenly virtues but also a
transfiguration of the common task.'[14] Love to God and
man is the goal of the moral life; prayer is a means of its
attainment. In his account of Clement's teaching on
prayer, it is clear that A. L. Lilley's chapter in *Prayer in
Christian Theology* has become part of Flew's inmost mind;
for once he does not acknowledge the debt in this place.
Prayer is a constant conversation with God, which is not
to be thought of as pagan incantation to call down
earthly blessings or divorced from the pursuit of knowledge. Flew describes Clement's conception of the end in
words of Charles Wesley:

> The o'erwhelming power of saving grace,
> The sight that veils the seraph's face;
> The speechless awe that dares not move,
> And all the silent heaven of love.

Clement is a philosopher and makes no extravagant
claims, but it follows that his Christian gnostic ought to
be sinless and filled with love for Lord and brother. Yet
Clement cannot be acquitted of the charge of 'disparag-
ing the sweet human affections and the common joys
of men. Thus marriage is said to be superior to celibacy
merely because it offers so many more temptations to

[13] *Ibid.*, p. 121.
[14] *Ibid.*, p. 139.

surmount. . . . The human life of Jesus is emptied of the emotions of courage, fear, anger, zeal, joy, desire.'[15] At times his view of God is of the Greek Apathetic and Impassible, but this dwells uneasily and in contradiction with the Hebraic notion of the Living God, 'prevenient, active, forthgoing, infinitely persevering in His love for his children'. But ultimately Clement takes his stand 'on the gospel of infinite and inescapable Love that will not let us go'.[16]

Origen is more of a theologian of the Cross than Clement, but his doctrine of grace is defective in his mingling of mysticism, asceticism and Stoicism.[17] The perfect Christian has renounced the outward and visible world and the emotions of mankind. Origen is the philosopher of the mystic ascent and the precursor of monasticism. But he makes an interesting distinction between 'to sin' and 'to be a sinner'. Conversion to Christ means that a man is no longer a sinner, though he may still sin. His heart will not become so pure that no thoughts of evil can stain it. The Jebusites still dwell with the sons of Judah in Jerusalem! Yet the prophets and apostles were perfect, though it is necessary to distinguish between that perfection which is a state of victory over carnal lusts and passions and that which is triumph in spiritual warfare against demonic powers. The latter is consummated in mystical union, which may be attained in this life, though perhaps only in the intermittent experience of that Divine intoxication, which is more sober than sobriety.

Flew's chapter on monasticism shows a deep sympathy with 'the boldest organized attempt to attain to Christian perfection in all the long history of the Church'.[18] But

[15] *Ibid.*, pp. 148–9.

[16] *Ibid.*, p. 151.

[17] For a study of *Origen and the Doctrine of Grace*, see the work of that title by one of Flew's pupils, Benjamin Drewery, (Epworth Press 1960).

[18] *The Idea of Perfection*, p. 158.

again, the attempt does not represent the fullness of the ideal of the first three gospels. As it evolved in the West under the dominating influence of John Cassian, monachism is a way of solitariness. There is a moving insistence on the centrality of the Cross and of communion with the Crucified which in its entire renunciation of the world is not blind to love of the brotherhood. But it is usually the monastic brotherhood which is meant. For the world or the Church outside, the monk has little time and it is impossible to avoid the conclusion that for many of the pioneers, monasticism was the honours school of holiness and the rest of mankind, even the baptised, had to be content with an inferior degree, if indeed they were not ploughed altogether. This was always the danger. Yet generalisation is ill-advised and courts refutation. Flew quotes those who, in solitude, came tenderly to observe and passionately to love nature, and ends with the tale of the two rich brothers who became monks. One gave away everything at once, learned a trade and devoted himself to asceticism and prayer. The other used his riches gradually, over a period, in works of personal philanthropy to help the afflicted. The blessed Pambo pronounced them both equal in holiness.

The Homilies of Macarius the Egyptian, beloved of John Wesley, are not free from those defects which Flew has exposed in monasticism as a whole. He lacked the Christian humanism of Clement of Alexandria. Yet his work is redolent of longing for the apostolic life of obedience and holiness. And his Christo-centric mysticism of communion with God, not absorption into the Infinite, would, according to Flew, have been a better way than that of Augustine.

Flew, following his master, Herrmann, charges Augustine with forgetting the humanity of Jesus when he draws near to God. This provoked a sharp footnote of refutation in John Burnaby's *Amor Dei* (1938). In his text,

Burnaby regards it as a mistake to see 'in Augustine's moments of contemplative exaltation his ideal of Christian life in the world'.[19] Earlier, Flew shows how the great Latin Father offers to the pagan world, weary with its wars and the chaos of its jaded sensuality, the fullness of the ideal of a Christian society. Can this be attained on earth? In many of Augustine's statements it would seem that the kingdom of peace belongs to the eternal order. 'Here we watch and struggle'. Yet although there is no respite from conflict in this life, there is a 'measure of human perfection' possible, but as Flew says 'this perfection is of those who are pilgrims and strangers on the earth, not of those who are in perfect possession of their promised home'.[20]

Augustine dominated Western spirituality in the Middle Ages. Most of it may be interpreted as the reinforcement or intensification of his ideas, although the intellectual climate is as much responsible as his direct influence. Pseudo-Dionysius, the Areopagite, was a Neo-Platonist and his amazing vogue, from the sixth century to the sixteenth, contributed to the development of Augustines' mysticism. For him perfection is the plunge into the 'Darkness of Unknowing'. Flew dismisses his ideal as non-Christian. It has virtually no place for Christ.

Bernard of Clairvaux's spiritual teaching is centred on Jesus and the Passion. Yet when he comes to describe the higher attainments of contemplation, he deserts the Sacred Humanity. This is symptomatic of the two-fold weakness of the monastic ideal – it cannot really believe that there is true goodness in this world, and it sets the goal of the Christian life in so rarefied an atmosphere that it eludes almost every seeker. St Bernard's fourth stage of love is to love oneself for God's sake alone. 'If there be

[19] *Op. cit.*, p. 73.
[20] *The Idea of Perfection*, p. 209.

any who have experienced it, let them speak; for myself, I confess, it appears to me impossible.' [21]

And so we come to St Thomas Aquinas, of all theologians, the one 'most dominated by the thought of the ultimate perfection of mankind'.[22] As Flew searched the Latin pages of the *Summa contra Gentiles* and the *Summa Theologica* he would think of the boy going up from his native village to Monte Cassino. He abstracted four theses:

(1) The Contemplative is superior to the active life.
(2) Christian perfection consists in love and is attainable in this life. (Flew thinks that the discussion is vitiated by the neo-Platonic tendency to identify evil too exclusively with bodily desires and by discussions of the relative merits of those in religious orders.)
(3) God must be loved for his own sake (Cf. Bernard of Clairvaux).
(4) Full perfection is in the life beyond the grave. (Flew notes that Aquinas seems to contemplate a *solus cum solo* beatitude rather than the communion of saints, though this is corrected by other passages in his writings of which he does not seem to have realised the full consequences. 'The ideal which he sketches as realizable in the present life is, in this one respect at least, superior to the fuller beatitude in the life beyond.' [23]

The Reformation reacted strongly against what it regarded as the false monastic idea of perfection. Calvin denies the possibility of perfection in this life and thinks that the search for it is a dangerous delusion. The word may be applied to the virtue of the saints, only if it is qualified, as with Augustine, to include a recognition of their own imperfection. Luther is fundamental to

[21] In cant., Sermo 15.39 quoted by Flew, *The Idea of Perfection*, p. 223.
[22] *Ibid.*, p. 225.
[23] *Ibid.*, p. 243.

Protestant spirituality. True, he emphasises faith rather than deliverance from sin, but his rediscovery of the historical Jesus, his debt to Tauler and the mystics, for whom union with Christ implied moral purification, and his liberating assertion that the Christian life is to be lived in secular callings and ordinary human relationships, constitute a revolution in Christian understanding. Calvinism carried this forward to victory. Flew contrasts the end of Dante's *Divina Commedia* with that of *Paradise Lost*. 'The soul is left by Dante in Paradise at the summit of contemplation; all speech fails; the vision itself is the momentary intuitive gaze of a soul laid to rest and despoiled of its own powers.' Milton, on the other hand, sees Adam and Eve sent out from Eden to an active life through which they may find 'a Paradise within'.'The world was all before them' and this is no barren wilderness, but a providential way.[24]

Flew discusses Ritschl's contention that there is a Lutheran doctrine of perfection. He finds this the product of what a later generation called 'wishful thinking'. Lutheranism marked a great revival of *religion* and of rediscovery of the givenness of faith, the undeserved, free mercy of God. But it neglected the command *Be ye holy, for I am holy*.

For the rest of his study, Flew becomes more selective. He does not consider the Counter-Reformation as such, though he has a section on the winsome St François de Sales, whose 'devout humanism' appeals to him. He refers to the great Carmelites only in passing. Quietism is one more instance of the pernicious effect of neo-Platonism. One feels that he is hurrying on to Methodism and discusses Fénelon, the Pietists, and William Law because they anticipate certain themes which Wesley was to take up and correct and harmonise. They are each, in some sense, a *preparatio Methodistica*. Quakerism

[24] *Ibid.*, pp. 253–4.

receives fuller treatment and, deservedly, because, unlike
the orthodox Reformers, it taught a holiness which was
not imputed but real, and 'returned wholeheartedly to
the attitude of the New Testament'.[25]

Flew observes that Quakerism is not *sui generis*. It arose
'out of the comparison between the prevailing poverty of
the contemporary religion and the riches of the New
Testament experience'. Also it 'was indebted, far more
than its leaders were aware, to the mystical tradition of
the Church'. Flew finds even in George Fox, and certainly
in the systematic formulations of the Quaker theologian,
Robert Barclay, the difficulty of reconciling the doctrine
of the Inner Light with the accepted dogma of Total
Depravity. There is a 'vicious dualism' as a result of the
disparagement of man's own natural powers. Reason is
helpless and man must receive the Light in entire
passivity. O for an hour of the Cambridge Platonists!

Yet Flew is able to summarise the distinctive Quaker
contribution in his characteristic way. There is, first, a
sense of victorious living; we need not be the slaves of
sin. Second, there is a social holiness, as relevant to the
fixing of farm-labourers' wages as to individual morality.
Third, the recognition of the divine seed in every man,
led, in spite of a misguided anthropology to 'a catholicity
of spirit, a desire to discover the good in other races and
other faiths and a new sense of the sacredness of human
personality'. Fourth, the Cross was central; and it was
' "no dead fact, stranded on the shore of the oblivious
years", but an inward living experience in the heart of
the believer, refashioning his life into perfect love'.[26]

One of Flew's longest historical chapters is on
Methodism. But it must not be imagined that as he
examines the teaching of his own communion he is blind
with self-satisfaction, as though all that had gone before

[25] *Ibid.*, p. 282.
[26] *Ibid.*, pp. 290–1.

was desert until Wesley came to teach the perfect doctrine of perfection! There have been Wesleyan theologians who have been guilty of the uncritical adulation of their founder and his works; but not Flew. Yet he does not go to the other extreme and, after the fashion of some – and not only Methodists – become hyper-sensitive to the faults of his own spiritual family. He was no man to be embarrassed by his own mother.

He relates Methodism to its past and shows how the doctrine derives from the catholicity of the Wesleys and gathers up the whole mystical tradition of the great Church. But it was the experiences of the early Methodists themselves which were the raw material of Wesley's teaching. Here Flew returns to the sources of his first paper to the London Society for the Study of Religion in 1918.[27] He gives extracts from some typical testimonies all of which show that the experience, which is communion with God, is never independent of the Jesus of the Gospels. It is communicable, 'but only by those who already have it'. There is nearly always a preliminary period of acute distress. In the case of John Haime this lasted for twenty years, during which time he still preached, and fruitfully; but so long an agony is exceptional. The experience is not, *pace* Pusey, 'justification by feeling'; it has an intellectual as well as an emotional content. It is followed by ethical results.[28]

The above is a description of the regenerate life according to the experience of the early Methodists. It seemed to Wesley that it was a sheer implication of that experience that those who shared it must not remain satisfied with their present state but must press on to perfect love. Wesley's works leave one in no doubt that Christian perfection is love, which includes the keeping of all the commandments.

[27] See above, p. 43f.
[28] *Ibid.*, p. 316–23.

So far, no one could legitimately quarrel with Wesley. Where difficulties arise is in Wesley's statement that 'A Christian is so far perfect as not to commit sin'.[29] There is ambiguity here and inconsistency. In this context Wesley means by 'sin' the 'voluntary transgression of a known law of God, which it was within our power to obey'. Wesley never deals satisfactorily with the problems, for his perfectionism, of involuntary transgressions and mistakes. Worse still, he not only claims that the experience of 'the Great Salvation' is instantaneous, he implies that, if a man has received it, then through a particular testimony of the Holy Spirit in his heart, he will be assured of the fact:

> If a man be deeply and fully convinced, after justification, of inbred sin; if he then experience a gradual mortification of sin, and afterwards an entire renewal in the image of God; if to this change, immensely greater than that wrought before he was justified, be added a clear, direct witness of the renewal; I judge it as impossible this man should be deceived therein, as that God should lie.[30]

Wesley never claimed this 'great salvation' for himself. 'Was it some fastidiousness', asks Flew, 'some half-unconscious suspicion that avowal would be perilous to the health of his soul?'

The strength and impressiveness of the doctrine lie in its universality. 'This is no esoteric message for the few.' It is a gospel for ordinary, suffering men and women. More than in any other teaching, with the possible exception of Quakerism, it is related to the Crucified. And it is not merely individualistic.

But there are defects. One is an inadequate analysis of the nature of sin. Wesley's psychology is at fault here, for he seems to disregard the unconscious. Sin, to him,

29 *Works*, xi 376, quoted by Flew, p. 325.
30 *Works*, xi 401–2, quoted *Ibid.*, p. 328.

is a *thing* 'which has to be taken out of a man, like a cancer or a rotten tooth'.[31] But he ignores the sin which we *are*.

Flew blames Wesley's Augustinianism. There is a paradox in the doctrine of total depravity. In its whole-sale condemnation of human nature it does not pay sufficient regard to the subtlety of self-will. It identifies sin 'too exclusively with concupiscence'.[32]

Flew finds a confusion in Wesley's use of the word 'assurance'. In the New Testament it applies to our certainty about God and his fatherly love for us in Christ. We dare not be as sure of ourselves as we are of him. The distinction is illustrated in the last words of a Methodist minister, unknown to Flew, who died in 1943. Asked if he had any doubts, he replied, 'I have plenty about myself, but none about my Saviour'.

At the end of his chapter, Flew returns to his constant criticism of evangelical asceticism, that it was blind to the beauties of this world and of ordinary human life. This led to a damaging division between sacred and secular. Even the Wesley hymns explore the intercourse of the soul with God more successfully than they do the relations of men with one another. And so to a favourite gobbet from Maltby!

Flew continues with studies of Schleiermacher and Ritschl, for which his German training had equipped him. He claims that Schleiermacher carried over the achieve-ment of eighteenth-century Methodism in the everyday life of the Church, into the realms of systematic theo-logical thought.[33] Yet his doctrine of sin is inadequate, though for the opposite reason from Wesley's; it is too optimistic, owing, we may suspect, to a deficient sense of the holiness of God. Nor does he make the Cross central.

---

[31] E. H. Sugden, *Standard Sermons*, ii. 459.
[32] *Ibid.*, p. 335.
[33] *Ibid.*, p. 373.

Christ is much more the supreme ideal than a historic person, and Flew is quick to see the explanation in his disparagement of the first three gospels and concentration upon the fourth! Schleiermacher's account of prayer is strangely unsatisfying and narrowed down to thanksgiving and resignation. There is no understanding of an active adventure of communion with the living and transcendent God.

With Ritschl we are back to a theology of the Kingdom of God, which, for him, is the *summum bonum*; for the individual, perfection is dominion over the world, which Flew expounds sympathetically on the grounds that man is greater than nature, the son of God revealed out of the groaning and travail of the whole creation. This lordship is expressed in patience, humility, prayer, which, for Ritschl, is thanksgiving alone, and moral fidelity to one's vocation. Perfection is no barren search for sinlessness. 'It rather means that our moral achievement or life work in connection with the kingdom of God should, however limited in amount be conceived as possessing the quality of a whole in its own order'.[34]

Flew maintains that Ritschl's is the most systematic of all the doctrines of perfection considered. It suffers from his denial of any place to metaphysics in theology. Flew says that 'if the activity of the mind on ultimate questions is banished from our conception of the ideal for the life of man on this earth, the ideal itself cannot be kept sweet or pure'. This is extremely interesting in view of the anti-metaphysical writings of Paul van Buren and others in the 1960s. Ritschl does not understand human despair or the need for great deliverance from intolerable distress, that is, his doctrine of sin is defective; similarly with his doctrine of grace, the kingdom depends too much on human effort. Above all, his doctrine of communion with God is inadequate. He suspected the

[34] Quoted *ibid.*, p. 387.

erotic piety of the middle ages, the mysticism of Bernard of Clairvaux. Metaphors of union with God are anathema to him and the notion of immediacy is disallowed. God reveals himself through the historical Jesus and in the law and promise contained in his word, but in all this there is lack of passion, lack of love to God and Christ. It is all of the will, cold and ethical.

In his conclusion, Flew refers to P. T. Forsyth and his exhilarating but dangerous epigrams:

> Perfection is not sanctity but faith.
> It is not sins that damn but the sin into which sins settle down.
> It is better to trust in God in humiliated repentance than to revel in the sense of sinlessness.

Do these really take account of the facts of sin in believers? 'A Church dignitary may be irritable; a life-long Christian deplorably egoistic. The main problem is whether the Christian religion is to promise release from such ingrained habits of mind, or whether, under cover of some fine phrase or delusive epigram, it is to acquiesce.' [35]

Forsyth was a disciple of Ritschl, but transcended his master in 'his overwhelming sense of power of the Cross'.

Flew's broad conclusion is that 'the seeking of an ideal that is realisable in this world is essential to Christianity'.[36] The English Church in its privileged, respectable piety had failed to inculcate this longing, which is why Quakerism, Methodism and the Oxford Movement reacted against it in their different ways. Flew then establishes eight principles of a positive doctrine:

[35] *Ibid.*, pp. 395–6. The quotations are from P. T. Forsyth's *Christian Perfection* (1899).
[36] *Ibid.*, p. 398.

*At Lund with the Metropolitan Juhanon of the Mar Thoma
Syrian Church* (left), *whom he had taught at Bangalore in 1921*

The Chapel, Wesley House, Cambridge, as it was from 1930 to 1968

(1) The Christian ideal must span both worlds and must recognise their true inter-relationship.

(2) The Christian life is the gift of God.

(3) No limits can be set to the moral or spiritual attainments of a Christian in the present life. There must always be a 'beyond'. 'The one person who cannot be perfect is the person who claims to be.'

(4) The good life has many realms; it is a social life and includes the pursuit of truth and beauty as well as moral goodness.

(5) Daily work is a divine vocation.

(6) The ideal life is 'moment-by-moment holiness'. Here Flew introduces a theme prominent in Caussade's *L'Abandon à la Providence Divin*. The English Benedictine Dom John Chapman made this discovery towards the end of his tortured course.

(7) There must be a sense of personal unworthiness.

(8) There is no escaping the Cross; the 'dying out of the temporal realm into the eternal'.

Flew ends with a further assertion of the supremacy of the first three gospels.

The foregoing should give some indication of the book's impressive scope. There is vast technical knowledge, yet somehow it is all related to the Methodist grocer at the corner shop in the 1930s struggling with his financial as well as spiritual accounts, trying to conquer his jealousy of his son or his dislike of his minister, wondering whether or not his following of Christ allows him to go to the theatre. There is also an understanding of theologians as men, an eye for human details and an instinct for beautiful passages.

Some particular judgements may need to be revised or supplemented in the light of more recent scholarship. Owen Chadwick's work on John Cassian implies that the desert father could have been treated even more amply and that his doctrine of perfection is of greater interest than Flew specifically states, in its denial of sinlessness in this life and its realisation that the 'perfect' who have overcome the grosser faults are more conscious than the rest of the gravity of sin and of the need of unceasing penitence, though not as a constant bringing back into the memory of old sins of the flesh, like a dog returning to his vomit.[37]

Werner Jaeger has shown that the so-called *Homilies of Macarius the Egyptian* were not from a fourth-century Egyptian 'desert father' but a fifth-century Syrian monk, whose teaching has close affinities with Gregory of Nyssa. As Albert Outler excitedly infers, this gives Wesley a 'somewhat curious and roundabout linkage' with Orthodox monasticism which Flew was in no position to exploit, but even more it makes one wish that *The Idea of Perfection* had found room for a chapter on Eastern spirituality.[38]

Among others, Flew's own pupils Gordon Rupp and Philip Watson have carried Luther studies far beyond the stage of 1934. Flew's chapter on 'The Reformation' would be larger now, and, had he himself been writing twenty years later, would have included some of the material on the Protestant understanding of justification and sanctification presented in the report on *The Catholicity of Protestantism*.[39] There might have been more stress on Luther's insistence on movement and growth in the Christian life. 'Faith for Luther is, as in the New Testament, not one of a long agenda of virtues, but a whole dimension of Christian existence, with hope and love the fountain from which the Christian life must

---

[37] Owen Chadwick, *John Cassian* (Cambridge 1950 and 1968). See 1968 edn., pp. 103–4.

[38] W. Jaeger, *Two Rediscovered Works of Ancient Christian Literature: Gregory of Nyssa and Macarius* (Leiden 1954). See A. C. Outler ed., *John Wesley*, p. 9, n. 26 (Oxford 1964).

[39] Edited by R. Newton Flew and Rupert E. Davies and published by Lutterworth Press in 1950.

spring.' [40] But it is doubtful whether the judgement on Lutheranism, which is that of Harnack, would have been radically altered even in view of the questions raised by the example of Dietrich Bonhoeffer.

Puritan studies, too, have advanced since 1934, and again Flew's pupils have had some modest, though in no sense a pre-eminent, share in them. Richard Greenham, Vicar of Dry Drayton in the reign of Elizabeth I, was convinced that there could be no absolute unspottedness in this life. 'Albeit to that perfection which the Scripture taketh for soundness, truth and sincerity of heart, which is void of careless remissness we may come.... Let us not seek to be more righteous than we can be. But let us comfort ourselves in the truth of our hearts and singleness of our desires to serve God, because he is God; and so shall we be accepted of God.' William Perkins, the most eminent Puritan theologian of the Elizabethan period, like Bernard of Clairvaux, distinguished four degrees of God's love – 'an effectual calling' which unites the repentant sinner with Christ's mystical body; justification, sanctification, 'whereby such as believe, being delivered from the tyranny of sin, are by little and little renewed in holiness and righteousness'; glorification, which begins at death, 'but is not accomplished and made perfect before the last day of judgement'.[41] This caution is very different from the passionate immediacy of the Methodist ideal. John Preston, 'Prince Charles's Puritan Chaplain', to quote the title of Irvonwy Morgan's account of him, is a theologian of the Divine love and argues, from the Geneva Bible version of the command to Abraham in Genesis 17:1, that perfection is integrity of heart and can co-exist with those infirmities which are an inevitable part of our humanity. Otherwise the second

[40] Gordon Rupp, *Luther's Progress to the Diet of Worms* 1521 (SCM 1951), p. 73.
[41] *William Perkins*, ed. Ian Breward (Sutton Courtenay Press), pp. 224 ff.

Adam would be less powerful to instil grace than the first to communicate sin, and the work of God in the new creation would come short of that in the beginning, when the Lord looked on everything that he had made, and behold it was very good. Christ implants in the heart a perfect seed, which wants only growth to become a perfect flower. Its growth will be menaced by the hazards of climate and many pests, but it will be strong enough to resist them all, unless we are to make nonsense of our claims for Divine grace. The perfect man is cleansing and purifying himself throughout his whole life and repents radically from each lapse, whereas the one in whom evil reigns wallows in his sin 'as a swine in the mire'.[42]

The main difference is between those Puritans who are cautiously realistic and dread even the semblance of human presumptuousness, and those so possessed with the love of God that their longing for him and his goodness breaks all bounds and they will set limits neither to their desire nor to his redemption. The whole issue is that of the place of love in Puritan theology. Of course, not all those who have been on fire with the love of God have shown that concern and compassion for their fellow-man, which, according to St John is its essential principle of verification, while, in theory – and this is Luther's doctrine – a change of status through faith in God is the only possible source of good works and the boldness of faith itself should free us from any inhibitions in the quest for perfection. But it was in 1628 that John Earle wrote of the 'she precise hypocrite . . . so taken up with faith she has no room for charity' and so sympathetic a scholar as Dr G. F. Nuttall admits that the criticism has force against Puritan piety as a whole.[43] It is in the

---

[42] For a fuller account of Preston's teaching see Gordon S. Wakefield, *Puritan Devotion* (Epworth 1957), pp. 137–9.

[43] Geoffrey F. Nuttall, *Visible Saints* (Blackwell 1957), p. 162.

mysterious underworld of the sects, the spirituality of which still needs to be studied, and which erupted in the Parliamentarian armies, that we may find a gospel of perfect love.

W. F. Lofthouse in a review of *The Idea of Perfection* in the *Journal of Theological Studies*, which is a brilliant pastiche of percipience and obtuseness, argued that 'the perfection considered is that of a man, of a Christian' and there is insufficient regard paid to the Christian society, the Church, or indeed to the social aspect of the question as a whole. It is difficult to see 'how a man can be good apart from a good society, or even nourish a genuinely good will. How can a statesman be unselfish when he has to press the interests of his country against her rivals or a tradesman when he has to gain the custom for which his competitors are scheming?' If these questions are outside the range of Flew's authors, are not they and their answer implicit in the synoptic teaching about the Kingdom of God? Lofthouse seems to suggest that Flew should have developed still further the principal doctrines of those writings by which he sets such store.

There is irony in the criticism, since the rest of Flew's theological life was to be devoted to the study of the nature of the Church. It also seems unfair since throughout *The Idea of Perfection*, it is treated as axiomatic that there is no holiness but social holiness. Yet Lofthouse's question remains to nag the theologian of the present day, heir of Niebuhr. He regards it as 'significant' that the Council of Trent is not mentioned and, at the risk of seeming churlish, we may agree that the complete study of the subject demands some treatment of the Counter-Reformation. The most recent scholarship would seem to distinguish between the Catholic Reformation, the Counter-Reformation and the Council, and in his Birkbeck lectures, Outram Evennett managed to avoid all reference to the last.[44] But it would have been

---

[44] H. Outram Evennett, *The Spirit of the Counter-Reformation* (edited

good to read Flew on St Teresa, St John of the Cross and the Ignatian *Exercises* as well as on the underlying concept of the Church.

The reason may well be, apart from limitations of space and time, that Flew deliberately regarded his *magnum opus* as the Protestant counterpart to Kenneth E. Kirk's *The Vision of God* and that he was content to leave sixteenth-century Catholic piety to him. More than once Flew refers to Kirk's 'great book', and there is much agreement between the two works.

The Vision of God, a writing up of the Bampton Lectures of 1928, was published in 1931, three years before *The Idea of Perfection*. Kirk's scholarship is phenomenally massive and his style flows with a consummate ease, which might make the literary critic prefer it to Flew's, who wrote as a preacher. But though Kirk's volume must be ranked as one of the outstanding works of twentieth-century British theology, and has a grandeur which cannot be denied, it may suffer in comparison with *The Idea of Perfection* on two counts. Kirk is a canonist and his mysticism has – perhaps inevitably and rightly – to compete with his moral theology; what is more he does not like Protestantism and finds it hard to write with sympathy of any Protestant author. Flew, on the other hand, though Protestantism is his particular field and he judges all his authors by his interpretations of the synoptists and Paul, rather than by later ecclesiasticism, has an intense and personal love for the Catholic tradition. *The Idea of Perfection* is more genuinely and nobly Catholic than *The Vision of God*.

It may also be questioned as to whether Kirk is justified in defining the *summum bonum* as 'The Vision of God'. He makes out a strong and plausible case. The concept is anti-Pelagian, since God alone can 'present

---

with postscript by John Bossy, Cambridge, 1968). For an explanation of the omission, see pp. 133 ff.

himself to the clarified vision' and supply 'the light wherewith he may be seen'. It carries the mind inevitably back to Christ, 'who brought God more vividly before the eyes of his contemporaries than any other has ever done' and in whom the Divine glory is revealed, while the rules of worship and of conduct which it inspires are delivered both from rigorism and formalism. Kirk is, however, somewhat embarrassed by the fact that the beatitude of the pure in heart stands without echo in the synoptic tradition, and some may wonder whether the concept of the vision of God as the *summum bonum* does not belong to neo-Platonism rather than to the New Testament. Flew does not make this criticism of Kirk. That was left to his pupil, A. Raymond George, who after a most careful examination of passages concludes that the metaphor of vision is discouraged in the synoptic gospels and that it is better to speak of 'personal intercourse' or, as George himself prefers for the New Testament as a whole, 'Communion with God'.[45] Flew's terminology leaves him free to instance the varieties of language used in Christian history to describe the *summum bonum* and to construct his conclusions by doing justice to them all.

All the same, the title of Flew's Cambridge University sermon in 1942 is *The Vision of God* and in it he accepts Kirk's thesis without demur.[46] He begins with a striking illustration from C. F. Andrews, which had come via T. R. Glover. It tells of an Indian woman, measuring herself along one of the great Indian trunk roads in a series of prostrations, eight-hundred to a mile. When she was asked where she was going, she named a shrine in the distant Himalayas (Flew would say Himlāayas), a thousand miles away, 'where from a cleft in the valley

---

[45] A. Raymond George, *Communion with God in the New Testament*, (Epworth Press 1953) pp. 93–105; also 166–8. See Kenneth E. Kirk, *The Vision Of God* (Longmans 1931), pp. 94 ff.

[46] See *The Cambridge Review*, 2nd May, 1942.

a breath of natural gas would burst into flame and vanish – a fleeting appearance of divinity'. She gave her reason for the agonising pilgrimage in two words: '*Uski* (sic) *Darshan* – Vision of Him!'

Flew admits that 'we may call (the Christian vision of God) the Christian experience if we will'. He describes five marks of it— it is mediated, not immediate; it is for the pure of heart, i.e. the forgiven who incessantly seek holiness; it is shared; it is met in the common encounters and decisions of daily life, most of all through suffering; and it is sealed with the mark of victory. He then goes on to ask: 'Is it for all, or only for the few?', and concludes that it must be universal because of the very nature of the ministry of Jesus, the cry 'Abba, Father' and the seeking of the lost sheep until it is found, and because the response which Jesus requires is faith, which is no esoteric attitude, but a necessary concomitant of human relationships in everyday life. 'The very comprehensiveness of the Christian experience becomes an argument that everyone is capable of it.'

The sermon cannot confine itself to metaphors of vision and would seem susceptible to Raymond George's argument that since other words are not only available but necessary to do full justice to the Christian experience and this language is used sparingly in the foundation documents of Christianity, it cannot bear the weight put upon it by Kirk and the Catholic tradition. Kirk's statement that 'Christianity had come into the world with a double purpose, to offer men the vision of God and to call them to the pursuit of that vision',[47] is historically wrong on the evidence of the earliest preaching.

In spite of Kirk's disclaimers, the language of vision carries with it some of those perils which Flew has noted in *The Idea of Perfection*. The emphasis may be on the human search rather than the Divine gift, it encourages

[47] *The Vision of God*, p. 1.

a piety of mystical purgation, sometimes of harsh and rigorist renunciation of the world God made, and may repudiate human relationships and love of neighbour in search of a solitary salvation in which the work of Christ is but an elementary stage. The fact that the introductory illustration to Flew's sermon is from Hinduism and that the concept of the Vision of God is compatible with religions very different from Christianity should serve as warning. The Hebraic background of the New Testament with its priority of the Word and of hearing, demands a more dynamic concept and the Christianity of our age, with its antecedents in Biblical theology and repudiation of idealism, has, without altogether being aware of it, made common cause with contemporary philosophy to dethrone certain presuppositions which Flew and Kirk both shared.

> Moore was wrong (his critics continue) to use the quasi aesthetic imagery of vision in conceiving the good. Such a view, conceiving the good on the analogy of the beautiful, would seem to make possible a contemplative attitude on the part of the moral agent, whereas the point about this person is that he is essentially and inescapably an *agent*. The image whereby to understand morality, it is argued, is not the image of vision but the image of movement.[48]

This passage is from Iris Murdoch's *The Sovereignty of Good*, from a paper called, significantly in our context, 'The Idea of Perfection', in which she seeks to rehabilitate the metaphor of vision. It is, she claims, the metaphor which anyone without philosophical prejudice would use to describe say, the change in a woman's attitude to her daughter-in-law from contempt ('my poor son has married a silly vulgar girl') to love and admiration. The

---

[48] Iris Murdoch, *The Sovereignty of Good* (Routledge and Kegan Paul, 1970), p. 3. The reference is to the Cambridge moralist, G. E. Moore.

change is not in will, movement, outward activity as the existentialists-behaviourists would say. 'M *looks* at D, she attends to D, she focuses her attention . . . M stops seeing D as "bumptious" and sees her as "gay", etc.' [49]

The metaphor of vision and the idea of perfection are closely related. 'Where virtue is concerned we often apprehend more than we clearly understand and *grow by looking*.' 'What M is *ex hypothesi* attempting to do is not just to see D accurately but to see her justly or lovingly.' [50]

Iris Murdoch is writing as an agnostic philosopher but it would be easy, in this argument, to dismiss her as a Platonist and therefore as representative of that school, which among Christians has obscured the Biblical testimony with ideas leading to some of the worst excesses of spiritual history. But before we do this, we should bear in mind that she is seeking to refute those linguistic philosophers, who, however cathartic the astringency of their analysis, have, in the extremes of their logic, been the progenitors, not simply of anti-religion, but of nihilism and 'meaninglessness'. Also she is trying to base her moral philosophy on a truly human psychology in a counter to behaviourism and she draws from aesthetic experience and not simply from science. The notorious defect of Biblical theology has been its distrust of *analogies*, and its repudiation of any point of contact with the richness of metaphysical speculation and the wider life of man. The metaphor of vision may not have been paramount in the first Christian preaching; but it was there, waiting to be used as Christianity broke out into the classical world and it could be refurbished for our time. Any one set of symbols may be abused and needs correction by others, as is equally the case with the more activist language of the Bible. Perhaps a task of the future will be to provide what J. E. Fison once

[49] *Op. cit.*, pp. 22-3.
[50] *Op. cit.*, pp. 23, 31.

desired – 'a synthesis of Dr Kirk's *The Vision of God* and Dr Newton Flew's *The Idea of Perfection*'.[51]

Those with whom Iris Murdoch is arguing are evidence that the ideas of perfection and perfect love have received short shrift in the prevailing philosophical climate. Freudian psychology has made us suspicious of claims of individual sanctity; we know, as Lofthouse did, that the perfection of each in some sense demands the perfection of all, while existentialism is not congenial to teleology or an undue examination of motive and intent. Many have been haunted by the awesome example of Dietrich Bonhoeffer and his 'involvement' in the plot to kill Hitler:

> I remember a conversation I had in America thirteen years ago with a young French pastor. We were asking ourselves quite simply what we wanted to do with our lives. He said he would like to become a saint (and I think it is quite likely that he did become one). At the time I was very impressed, but I disagreed with him, and said, in effect, that I should like to learn to have faith. For a long time I did not realise the depth of the contrast. I thought I could acquire faith by trying to live a holy life, or something like it. I suppose I wrote *The Cost of Discipleship* as the end of that path. Today I can see the dangers of that book, though I still stand by what I wrote.
>
> I discovered later, and I am still discovering right up to this moment that it is only by living completely in this world that one learns to have faith. One must completely abandon any attempt to make something of oneself, whether it be a saint or a converted sinner, or a churchman (a so-called priestly type!), a righteous man or an unrighteous one, a sick man or a healthy one. By this-worldliness I mean living unreservedly in life's duties, problems, successes and failures,

[51] *Scottish Journal of Theology*, Vol. 7, No. 2, June 1954, p. 202 in a review of A. Raymond George, *Communion with God in the New Testament*. Cf. J. E. Fison, *The Christian Hope* (Longmans 1954), p. 244 for a comparison of Kirk and Flew.

experiences and perplexities. In doing so we throw ourselves completely into the arms of God, taking seriously, not our own sufferings, but those of God, taking in the world – watching with Christ in Gethsemane. That, I think, is faith, that is *metanoia*; and that is how one becomes a man and a Christian (Cf. Jer. 45!). How can success make us arrogant, or failure lead us astray, when we share in God's sufferings through a life of this kind?[52]

This extract from a letter written on 21st July, 1944, the day after the unsuccessful assassination attempt, is one of the most characteristic passages of twentieth-century spirituality. To say that only a man from a Lutheran background could have written it, is not to try to evade the 'Copernican revolution' which it represents. It seems far from the preoccupation of an Ignatius Loyola or a Wesley with the saving of an individual soul, the finding of the way to heaven. To relate it to Flew's approach we may make four comments.

First, the whole direction of his argument in *The Idea of Perfection*, as of all his teaching, would make him sympathetic to the plea for 'worldly holiness' and for an unselfconscious moment-by-moment abandoning of the self to God in the midst of life. Second, he would have wanted to emphasise perhaps more than was possible for Bonhoeffer in the crisis of the Nazi *Gotterdämmerung*, the ambiguity of the New Testament, particularly the Johannine term *Kosmos* (world). The world is God's, he loves it, gave his Son to lead a fully human life within it, and yet the world is very evil and arrayed against God. The Nazis were 'of the world' in one sense, to oppose them in a worldly way meant using some of their own weapons of violence and annihilation. The fact that Bonhoeffer was put to death, and has become so symbolic a figure, does not free us from the appalling dilemma.

[52] Dietrich Bonhoeffer, *Letters and Papers from Prison* (SCM Press, 3rd ed., 1967), pp. 201–2.

Perhaps this is what constituted his Gethsemane. Ours may lead to a different issue. It in no way disputes the 'massive heroism' of his character to say that his action would have been wrong in almost any other context than his own and that the reasoning which led to it is not to be applied without question to situations which are vastly different from his.[53]

Thirdly, though this was not true of his life and personality as a whole, one feels that in the letter quoted, there may be too much emphasis on suffering and insufficient on love. In Bonhoeffer's circumstances, this was inevitable. In another's, the result could be masochism rather than Christianity. The purpose of the Christian life is not to suffer with God in the world, but to be united with Christ in the continuing work of his love and goodness. That this will almost certainly mean suffering is obvious; but to be preoccupied with suffering, except when its imminence and intensity expel all other thoughts from the mind, is the road back to absorption in the self.[54] Dare we say, in spite of the interpretation of Luther noted above, that Bonhoeffer *in his thoughts* is too much dominated by faith at the expense of love?

Fourthly, Flew would undoubtedly have agreed with the Archbishop of Canterbury that, in spite of some of his assertions, Bonhoeffer's witness was sustained by the 'holy tradition'. 'Again and again in letters he is expressing dependence upon God through the medium of his own memory of hymns and psalms and music, the rhythm of the Christian year, the stuff of the worshipping tradition. . . . The religious language is the servant and the medium of the heroic faith which is finding God in the suffering, and the religion seems to pass beyond words

---

[53] Cf. Alasdair MacIntyre, 'God and the Theologians', *Encounter*, September 1963, pp. 3 ff. '. . . in our sort of society it becomes a form of practical atheism for it clothes ordinary liberal forms of life with the romantic unreality of a catacombic vocabulary.'

[54] Cf. Iris Murdoch, *The Sovereignty of Good*, especially p. 68.

into wordless contemplation. We are near to the mystical tradition and to what some older writers called "the terrible strength of the saints".' [55]

Bonhoeffer, the critic of 'religion', the Lutheran who would not have much patience with Methodist teaching about Perfection, has himself to be ranked with the saints and would illustrate some of Flew's contentions in any revised version of his treatise. Perhaps the last word should come from the wayward Lofthouse's review:

> Perfection is an attitude of mind; and if so (as every saint and lover really knows) attainment and non-attainment imply each other; they are one and the same thing; it is not a matter of 'relative here; perfect later on' –
> . . . To fill up his life, starve my own out I would – knowing which, I know that my service is *perfect*.

The Church

The Fernley-Hartley lecture, given annually at the Methodist Conference, is the fruit of the amalgamation at Methodist union in 1932 of two trusts, the Fernley, deriving from the Wesleyan Methodist Church, the Hartley from the Primitive Methodist. The lecture itself lasts for an hour or so, and is expected to be but the synopsis or section of a considerable book. When Flew was invited to lecture at the 1938 Conference in Hull, he had already been Convener of a Conference Committee, set up in 1935, which reported to the Bradford Conference of 1937 on the nature of the Church. He was also fully engaged on the Faith and Order side of the ecumenical movement and was aware that until recently there had been a neglect of any consideration of the Church on the part of non-Roman scholars though the

[55] A. M. Ramsey, *Sacred and Secular* (Longmans 1965), pp. 52–3.

arrears were being made up.[56] The fundamental question was 'Did Jesus intend the Church?'. This he set himself to answer.

Before doing so, he restated it in more realistic form. On the New Testament evidence Jesus could hardly have worked out the relationship to Judaism of any community he gathered around him, much less devised its detailed organisation or forms of worship.

> Instead of asking 'Did Jesus found the Church?' or 'Did Jesus organize a Church?' we should ask whether Jesus directed His teaching to a particular community, and whether His ministry had in view the formation of a community as one of His dominant aims. If we are driven by the facts to an affirmative answer, we should also inquire whether His teaching enables us to descibe the community which He has in view with any degree of definiteness, so as to determine its characteristic marks, its essence, and abiding idea.[57]

But, first, it is necessary to consider one of the most prominent of all the ideas of Jesus. The word for Church occurs but twice in the four Gospels, both times in *St Matthew*; but the phrase 'the Kingdom of God', or 'of Heaven' is in constant synoptic use. Traditional exegesis, both Catholic and Protestant, has identified the Kingdom with the Church. But this is not justified by the Hebraic background of the phrase, in which the

---

[56] In an article in *Christendom* Vol. IV, 1, he was able to list William Adams Brown, *Your Church and Mine* (1935), A. C. Headlam, *The Doctrine of the Church and the Christian Reunion* (1911), H. L. Goudge, *The Church of England and Reunion* (1938), A. M. Ramsey, *The Gospel and the Catholic Church* (1936), and three Cambridge Presbyterians, John Oman, *The Church and the Divine Order* (1911), C. A. Anderson Scott, *The Church: Its Worship and Sacraments* (1927), and P. Carnegie Simpson, *The Evangelical Church Catholic* (1934).

[57] *Jesus and His Church* (Epworth Press 1938 edn.), pp. 25–6.

Kingdom of God means his kingly rule, not the sphere or territory of his government; nor was it so understood by the Christians of the first four centuries. In the first three gospels, the overwhelming majority of the sayings imply reign or rule, rather than a community. Yet Jesus does speak of entering the Kingdom, and one of his most authentic parables is that of the mustard seed, which flourishes into a tree with birds lodging in its shadows. For this usage Flew suggests 'domain', which etymologically, 'preserves the sense of the sphere in which a Lord exercises his dominion rather than the actual people who live in the domain'.[58] The other kingdom sayings have a more specifically eschatological reference to the future consummation of God's rule and the joy of the Lord's disciples and the elect within it.

Flew's second chapter confronts the eschatological problem. If Jesus thought that the Kingdom was coming soon, bringing with it the end of human history, how could he have envisaged any kind of new community? Flew disposes of this, perhaps too easily, as irrelevant:

Whether the days be swifter than a weaver's shuttle or prolonged through immense vistas of time, the obligation of the Christian to live every moment in the perfect love of God is categorical. The words of Milton's Archangel:

What thou liv'st
Live well; how long or short permit to heaven
are as valid for this community as for the individual life.[59]

There is no doubt that it is just here that later theologians would want to press him hardest. The chapter is very brief and does not consider such a saying as:

Verily I say unto you, There be some here of them that stand

---

[58] *Ibid.*, p. 34.
[59] *Ibid.*, p. 46.

by, which shall in no wise taste of death, till they see the kingdom of God come with power (Mark 9:1).

This brings Flew to his longest chapter and the heart of the book. In 'The Idea of the Ecclesia in the Mind of Our Lord', he develops his famous five-fold argument:

First, there is the conception of a new Israel which appeared in His teaching and actions.

Second, the fact that He taught His disciples, as the nucleus of the new Israel; the ethical teaching of Jesus presupposed a new community, and the power to fulfil the new demands.

Third, His conception of Messiahship.

Fourth, the conception of the 'Word of God' or 'Gospel' as constituting the new community; the fact that He preached and that His message was of a certain kind, inevitably marked off those who accepted it from those who did not.

Fifth, the fact that He sent out His disciples on a certain mission. That mission governed His conception of apostleship.[60]

These points are substantiated with a wealth of exegesis. Only when he has successfully proved that Jesus thus intended the *ecclesia* does he turn to the promise to Peter in Matthew 16:17–19.

' . . . thou art Peter and on this rock I will build my church . . . '

Grave suspicions notwithstanding, Flew is inclined to accept the passage as authentic, though it does not belong to Peter's confession at Caeserea Philippi. There is richness both of scholarship and experience in his interpretation which must have been for some readers worth the price of the volume and formed the basis of countless sermons. Peter is the Rock, though others to

[60] *Ibid.*, p. 48; summarised also at the end of the chapter, pp. 121–2; also in the introduction, p. 16.

whom the same revelation is given, may become the
foundation of the Church too. (Ephesians 2:20) It is also
important to remember that in one sense Christ himself
is the foundations (I. Corinthians 3:11) and the rock
(I. Corinthians 10:4). It is unnecessary to bandy the
different analogies of the New Testament one against
the other. The power of the keys is the power

> for the communication of the open secret which has now
> been revealed. This is entrance to the Kingdom. The power
> of the keys is thought of primarily as the power to admit,
> as when a modern Christian says of another to whom he
> owes his very soul: 'he has the key, and he opened Christianity
> to me as by an inner door'. Doubtless the power to admit
> may also involve the power to exclude, which is implicit in
> the story of the Council of Jerusalem. But this power to
> exclude is in the background, and secondary. Those who
> accept Peter's message and Peter's Lord enter the kingdom.
> That is the authority entrusted in Peter.[61]

This concludes part One of the treatise. Part Two
deals with the Primitive Church and is a study of the
Acts of the Apostles in which the author finds reflected the
five points he has discovered in the synoptic gospels. The
section ends with a lengthy and learned chapter on
'The Ministry of the Ecclesia'. Words written in 1938 have
a melancholy fall as Flew notes the 'singular dispro-
portion' in English work on the Church, which, for
historical reasons, devotes far more space to the ministry
than to the ecclesia itself. He pleads for the 'better way'
of the New Testament – to concentrate 'on the essential
nature of the Church which the ministry serves, and only
after that, on the relation of the ministry to the Church'.[62]
The lesson has hardly been heeded.

The chapter reviews the different kinds of ministry

[61] *Ibid.*, p. 133.
[62] *Ibid.*, p. 180.

mentioned in the *Acts* and the rest of the New Testament. The Apostles are accorded a certain pre-eminence because of their unique relationship to Jesus, but the nature of their authority is undefined. The appointment of 'the Seven' marks a development in Church organisation, making the ecclesia, in Hort's phrase, a 'true body politic'. They are probably not the precursors of the later diaconate, but a charismatic order of preachers. They arise in fulfilment of the Church's mission (to this extent we may say, paraphrasing Flew, that their appointment is pragmatic) and as a sign that Christianity is bursting the bounds of Judaism. Presbyters are all bishops, elders, several in each Church of equal rank, overseers of the local community. They and all the other ministries are contingent upon the Church's mission. Nowhere is the celebration of the eucharist singled out as the prerogative or supreme task of any of the ministers.

Some of the most important words in the whole of *Jesus and His Church* occur at the end of this chapter when Flew, following Hort and Weiss and others, stresses the uniqueness of the Church in the ancient world. There was nothing in any way comparable to this community, with its universal mission and love of the brethren for Christ's sake. No other religion had a Church in the Christian sense.

Part Three is comparatively brief and simply shows that in the rest of the New Testament the main outlines of the Church summarised in the five-fold argument, may also be discerned. As in *The Idea of Perfection*, the Fourth Gospel is relegated to the end.

By any standards, *Jesus and His Church* is an impressive achievement. Again, in addition to the texts of Scripture themselves, one feels that all the other authorities have been mastered and marshalled rather as 'biggie-Flew' drilled his rugger team at Christ's Hospital.

Perhaps the abiding value of the book is in its re-creation of the New Testament Church as a *koinonia*, warm and living and for all men, a new fact in human history. One who was *anima naturaliter Methodistica* was needed to describe this in the attempt to free debates between churchman from their obsession with order. Flew believes that the concept of the Church in the sub-apostolic age shows a decline from that of the New Testament. He quotes J. B. Lightfoot's comment on the Ignatian doctrine of episcopacy:

> It need hardly be remarked how subversive of the true spirit of Christianity, in the negation of individual freedom, and the consequent suppression of direct responsibility to God in Christ, is the crushing despotism with which this language, if taken literally, would invest the episcopal office.[63]

Two thousand copies of *Jesus and His Church* were printed in July 1938. In the stringent conditions of wartime a further 1,000 were issued in 1943 and again in 1945. Thereafter followed editions of 2,000 in 1950, 1956 and 1960, making 10,000 in twenty-two years. These are far from being *Honest to God* figures, but they do betoken a persistent influence, and are significant, for a book of its kind in its day, when there were fewer theological students than in the proliferating faculties of the 1960s. The fact that no reprint was undertaken in the boom years and that copies are now obtainable only from the shelves of second-hand shops shows that *Jesus and His Church* is no longer in fashion. Will it ever return?

Certain criticisms were made on its first publication. Part of its strength lies in the fact that it is a Methodist contribution, but may it not read something of the Wesley's idealism of the primitive Church into the original documents? Were not Christian origins more shabby and more sordid than, not only the Wesleys, but even the *Acts of the Apostles* pictured them? Though Flew

[63] *Ibid.*, p. 257.

was a liberal theologian, his conclusions tend to be somewhat conservatively safe. More than once in *Jesus and His Church*, he remarks on this. 'The result of the argument may seem surprisingly conservative to those who are acquainted with criticism of the fifty years since Hort wrote his famous lectures on *The Christian Ecclesia*. But the conservative result has not been reached by the traditional route!' [64] Again, in his acknowledgement of Gerhard Kittel's *Theologisches Wörterbuch zum Neuen Testament*, he refers to 'the surprisingly conservative conclusions to which these philological studies frequently lead'.[65] But philology nearly always does lead to conservative results, unless it is the slave of the phantasies of a J. M. Allegro. It is form and redaction criticisms, awkward comparisons of differing blocks of material, the attempt to reconstruct the historical background without pious presuppositions, which tend to radicalism.

The five-fold argument itself came under fire of an admiring but severe critic in an unpublished paper in 1940:

It is possible to feel that this symmetry is a little too beautiful, that it fits together a little too neatly like the jigsaw puzzle which fits together only because it was a whole before it was cut into pieces: such a whole exists more easily in the academic mind than in the natural course of active living.[66]

Another theologian, then at Cambridge, George Johnston, criticises the argument not on grounds of method, but on the Gospel evidence.

The weakness of this is its failure fully to do justice to the necessity of Jesus' death for the constitution of the new Israel. Messiahship, it is true, involves a community; so does the ethical teaching by its very definition; yet the 'Messianic'

[64] *Ibid.*, p. 17.
[65] *Ibid.*, p. 11.
[66] G. F. Nuttall; quoted by kind permission.

dignity won recognition for what it was only through the glorious exaltation which followed the final humiliation.[67]

We may observe in passing that a fuller examination of the Fourth Gospel might have brought Dr Flew nearer to Dr Johnston's position. *St John* is in some respects damaging to the view that Jesus founded the ecclesia in his lifetime. The Spirit was not given because Jesus was not yet glorified, while it may be argued that the conception of the Church, which is brought to birth by the insufflation of the Spirit in the Upper Room on Easter evening, takes place by the dying act of the Crucified when he gives his Mother and the Beloved Disciple each to the other. Johnston maintains that the title Church, or ecclesia, should be reserved for the post-resurrection community. 'The disciples are potentially the Church. They are and yet they are not the ecclesia. This may be called an adoptionist ecclesiology; they become the Church *through the Baptism of the spirit. Without the Cross and the Resurrection there is no Church.*' It is the creation of the Redeemer.[68]

C. K. Barrett thinks that Johnston has made his point, though he recognises that the difference between him and Flew is not irreconcilable and that both are agreed that 'in the sense of being redeemer, Jesus founded the Church'.[69] His own criticism of the five-fold argument is that there is nothing in it 'which makes us think of a community living on in earthly conditions of space and time rather than of a glorified Church in heaven with God, after the complete and final consummation of the Kingdom'.[70]

[67] George Johnston, *The Doctrine of the Church in the New Testament* (Cambridge 1943), p. 50.
[68] *Ibid.*, p. 56.
[69] C. K. Barrett, *The Holy Spirit and the Gospel Tradition* (SPCK 1947), p. 137.
[70] *Ibid.*, p. 138.

Whether or not we agree with Barrett, there is no doubt that the increasing tendency to give full weight to the eschatological passages of the gospels has made scholars less interested in Flew's original question: 'Did Jesus form a community, which was to continue in the existing order after his death?' This has been combined with an increasing unwillingness to be confident that it is possible to reconstruct from the gospels any definitive picture of the Jesus of history. Flew made his theological and spiritual home in the late nineteenth-century climate of Heinrich Weinel's claim 'We know Jesus right well'.[71] Now the New Testament critic is not so sure and is inclined to regard any full portrait as deserving the strictures of Henry J. Cadbury's title – *The Peril of Modernizing Jesus*. The Jesus of the 'new Quest' is far too much of an existentialist to be an authentic figure of the first-century, as is the Jesus of the revolutionaries, a Che Guevara before time. But Flew's Jesus too may not altogether survive Cadbury's cautions:

I am doubtful whether we do not read into Jesus' life more of a campaign than existed. . . . The sense of purpose, objective etc. as necessary for every good life is more modern than we commonly imagine. Some men in antiquity lived under it, (but) . . . my impression is that Jesus was largely casual. He reacted to situations as they arose but probably he hardly had a programme at all. . . .
Almost everything that Jesus said can be associated with the kingdom. But I must express my feeling that a term like that was so conventional and so inclusive that it would be a mistake to find the key to Jesus' interests by our own attempt to narrow the term down to some special implications of the term. . . . Whatever be its most probable or persistent meaning it provides in the parables no centralising subject, but rather a convenient way of doing what we do when we

---

[71] Quoted by Dennis Nineham, 'Jesus in the Gospels' in N. Pittenger (ed.), *Christ for us Today* (SCM 1968), p. 51.

say 'Life is like this'. 'Truth or duty may be illustrated by
this.' 'Here is the way it seems to me.' [72]

We shall consider below the implications of this for
Flew's whole approach to the New Testament. Meanwhile, scepticism about the historical Jesus has resulted
in what we may describe as a new high Churchmanship among some scholars of a liberal Catholic bent.
For everything that we know about Jesus, we are
scandalously dependent upon the early Church. John
Knox has gone so far as to say:

> The career of Jesus of Nazareth, simply as a human career,
> was, for all its intrinsic greatness, a relatively unimportant
> incident in Jewish history. The event of Jesus Christ the Lord
> was historically the important thing; and this event happened
> only in the life of the Church.[73]

Scholars such as John Knox and Dennis Nineham would
see the saving event of God in Christ as consisting of the
life and activity of Jesus as refracted by the response of
those who received him. At its simplest the Church is the
company of those who remember Jesus. Whatever may
have been Jesus's own thoughts about the future, we
may say without hesitation that God intended the
Church.

On the other hand, there are those who would feel
that in the last decades of the twentieth century, the
important question is not so much 'What is the Church
and did Jesus conceive it?' as 'Where is the Church?'
Is it to be found in the Sunday assembly or the fellowship
of the baptised any more than in the hierarchical

---

[72] H. J. Cadbury, *op. cit.*, pp. 140–2, quoted by Dennis Nineham,
op. cit., pp. 59–60.

[73] John Knox, *The Early Church and the Coming Great Church* (Epworth
Press, 1957), p. 47. Cf. Dennis Nineham, 'History and the Gospel',
The London Quarterly and Holborn Review, April 1967, pp. 93–105.

institution? There is a new sense that continuity is a myth, whether in the form of apostolical or evangelical succession. The New Testament Church cannot now be our 'model' – 'what we see in the Bible is the kind of Church which it was historically possible for men inspired by Jesus to create in the first century of our era', not a pattern laid up in heaven for all time.[74] In some ways that is the most serious fact militating against the kind of effort Flew so powerfully made.

There remains the question as to whether he was justified in giving the place he did to the first three gospels. The supremacy of Matthew, Mark and Luke is vital to the argument, not only of *Jesus and His Church* but of *The Idea of Perfection* too. More recent scholars would not distinguish so sharply between the synoptics as accurate historical records and St John as largely interpretation. Indeed the tendency is for the New Testament to be judged much more as a whole and for the distinction, so prominent in liturgy, between 'epistle' and 'gospel' to be suspect. Is not Romans 8, I Corinthians 13, or John 14 as authentic a document of 'the things concerning Jesus' as the Parable of the Prodigal Son or the Sermon on the Mount or even perhaps the Passion narratives? Nor do the first three gospels necessarily present a Jesus of more universal attractiveness than the rest of the New Testament. Albert Schweitzer, E. C. Hoskyns and R. H. Lightfoot have come into their own in emphasising the strangeness of Jesus, his remoteness from our age, his inability to think in our categories and the perils of making him in our image.

The pendulum may swing again in Flew's direction. Just as Wolfhart Pannenberg has revived some of the

[74] Cf. J. H. S. Kent, 'The British Non-Conformist Ministry' in N. Lash and J. Rhymer, eds., *The Christian Priesthood* (Darton, Longman and Todd 1970), p. 86. In different terms G. F. Nuttall applies a similar criticism directly to Flew in the unpublished paper referred to above.

old liberal arguments for the historicity of the empty tomb, so it could be that the time of some of Flew's basic ideas will come again. In a book, interestingly called *The Church and Jesus* (SCM 1969), F. G. Downing, while emphasising as against Flew's generation the diversity of the New Testament and the difficulty of the quest for the primitive Church, has presented an irreducible minimum of genuine sayings of Jesus and insisted on (what Knox and Nineham would not deny) the presence of a real man of flesh and blood as the inspiration of all subsequent activity. Already there are signs that his claims for the uniqueness of the Christian community in the ancient world, reinforced as they were by classical scholars (who tend to be more conservative about the New Testament than many modern specialists) are being taken up once more; while it is probably true that the synoptic gospels still have most power to convert the enquiring layman. Archbishop Anthony Bloom and Sir John Lawrence were both brought to Christ by reading *St Mark*.[75]

Of course, the vital question is not 'Who is right?' but 'What is right?'. Scepticism is not necessarily impiety and too many Christians have fled the blizzards of exploration for the cosy homestead of an illusory faith which does not answer doubt, but simply excludes it and is as deaf to the winds of the age as it is blind to the offence of the Cross. Yet scepticism may be a form of one-upmanship and doubt, a pathological condition based on parental complexes and God knows what. Is it so very misguided to settle on that vision of Jesus which most inspires us, provided we realise that it is but a 'broken light' and that it needs to be refracted through the prisms of other Christians and of critical honesty and that, only at the last, shall 'we see him as he is'?

Be that as it may, the theology of Robert Newton Flew,

[75] See Rupert E. Davies, ed., *We believe in God* (Allen and Unwin 1968), pp. 26, 115.

good in its time, may still preserve some essential elements of the gospel, which must not be lost by future generations. The belief that Christ offers not only a doctrine but a way of life, which is possible for all men, that the Church should be the community in which this is realised and shared, that this transcends the divisions of 'names and sects and parties', that it is to be at once preached and prayed for and sought earnestly, yet, in the end, received as a gift is not antiquarian sentimentality. And if it be said that for Flew, theology was less of a tough-minded professionalism than an aspect of Christian devotion, he would, with all his lifetime's labours and superb linguistic and bibliographical equipment, have accepted the charge as entirely true of his interpretations. One tradition affirms that *lex credendi* is *lex orandi*, and Flew himself said that 'the *Theologia Dogmatica* of the future which may be different from previous structures must be built on the *Theologia Spiritualis* of the past?' [76] Both his leading books end with prayers from the ancient sacramentaries and like his classical predecessors he would regard these as the beginning and the end of the argument. The struggle with doubt is at once intellectual and moral, a part of the discipline and chastening of the Christian man.

He wrote as a lover. The objects of his desires were equally Jesus and his Church. He believed that neither would betray whatever loyalty or love a man might give to them.[77]

[76] *The Idea of Perfection*, p. xi.
[77] This embodies a much used phrase of Flew's. See, e.g., in relation to the Church, his introduction as Moderator of the Free Church Federal Council to Sir James Marchant, ed., *Has the Church Failed?* (Odhams Press 1947), p. xiv.

6

The Methodist

On the fly-leaf of his copy of Volume One of Wesley's *Sermons on Several Occasions*, Flew wrote:

> This book is a family heirloom and was purchased by my Grandfather, Robert Flew, senior Clerk at Her Majesty's Prison in Portland. It is his signature that is almost wholly obliterated when the next page is turned over. (This 'improvement' was carried out in 1928, when the improver was five years old.) So there are four generations who have left their mark on this book:
>
> | All these three | Robert Flew, born 1832 d. 1901 |
> |---|---|
> | accredited local | Josiah Flew, born 1859 d. 1925 |
> | preachers (two | Robert Newton Flew, born 1886 |
> | ordained ministers | |
> | ordained 1883 and | Antony Garrard Newton Flew |
> | 1914 respectively) | born 1923 |

The refrain of almost everything we have so far told is that Flew was a Methodist and the son of a Methodist. He cannot be understood apart from this pedigree.

'I never liked a man so much, who had so much unction', said a Cambridge Anglican. The 'unction' was perhaps very unAnglican. It had something in it of the old time prayer-meeting Methodist, who *felt* his relationship to God and used language to express his feelings and move others;[1] but it was in part parody; just as in the privacy of the Lodge when there were no students within earshot, he would imitate Paul Robeson and sing,

> Mighty mountain
> Toiling upwards!

so he sometimes, in public, affected the part of the paternalistic divine. 'The natural man has been overcome', he would say when a student's request, refused perhaps with annoyance at the first time of asking, was at

---

[1] The following very interesting undated letter was received from Dr H. L. Goudge, Regius Professor of Divinity at Oxford (and father of the novelist, Elizabeth Goudge) in reply to some comments Flew had made on his book *The Church of England and Reunion* (SPCK 1938).

Christ Church,
Oxford.

Dear Dr Flew,

Thank you so much for your kind and careful letter, which is a great encouragement to me, as your words habitually are. I think you misunderstood me in one point and it is rather an amusing instance of the different *nuances* attached to words in Methodist and Anglican minds. I said 'It will be felt that if what has been written rightly represents the mind of the Church of England, its view of the Church is substantially the same as that of Rome and of the Christian East etc. etc', not 'seen that' and I proceeded to show that the feeling would give an erroneous impression. But you took me to mean that the CofE view *was* substantially the same as that of Rome and the East. The reason was, I think, that when you say 'I feel that' you are accustomed to refer to your personal judgment as a whole, not to *mere* feeling as instinctive reaction. The Anglican would say 'I think that' in a similar case. You may *think* one thing and *feel* another inconsistent with your thought; it is most uncomfortable, but it may happen, especially if your present convictions cut across the ideas in which you were brought up. Isn't it so?

Ever yours,
H. L. Goudge

length granted. He could laugh at himself and he did not object to amiable teasing and was referred to as 'the man of God' by his own family. Mimicry did not always displease him and he would tell a slightly un-Methodist story of one of his Christ's Hospital masters who, himself unseen, watched members of a class 'taking him off' for several minutes before he could stand it no longer and cried, 'My God! am I really as bad as all that?'

Flew was undoubtedly as much of a Methodist as he was a Flew. He would have as soon left the communion into which he had been born, as denied his parentage or been unfaithful to his wife. He saw his vocation as within the Methodist Church, refused an academic appointment in Canada as a young man, and was for ever loyal to Conference and its disciplines. He felt that its system was the best in Christendom and the envy of those Anglicans who had troubled to discover it. Though a Wesleyan he was never partisan and entered fully into the union of 1932. He was perhaps fortunate in that he was not sufficiently senior to have been closely concerned with the controversies which preceded union, and he entered the new Church with a reputation in ecclesiastical statesmanship still to be made. He was never heard to speak contemptuously of the other denominations of the united Church and deplored criticism of the 'ex-Primitives' and their supposed lack of Churchmanship and non-liturgical ways. He knew that his ministry was to serve Methodists of all shades and he liked to be regarded as the friend of all.

He was never Athanasius *contra mundum* either in his own Church or outside. His causes were the causes of his time, and he was but one of a company of scholars and leaders who advocated them. He was resolute in his advocacy and eloquent, at his best when refuting the opposition; and perhaps never in a minority. He was often the man for his Church's hour. As well as helping to make Methodist scholarship a force to be reckoned with and training many of the leaders of the next generation, he sought to recover for Methodism a true spirituality, to continue the work of Lidgett, Wiseman and Lofthouse and bring her into the ecumenical movement, and to give her a doctrine of the Church.

The first two of these aims we have already considered, the third will be the subject of the next Chapter, the fourth, though *Jesus and His Church* is one of its monuments, demands fuller exposition.

From Methodist Union until 1937 the Secretary of Conference was a Wesleyan Minister named Robert Bond. He was a quiet, gracious competent man, and though not a theologian himself, remarkably sensitive to the needs of the times. In 1935, he induced the Methodist Conference to appoint a representative committee to produce a statement on *The Nature of the Christian Church, according to the Teaching of the Methodists*. W. F. Lofthouse presided but Flew was convener and wrote the report, which in its day was unique. 'I have been unable', said Flew, 'to find any other modern statement on this subject, which has been given the imprimatur of a great church'.

Much of the document deals with the New Testament and bears the mark of Flew's Cambridge studies and preparation for his Fernley-Hartley lecture. It also is stamped with his clarity of presentation. After a brief examination of the word *Ecclesia*, there is an account of the metaphors used to describe the Church, sections on its origin, fellowship, allegiance, message and mission, and more than four pages on the ministry, which include such pertinent sentences as these:

. . . we cannot speak of 'the threefold ministry' as claiming the authority of the New Testament. Further, there is no evidence that definite prerogatives or powers are to be transmitted. . . . We may conclude that though it is highly probable that the laying on of hands was largely practised in the apostolic age as a rite introductory to many of the varied ministries to which members of the Churches might be called, the New Testament tells us little, and therefore it is difficult to believe that any principle essential to the Church, or constitutive of the very being of the Church, was involved in that rite. . . . In I Corinthians and Romans the ministry is not created by the Church. It is created by the Spirit, whose divers gifts (*charismata*) mark out this man and that for special functions. Thus we may say that in the New Testament the ministry of the Word and Sacraments is a divine gift to the Church, and was in those early days an integral part of its organic life.

The loyalty of the Methodists to the teaching of the New Testament is affirmed.

We join with Christians of all communions in the confession that the history of the Church, including that part of it to which we own our loyalty, has fallen far short of the ideal outlined in the New Testament. . . . We do claim that none of the forms of organization taken by the Apostolic Church should be determinative for the Church for all time. . . . Christ constituted a community of disciples and believers. They had two simple rites. He gave them what the early Church passed on, a new life in the Spirit, an experience of God, a store of teaching, a gospel, and a mission. The Church did not die. The Church, as we believe, cannot die. 'The gates of Hades shall not prevail against it.' The historic continuity of the living Church is vital to Christianity.

Methodism, it is claimed, is jealous of its continuity with the Church of the past in experience, allegiance to Christ, in message and in mission. ' "Christians trace their genealogy from the Lord Jesus Christ.". . . This is our doctrine of apostolical succession.' There follows a summary of the principles of the Protestant Reformation, which antedates the revived Protestant confessionalism of the war and immediate post-war years and marks something of a transition from Flew's earlier emphasis on the glories of Catholicism to his later battles to demonstrate Protestant Catholicity. The Reformation stressed that salvation is by faith (i.e. trust in God) alone, it 'introduced into the world a deeper understanding of the Personal Work of Christ than had prevailed since the apostolic age' and it rediscovered the priesthood of all believers. The last is illustrated by a particularly fine quotation from Luther:

'At the Eucharist,' says Luther, 'we all kneel beside our priest or minister, and around him, men and women, young and old, master and servant, mistress and maid, all holy priests together, sanctified by the blood of Christ. We are there in our priestly dignity. . . . We do not let the priest proclaim for himself the ordinance of Christ; but he is the mouthpiece of us all, and we all say it with him in our hearts with true faith in the Lamb of God who feeds us with His Body and Blood.'

Since the Reformation there have been a number of separated 'confessional' Churches with their faith defined in documents. The Roman Church itself became a community of this type by the adoption of the decrees of the Council of Trent. Methodists have Wesley's *Notes on the New Testament* and the first four volumes of his sermons. And so a place is claimed for Methodism within the one Church of God by arguments reminiscent of Flew's 1933 essay on 'Methodism andt he Catholic Tradition'. Methodism 'was guilty of no "schism" '. But it 'cannot be content with the present broken communion of Christendom'.

Not one of these communities can legitimately claim to be the whole of the Catholic Church on earth. Neither are these separate communities analogous to the local 'churches' in primitive Christianity. Today the Church of Christ on earth means all the believers, in whatever community they are found, who confess Jesus as Lord, to the glory of God the

Father. We acknowledge that all the communities which make this confession and maintain it among their members, whether the Roman Catholic, Orthodox Eastern, Lutheran, Reformed, Presbyterian, Anglican or Free Churches may humbly claim to belong to the Body of Christ.

The Statement ends with seven affirmations, which gather up the preceding argument and extend it to include both social witness and the communion of saints. 'The Church is of necessity set under our Lord to be both the critic and the saviour of the world. . . . The Church on earth looks forward to the vision of God, the perfect consummation of its present fellowship in the light of heaven.'

Flew was one of the band of theologians, college tutors and administrators, who, in the twenty years after Methodist union, contended for a strong and confident Methodist Churchmanship, based on belief in the Church as a Divine Society, greater than the sum of its separated parts. Within this Church, One, Holy, Catholic and Apostolic, Methodism had an indisputable place, faithful as it was to Scriptures, Creeds and Sacraments, and having as it did a ministry representative of the whole Church among the local societies and set apart by the laying on of hands, which set the seal of Christ and his people upon individual vocation. To these marks of Catholicity, Methodism also brought its passion for personal and social holiness and its distinctive warmth of fellowship. All were enshrined in the Wesley hymns, which, with their rapturous orthodoxy and intense devotion, had made ordinary people free of Catholic truth and were both the sustenance and expression of authentic and distinctive Methodist churchmanship.

Flew and his colleagues stood on the ground just to the right of centre. They were not happy with what one of them called 'saccharine Hymns', some of which had been included in the 1933 Methodist Hymn Book, and which were replacing Wesley in the Methodist people's affections. They had no objection to Moody and Sankey, who taught the full gospel to simple people; but they deplored the somewhat insipid and precious piety of hymns like Benjamin Waugh's *Now let us see Thy beauty, Lord* and the spinsterish and selective 'Holiday Home' religion of *Yes, God is good!* and *All things praise Thee, Lord most High*. Charles Ryder Smith, who was Principal of Richmond College, Surrey, until 1940, and President of the Wesleyan Conference in 1931, said that to the words of the last, which includes a line about 'Rustling leaf and humming bee', he wanted to add:

> Snarling wolf and leaping flea;
> All things praise Thee; Lord may we.

There is no doubt that the protest against such hymns by the more Wesleyan – and the epithet does not necessarily refer to former denominational allegiance – of the College tutors and their positive teaching, together with the books of Bernard Manning, F. L. Wiseman, J. E. Rattenbury and, at the end of his time, of Flew himself, helped to promote something of a Wesley revival during the second world war and in the first decade and a half afterwards.

These teachers were also disturbed by the lack of sacramental understanding and the failures in sacramental practice in the Methodist circuits and societies. Indiscriminate baptism, infrequent communion, and deficient rites for both ordinances were far too common. They were not happy with lay administration of either sacrament except in rare emergencies, not because they attached any magical efficacy to ordination, but because they believed that the sacraments were particularly related to the pastoral office and to the men commissioned to exercise it on behalf of the whole Church. They discouraged their students from administering baptism in the course of their week-end preaching visits, because such baptisms might well be without preparation and the young men, there but for the nonce, were not likely to be able to enter into any genuine pastoral relationship with the candidates and their families.

In 1947 when Flew was President of the Conference, the Leaders' Meeting of a rural society and its minister asked him to arbitrate in a dispute between them on Holy Baptism and agreed, in advance, to abide by his judgement. A woman had quarrelled with the local Vicar and had thereupon transferred her children to the Methodist Sunday School, 'but not her hassock to the Chapel'. A new baby arrived and she asked the Methodist minister to baptise him. Since she had no idea of the meaning of Baptism and had no intention of attending either Church or Chapel, the minister gave her the service book to study. She was insulted by this and went off and composed her quarrel with the Vicar, who 'did' the baby.

The Leaders' Meeting was upset by its minister's scruples and felt that he had driven a family away from the Chapel. Hence the submission to the President, which may also have been due to the fact that he was Flew and that there were memories of his father in the circuit. The President's sympathies were entirely with the minister, though he handled the matter with great delicacy and his memorandum was preceded by a personal letter so that it would not seem to be an *ex cathedra* pronouncement. But he set out the issues very patiently and explained the doctrine of Holy Baptism as a rite of the Gospel with solemn implications both for the candidates and for those who presented them.

This form of Churchmanship was not allied to the Methodist Sacramental Fellowship founded in 1935. Flew and his friends were sympathetic to its aims, but they did not want Methodist Churchmanship to become a party matter. They were anxious to avoid what is now called 'polarisation'. They wanted all Methodists to be churchmen in what they believed was the New Testament sense. A movement which made people smell Romanism – and however unfounded were such charges against MSF leaders such as J. E. Rattenbury and A. E. Whitham, one prominent member had defected – was to them a dangerous and painful distraction from the main issue.

The omnipresent figure who surveyed every aspect of Methodist Church life from over his spectacles, until he reached the age of 92 and was able to discard them and continue with the naked eye, was John Scott Lidgett. He was the great apostle of Catholicity, the 'inward Catholicity', which 'consists in the fellowship of a great experience . . . fellowship of the saints through common access to God'. His name must have appeared as a signatory to every letter to *The Times* from ecumenical Church leaders for forty years. Theologian, social worker, educationalist, statesman, he was 99 when he died in 1953. He was President of the Wesleyan Conference of 1908 and obvious choice as the first President of the united Conference in 1932. We have already seen Flew irritated by his ambivalence in a private discussion on the effect of the higher criticism, and citing with admiration his Presidential address on the Nicene creed and receiving with delight his congratulations on a broadcast sermon.

Lidgett undoubtedly remained 'in the active work' for too long so that he had to be prised out of the Chair of the London South District in 1948. He could be exasperating and unpredictable, and it was not always easy to determine whether he would appear in debate on the reactionary or the radical side. In 1942 he spoke in favour of dancing on Methodist premises to the distress of the narrower evangelicals. What were beyond dispute were his theological integrity, his versatility of achievement and his courage to speak for what he believed to be

right. Flew in conversation would contrast him with the
other great veteran of the early years of the united
Church, Frederick Luke Wiseman, musician, popular
evangelist and churchman too. Wiseman was magnanimous and generous to excess, but if he had pledged
himself to support a line in debate, he would sometimes
say to a younger speaker on the same side, 'You have
done so well, there is no need for me to add anything'.
Lidgett, on the other hand, would never withdraw, but
always strike some of his direct hammer blows in
reinforcement.

If Lidgett was the perennial elder statesman, the one
who remained amid all the changes of Flew's period,
his own closest friends were men nearer his own age.
He was always *en rapport* with Bardsley Brash, but his
greatest intimate, the one who meant most to him in the
whole brotherhood of the Methodist ministry, was a
former colleague at Clapham, Howard Watkin-Jones,
tutor in Church History at Headingley College, Leeds,
a Welshman and a musician, who was remarkable as the
possessor of a Cambridge Doctorate of Divinity, awarded
in 1928 for a work on *The Holy Spirit from Arminius
to Wesley*. It was not until 1955 that Cambridge was
again to give so high a degree to a Methodist. Watkin-
Jones became President of the Conference in 1951, and
although he had to follow W. E. Sangster, one of the
greatest preachers and personalities of the time, his
own winsome evangelism made his year memorable
and helped to revive Methodist confidence and increase its membership, so that it looked as though the
hopes of post-war consolidation and advance might not
be belied.

There is no record that Flew and Watkin-Jones spent
much time discussing each other's scholarly work. His
friend's name is not found in the prefaces or acknowledge-
ments of any of Flew's books; nor did Flew mention him
much in conversation, which, for one who talked freely

and enjoyed convivial gossip, is significant. The explanation seems to be that, of his contemporaries, Flew spoke with reserve of those whom he deeply disliked and of those who were closer than brothers. The first category was very small, the second may have been confined to Howard Watkin-Jones.

'Watkin', as he was known to his friends, though Brash puckishly called him 'Gwatkin' after the Cambridge Church historian, shared Flew's convictions about Methodist Catholicity. The two of them were Methodist representatives at the ecumenical conversations which produced the report on *Church Relations in England* in 1950, and, in the words of the Baptist, Dr E. A. Payne, 'appeared as "twin-brethren" very closely in accord with one another'.

It is generally accepted that during the 1940s there emerged one Methodist statesman of towering stature and formidable integrity. He was Wilbert Francis Howard, first New Testament tutor, and then Principal of Handsworth College, Birmingham. He was a New Testament linguist and theologian of outstanding gifts, whose youthful name Flew had heard quoted with approbation and a German accent in the lecture room at Marburg in 1910. Like Flew, Howard was a Methodist preacher before all else and his written work was sacrificed to his Church obligations. He wrote two important books on the Fourth Gospel and was much engaged in continuing J. H. Moulton's *Grammar of New Testament Greek*. He insisted on retiring from his college Principalship at seventy, partly *pour encourager les autres*, partly to devote his time to scholarship. Unfortunately, after but a few months in Cambridge, he died in 1952.

Howard was President of the Conference in 1944, but because Dr A. W. Harrison, his successor, died in office, he had to resume in January 1946, which means that, to date, his has been the longest occupation of John

Wesley's Chair since Methodist union. Even apart from this, which led to the sacrificial assumption of an additional burden in the year that his college had re-opened after the war, his strength of character was such that he was bound to be dominant, though he was in no sense power-hungry. He saw issues clearly and fought without compromise. His understanding of the Christian ministry may be illustrated by an anecdote he would tell about H. J. Pickett, a Primitive Methodist Minister, who had been Principal of Hartley College, Manchester. Once at an acrimonious meeting, Pickett was told by his people, 'Remember you are our servant'. 'Yes!' he retorted, 'I am your servant, but you are not my masters.' Howard would also emphasise the distinctive and transcendent nature of a minister's calling by pointing out that, whereas any other man was considered to be justified in seeking to better his social position, to obtain more money and greater fame, these things were instinctively deemed unworthy of a minister.

A lightness of touch went with his massive scholarship, he could use a rapier as well as a bludgeon and, before his years on the platform, used to contribute Conference impressions to the *Methodist Recorder*. He was a redoubtable mimic in private. In retrospect he seems a sterner, less gentle figure than Flew, who may have been somewhat afraid of him, and whom he would tease, perhaps even on one notable occasion, as we shall see, to excess. But he admired Flew sincerely, would often quote him in his lectures as the last word on the subject under discussion, and he shared both his ecumenical vision and his Methodist churchmanship.

The supreme governing body of the Methodist Church is the annual Conference. To have real influence in the Church at large it is necessary to master the intricacies of debate and to be sensitive to the moods of this six hundred and ninety strong assembly. Many a fine orator, lucid teacher and able preacher has failed in Conference, for it is more like a Parliament than a Church congregation or lecture-class; yet it meets in a great hall with the representatives seated in rows, district by district. Certain officials have permanent seats and some personalities return year after year, while others are elected but once in a lifetime and may almost be too bemused to know for what or for whom they are voting. A good Conference speaker needs a clear and preferably loud voice, a quick and well-ordered mind, a reasonable command of language and confidence both in himself and his arguments. He has to be particularly careful to know when or when not to be humorous and also what style of humour will be appreciated. The high table story, the donnish aside or an undue whimsicality may sink like lead to the bottom of that vast pond. If the speaker is an obvious expert in certain fields, he will be heard with great attention, and no restlessness, impatience or shuffling departures to the tea-room will interrupt his flow of words.

Flew's first Conference was at Plymouth in 1913, as a very privileged probationer. He was a representative of the Second London District when he was at Clapham in 1923 and sat by Joseph Rank, the millionaire miller, who, to Flew's disgust, spent most of the sessions studying the financial columns of *The Times*. Strangely enough, at both Conferences, George Jackson, Superintendent of the Edinburgh Mission, and afterwards Tutor at Didsbury College, whom Flew was nominated to succeed in 1928, was the victim of a heresy hunt by a conservative organisation, long since defunct, called the Wesley Bible Union which, it will be recalled, he also encountered during the discussion at Dr Workman's in 1917. In 1923, Flew had in his pocket some notes for a speech in defence of theological freedom. He was not required to speak on that occasion, but in the 1930s he became, before long, one of the outstanding personalities of the united Conference, intervening with great authority and incisiveness on matters of Faith and Order, (which committee he convened), ecumenical relations and education. In August 1939, the *British Weekly* commented:

> The man of the hour at the Liverpool Conference was undoubtedly Dr R. Newton Flew, Principal of Wesley House, Cambridge. He spoke brilliantly in the debate on education and has been the moving force behind the remarkable report on Sunday School organisation. His chief theme, however, was that of religious reunion, speaking as secretary for the Methodist group. He has a vivacious style and a voice so effective that Conference did not object when he turned away the microphone.

W. F. Howard wrote of him banteringly in *The Methodist Recorder*:

> There are two Dr Flews. There is Dr Flew the learned and charming conversationalist. He wears spectacles. There is Dr R. Newton Flew, who ascends the Conference tribune or the platforms of General Councils wearing eye-glasses with a broad black ribbon. That is the Conference potentate in whose presence I feel very small, before whom my knees tremble and my bones become as water.

It was this which provoked Flew to ask a riddle of his men at Wesley House: 'When is a scholar not a scholar?', with the answer 'When he becomes a journalist'! In a subsequent piece, Howard made a slight correction. The eye-glasses did not have a broad black ribbon, but a thin black double cord!

Flew was designated President of the Methodist Conference in 1945, to take office in 1946. He was in the course of his year as Moderator of the Free Church Federal Council, a sign that his ecumenical progress kept pace with his Methodist, if indeed it did not slightly exceed it. Never before or since has a Moderator been designated as President. Usually the Free Church dignity is conferred on one who is an elder statesman, or ex-President, of his own communion. At this time, however, orthodox dissent had burgeoned into its short-lived, war-time, second spring and was giving honour to its theologians, some of them comparatively young men, like J. S. Whale, who had been an exhilarating Moderator in 1942–3.

Throughout the war, the mood of Methodism had been one of hope deferred. There was less sense of shock, bewilderment and loss of direction than in 1914–18. The war, it was felt, had vindicated the Christian message. Theologically it could be explained as God's judgement on disobedient nations and faithless churches. Its message to Christians was, in the title of a popular book by D. R. Davies, a slightly shrill protagonist, who had his vogue at the time, *On to Orthodoxy*. For many, this meant the recovery of the faith of the Catholic creeds, as illustrated in the brilliant books and broadcasts of C. S. Lewis and the works of Dorothy Sayers and T. S. Eliot, that remarkable literary trio of high Anglicans; for others, the secret was 'Biblical Theology' as unfolded in the teachings of C. H. Dodd, J. S. Whale, and, at that time, A. R. Vidler and Nathaniel Micklem; for Methodists, the need was a return to the 'first works' of evangelism and holiness. Union had not resulted in the advances its supporters had dreamed of, but there were great expectations of what might be accomplished after the war.

In fact, Methodism may not have realised the extent of its war-time achievements. The Methodist Youth Department was formed, with, among much else, two decades of successful and pioneering youth club work ahead of it. Women's Fellowship was created. There was the herculean ministry of W. E. Sangster at Westminster Central Hall, with its combination of histrionic, practical, popular preaching and the mission of mercy and friendliness in the air-raid shelters in the vaults of the building. There was chaplaincy and canteen work wherever there were troops, and there was much patient discussion and teaching in local societies, especially when Howard and Harrison were Presidents. There were also the 'Christian Commando Campaigns'. These owed much to the inspiration of Colin A. Roberts, who had succeeded Flew at Muswell Hill in 1927, but was, from 1939 and for the rest of his active ministry, at the Home Mission Department. The name was topical and memorable. Perhaps it was more than a little exaggerated to imply any comparison in danger or tactics between the real commandos of the war and the advocacy of the gospel mostly by parsons. But the aim was to confront people with the claims of Christianity where they were, and the assignments took team members, quite often two-by-two, into factories, public-houses, schools, nurses' homes, department stores and the open-air. As well as direct testimonies, the technique of question and answer in 'open forums', patented by Donald Soper, was much used, while this was the period of the 'Brains Trust'. Flew himself went on the Commando Campaign to Norwich, and did a good deal of Brains Trust work among forces in the Cambridge area. A stock question was 'Why does not God stop the war?', and Flew's stock answer, which, he claimed, was always received with 'great guffaws', was 'Because he isn't an Almighty Hitler'.

The Commando Campaigns were to have several years of usefulness after the war. The greatest of them – the London Commando Campaign which involved a team of 3000 – was during Flew's Presidency, in April 1947. Well-disposed Anglicans and Free Churchmen often partnered the Methodists – an Anglican Franciscan, Father Gilbert Elliott, was prominent at the Albert Hall Rally, which inaugurated the London Campaign, and quoted the Wesley hymns like a Methodist – but even though some barriers had collapsed under war-time necessities, the normal Anglican attitude to other denominations was still one of cold and superior reserve. But, early in 1946, the Church of England published a report, which showed that it had the same concern as Methodists. It was called *Towards the Conversion of England*.

Methodist spokesmen had urged incessantly the need for 'advance'. Professor Eric Waterhouse, of London University and Richmond College, persuaded the Conference of 1941 to commit itself to a 'Forward Movement'. Flew contrasted the debate on this very favourably with one or two in which the pacificists had, in his view, behaved with considerable obtuseness and invalid logic. By the time he came to the Chair, the war was over, and the Church could resume its historic task in what were felt to be the more favourable circumstances of 'post-war reconstruction'. The one fear was that Methodism might not be equal to the hour, because of what the aged Maltby diagnosed as 'palsy'. It is easy in retrospect to regard this as an over-simplification. Flew, at any rate, was aware that the world and the Church were entering a 'new era'.

The Conference of 1946 met in London, for the first time since the uniting Conference of 1932. The 1944 Conference had been planned for the metropolis, but had been driven to Leeds by 'doodle-bugs'. It fell to Howard to induct Flew, owing to Harrison's death. He could not resist the opportunity to 'rag' amid his dignified periods of generous introduction. To quote the indirect speech of *The Methodist Recorder*:

Providence had dowered him (Flew) with many gifts, not the least of which was that it had moulded him, mentally and physically, on archiepiscopal lines (Laughter). Two or three days ago he (Dr. Howard) had received an American religious magazine, one page of which contained photographs of distinguished Churchmen; and one of the most interesting of them represented two divines in close conference at a table (Laughter). The legend beneath read: "The Revd. Dr. Newton Flew (left); the Archbishop of Canterbury (right)." He had never yet set eyes on his Grace of Cantuar; and had he not known Dr. Flew for many years he would have guessed that the correct description would have been "The Archbishop of Canterbury (left) discussing atomic energy with one of his Suffragans (right)". (Laughter).

The Conference, the first since the complete end of hostilities, met under the shadow of the mushroom cloud. Flew had already served on a sixteen-man commission of the British Council of Churches to consider the terrible new fact of atomic power. Its report, *The Era of Atomic Power*, was published shortly before his Presidency. Subsequent opinion has regarded the Report, in spite of its brave intentions, as too much the product of habits of moral judgement that had become ingrained in response to the Nazi terror. It was insufficiently aware of the ethical revolution which the new order and the old Gospel alike required. But this is the wisdom of hindsight.

Flew's Presidential address was on *The Atomic Bomb and the Eternal Gospel*. He began by referring to the British Council of Churches Report, and deplored the fact that the first use of atomic energy was in the crude form of a bomb. There were those who urged that the Churches ought to devise a political programme for the future of mankind. This they could not do; but they had three specific tasks:

(1) Let them study the facts about atomic energy, its uses and abuses.

(2) Let the Church deepen the sense of world community. The ecumenical movement gave an opportunity for this, while K. S. Latourette, the historian of Christian missions, had characterised

the period until 1914 as 'the great century' of Christian expansion.

(3) Let the Church do the proper work of the Church.

Flew's third point was expanded into the main theme of his utterance. The Church must proclaim, as Jesus did, that 'The Reign of God is at hand'. As he expounded the 'gospel of the Kingdom', Flew produced one of his most memorable phrases about the purpose of God: 'He planned the Cross before he packed the atom'. Of all the themes of Christian doctrine, Flew pleaded especially for the recovery of faith in the life everlasting. To the charge that this was otherworldliness, he retorted, 'We need something otherworldly when we stand by the graveside of our dead, or when we face the thought of the destruction of thousands of millions in Auschwitz or Belsen.' When man repudiates the eternal background, he becomes a secularist and the adequate definition of that is Chesterton's – 'dated'.

The President went on to outline an eight-point programme for the local Church. He had devised this after consultation with ministers and laymen in the circuits. We may summarise it as follows:

(1) To hold a weekly meeting for prayer and fellowship.

(2) To be open to newcomers.

(3) To care for members in transit, by trying to link them with the Church in the place of removal and being particularly solicitous of those coming into its own area.

(4) To engage in regular and habitual worship – 'the only way to nourish and sustain faith'.

(5) To make every effort to recover the lapsed.

(6) To regard daily work as part of a Divine calling.

(7) To engage in family worship and Bible reading.

(8) To make evangelism the aim of every activity, to ensure that every business meeting serves this purpose.

As was to be expected, Flew urged the quest for holiness. 'This is your real trouble – you are not producing saints.'

The peroration was as eloquent and powerful as anything Flew ever uttered. Taking up a quotation at the end of his penultimate paragraph – ' "Is not my word like fire?" saith the Lord', he spoke of the fire which purges and the fire which warms, and longed for 'a fire amid the ashes which will set the world ablaze'. And so into a verse of Charles Wesley's:

> In me thy Spirit dwell;
> In me thy mercies move:
> So shall the fervour of my zeal
> Be the pure flame of love.

The address ended in a 'silence which could be felt'.

It was a properly Methodist speech, which gathered up the convictions, hopes, self-criticism and longings of the best Methodist minds of the period. It sounded notes which were to be heard again and again in Methodist pronouncements of the next ten years. It enunciated the principal themes of Flew's Presidency, notably evangelism and *personal* evangelism.

To the Ministerial Session, which in those days met after the Representative, Flew spoke of Worship, both private and public. This was one of the subjects which he handled with particular *finesse*. In treating of it he was able to indulge his interests both in the theological and the practical, to raid his vast knowledge of the Christian traditions and to open his own heart. Because it gives the quintessence of his teaching in many places and over many years, it is reproduced in full as an appendix to this chapter.

After the responsibilities of presiding at the annual Conference itself, the Methodist President becomes the itinerant *par excellence*. He must visit virtually every

District in the Connexion, while towards the end of his
year, he must take the Chair at the Welsh Assembly and
the Irish Conference. In addition, he has to maintain
some link with the specific work of his particular
'station', in Flew's case, Wesley House and its Principalship. Gordon Rupp was appointed to Wesley House as
President's assistant and took Flew's classes for the year,
but in most weeks Flew spent one or two nights in
Cambridge to attend to College business and correspondence. From Saturday until Wednesday or Thursday
each week he might be anywhere in England, Scotland
or Wales, preaching sermons, addressing rallies, holding
the one man Brains Trusts which were a feature of his
Presidency, and liable at any moment to be called to
arbitrate in cases of discipline, or resignation, or high
policy. We have referred to the Baptismal dispute in a
country circuit, which was submitted to him; there were
also matters of mixed marriages, and of approaches
from Bishops about Methodist ministers who wished to
enter the Church of England. The President would have
frequently to be in London to preside at the major
Committees, such as Overseas and Home Missions,
Ministerial Training and General Purposes. His regular
letters to his mother at Hatch End were often written in
rolling, crowded trains, or hotel bedrooms late at night,
or between meetings. In all this Flew felt amazingly
exhilarated by his constant discovery of numbers of
Methodists who prayed for the President every day. He
also enjoyed his association with the Vice-President, the
Barnsley layman and former Member of Parliament,
R. J. Soper.

In October 1946, Flew spent six consecutive days in
Cambridge for the Silver Jubilee of Wesley House. For
the morning service at Wesley Church, Christ's Pieces,
on 20th October, he chose perhaps his favourite text,
I Corinthians 4:7, 'What hast thou, that thou didst not
receive?', and expounded it in terms of an aphorism of

the Scottish ecumenist, A. C. Craig, first General Secretary of the British Council of Churches, that, for the Christian, 'Religion is grace and ethics is gratitude'. It was not the easiest occasion of his Presidency and he was more nervous than usual. That evening he was at the Hills Road Church, and immediately afterwards he had to go back to Wesley Library to talk to the University Methodist Society, entirely without preparation, on 'Methodism and the Worldwide Church'. But on such a theme and in such circumstances he rarely failed – sometimes to a popular or semi-popular audience, he was more effective when he spoke spontaneously from his unique knowledge and experience than when he had deliberated his remarks and their effects – and this was a *tour de force*.

The next day saw a celebration lunch at the House and a lecture by Leonard Hodgson, Regius Professor of Divinity at Oxford, and Secretary of the Faith and Order Continuation Committee, on *Biblical Theology and the Sovereignty of God*. Flew, flanked by Hodgson and the Regius Professor at Cambridge, Raven, commented that to have the two senior Divinity Professors of the rival universities on the same platform was almost 'an eschatalogical event'. The court was thronged with old students and representatives of the University and Methodism, among whom was W. E. Sangster, for once strangely inconspicuous. There followed a dinner with the Vice-Chancellor, the Senior Proctor (Fred Brittain, author of memoirs of Quiller-Couch and Bernard Manning), the Bishop of Ely (Edward Wynn), the Dixie Professor (Norman Sykes), and several Heads of Houses among the guests as well as Michael Gutteridge's son.

December 5th was Maltby's eightieth birthday and a dinner in Leeds was held to honour him. There were fifty-two people present. The Bishop of Ripon (G. A. Chase, formerly of Trinity Hall and Selwyn) was the only non-Methodist. Twenty years later, a gathering for one so illustrious would have had a larger ecumenical presence.

By January 1947 it was clear that the winter would be one of the severest in living memory. Yet through blizzard, ice and flood, the tours went on. Only Exeter and Stafford were inaccessible, and the President's health remained excellent. The *Tavistock Times* had this to say, pointing out that he had visited that small town in April because a Conference in Geneva had been postponed:

Last year the President, Dr A. W. Harrison, died while on his travels and Conference passed a resolution enjoining future Presidents to take fewer engagements. Dr Flew's way of taking a possible rest is to offer to perform a sentimental journey, to visit his birthplace, his old college friend at Tavistock, a former Church steward of his is now retired at Rilla Mill and to preach on the 'Green' at Polperro on the anniversary of John Wesley's so doing. . . .

Flew thought that the local press served the cause of the Churches better than the national. Fresh from the *Tavistock Times*, he spoke to the spring meeting of the British Council of Churches and exhorted the London editors to remember that 'London is not England' and 'to trust the moral instincts of the people a little more, and remember that there is a great, though as yet perhaps undiscovered, wealth of religious interest among the people of this country'.

And so the months passed by with their kaleidoscopic view of Methodism in 'austerity', frost-bound England, emerging into a glorious summer as through waters of baptism. There was a daunting Holy Week which seems to have included journeys to Darlington, Manchester and Masham, in Yorkshire, and an Easter Day of five services in Harrogate. Some of the trains were so crowded that the Presidential suitcase in the corridor was the only seat he could find, if indeed there was always room to perch on that. The train from Manchester to Northallerton could not move out of the station. The carriages were so full that they were right down on their springs.

Holsworthy, his birthplace, gave him an illuminated address. He preached in Worcester Cathedral. He revelled in what he described as 'the debauch of holy oratory' at Cliff College on Whit Monday and was much fêted at the Irish Conference. In several places he had German Prisoners of War among his auditors and spoke to them in their own language. Everywhere he looked out for children and made a habit of asking them to line up and shake hands with him after his meetings. Mrs Flew was with him whenever possible and one of his gambits was to tell a story which included some description of a lady's hat. He would pretend to get stuck and appeal to Mrs Flew in the congregation. In Cornwall, the intervention of the President's lady excited considerable curiosity and necks were craned from the gallery. Flew called out 'That's right! Have a good look at her. I quite agree with you that she's worth looking at. I enjoy looking at her myself.'

One of Flew's celebrated addresses was on the theme 'What is the difference between a Christian and a very decent-living person who does not go to Church?'. He had summarised his seven point reply in his moderatorial address of 1945 to the Free Church Federal Council on *Evangelism and the New Order*. Here is a fuller recension which, in response to many requests, including one from Leslie Weatherhead, he had duplicated:

(1) *A Christian says: "As for me, 'Jesus is Lord' "*, and the non-Christian can't say it.

(This allegiance naturally also involves attention and

obedience to the *words* of Jesus (Luke VI. 46). Does the non-Christian give this attention?)

(2) *A Christian is a forgiven man; he knows what it is to take forgiveness from God.* There is a barrier between himself and God and Jesus has taken it out of the way. The other person doesn't know this.

(3) *A Christian 'walks with God'.* (One of the oldest and best of the many phrases used to describe the fact); he knows what prayer is. He takes everything to God, or, if he forgets, he is sorry about it. He knows quite well that this is the way to live. The non-Christian doesn't do this.

(4) *A Christian shares all these three convictions or experiences with other Christians;* He knows that there are others with him, and is glad about it. This is what is meant by the phrase: "the fellowship of the Holy Spirit". This sharing or fellowship involves the Church. The 'decent person' doesn't see any point in the Church for himself.

(5) *A Christian has a cause, which is the cause of the Church.* This is the reconciliation of all men and women and children (and indeed of the universe) to God and therefore to one another. (This clearly is a greater cause than Communism or Fascism, or the League of Nations. You may say "it is impossible" but you can't say "it isn't great".) The non-Christian hasn't this cause.

(6) *A Christian is never satisfied with himself.* If he is, he ceases to be a Christian. There are always 'heights beyond'. The non-Christian seems to be satisfied; "I'm as good as them as goes!"

(7) *The Christian looks forward to heaven;* he has a conviction and a message about life beyond the grave. Because this conviction is founded on Christ as Lord (see 1) as Saviour (see 2), and is giving him a life of communion with God (see 3), the Christian has a certainty of continued communion with God which the 'decent person' hasn't got.

On these Seven Ways of Difference, some additional notes are appended.

(i) The whole of the Christian creed is really contained or implied in them – i.e. the body of belief which is common to all the main communions of Christendom. Thus, the

Divinity of Jesus Christ is in No. 1; the Atonement and the great belief, on Grace, Man and Sin, in No. 2; the Christian doctrine of a personal and loving God, in No. 3; the doctrines of the Holy Spirit and the Church, in Nos. 4 and 5; the doctrines of the communion of Saints and the life everlasting in Nos. 6 and 7.

(ii) These Seven Ways point to a mode of life which in its motive, content, sanction and ultimate goal is vastly different (and ought to be) from the life of the decent living people who don't hold these convictions. What this Way of Life is may be discovered from the New Testament and in fellowship. There is no method of discovering it if you drift outside the fellowship.

(iii) The Seven Ways deny emphatically the commonest English heresy that religion is to be identified with morality. Christianity is inseparably linked with morality, but essentially it means walking with God, by His strength and not our own.

Some more modern Christians are so conscious of the 'hiddenness' of the Christian life that such statements embarrass them, but it is interesting to compare these points with Archbishop Ramsey's description, in his Scott Holland lectures of 1964, of 'three things' which constitute the 'something different' of Christianity. 'The first is a deep reverence for persons as destined for eternity with God. The second is a kind of heavenly serenity which is able to draw the sting of suffering. And the third is the humility of a man or woman who has known authentically the presence of God.'

On 15th July, 1947, Conference met at the City Hall, Newcastle upon Tyne and Flew had to hand over to W. E. Farndale, Chairman of the Lincoln District, in whom the Church honoured a different style both of personality and of Methodism, a pupil of A. S. Peake and a quietly acute leader. The Flews must have been especially gratified to receive this letter just before Conference opened:

at/
9 Montagu Avenue
Kenton Road
Newcastle-on-Tyne 3.
tel. 52593
July 15, 1947.

My dear Mrs. Flew,

This closing day of your husband's year of office must not pass without my sending you a brief note of warmest congratulations upon so successful a course, without the interruption of a single engagement lost through ill-health.

When I think of the incessant strain, coming so soon after The Moderator's itineration, with, the severest spell of wintry weather for 52 years to endure, I marvel at the buoyant courage that he has shown throughout.

I am sure that the courage was sustained in no small degree by the partnership which you have given him throughout this year of far wanderings.

You have given the comfort of your constant presence and must have inspired him to face with cheerful confidence the trials and tribulations of our English railway system.

It has been a triumphal progress that has left nothing but grateful memories all along the path of the pilgrimage.

Please do not dream of replying to this note.

Yours very sincerely,
Wilbert F. Howard.

The transition of power in Methodism from one President to another is swift and decisive. In a trice the chief dignitary of the Connexion inducts his successor, leaves his Chair and enters the shadowy existence of the ex-Presidents. *Sic transit gloria mundi.* Flew however had to intervene at least twice on important issues at the Conference of 1947. One was on atomic warfare. He felt that Christians needed to ask why the first atomic bomb had not been dropped on an uninhabited place instead of Hiroshima, and why the bomb on Nagasaki followed so soon afterwards instead of giving the Japanese government a chance to sue for peace. He also spoke powerfully in favour of the scheme for Church union in South India, due to be inaugurated that autumn, against a last-minute, rearguard attack from Dr Henry Bett, an ex-President and former Handsworth tutor.

Flew's consolation prizes, if he needed them, were a visit to the Methodist Ecumenical Conference at Springfield, Massachusetts, in the early autumn of 1947 and the delivery of the Cato lecture in Australia the following May.

Flew's first experience of world Methodism was when the Wesleyan Conference, meeting at Plymouth in 1929, appointed him, without his knowledge, as its representative to the centenary celebrations of Scandinavian Methodism in May 1930. This introduced him to the life and work of George Scott, who, converted at a love-feast in Edinburgh, went out to Sweden in 1830 and in twelve years, before he was driven home by a riot, made a permanent contribution to the spiritual life of the land. Flew was presented in Uppsala to the great Archbishop and ecumenist, Nathan Söderblom, preached at Gothenburg on 'Holiness without which no man shall see the Lord', lectured on John Wesley, and met many of the Methodist leaders from Europe and the United States, including Dr (afterwards Bishop) Sommer, of Frankfurt, to whom, on the eve of the war, he sent a copy of *Jesus and His Church*.

Springfield 1947 marked the beginning of the post-war movement of world Methodist confessionalism, which has run parallel to the ecumenical movement ever since and has sometimes seemed to be its rival. But in those days all was American generosity, hospitality and kindness to former enemies and impoverished friends. It was Flew's first visit to the United States. His reactions were the customary ones of wide-eyed fascination and amusement leading to affection and respect. 'This is the best Ecumenical Methodist Conference ever held. But some of the speakers are so slow that I can write letters and listen as well.' Flew himself had to speak at a meeting, which had begun one evening at 8 p.m., but his turn, delayed by 'devotions' of almost an hour, and a long-winded preceding speaker, did not come until 9.50. He was told that there would be great disappointment if he only spoke for twenty minutes, so he continued until 10.30, describing the marks of the Gospel, with some indebtedness to Maltby:

> Once for all
> All or nothing
> Here and now.

'I have been repeatedly assured since that this will be preached all over USA – which was exactly why I gave it.'

After the Conference, he delivered the Shaffer Lectures at Yale Divinity School. He chose as his subject 'The Ethics of Jesus', which he divided into four lectures: *The Ethics of Grace and Natural Ethics: The Gateway – 'Repent and Believe' : The Main Road – a Discussion of the Beatitudes: The Originality of the Ethics of Jesus.*

This theme had occupied Flew's thoughts ever since his Fernley-Hartley lecture in 1938. He wanted to follow *Jesus and His Church* with a companion study of *Jesus and His Way.* The opportunity seemed to have come when he was asked to deliver the Cato lecture in Australia in 1941. This lecture takes its name, as Flew pointed out to his old friend Roderick Macleod, not from the Roman senator who cried *Carthago delenda est,* but from an Australian magnate, Fred J. Cato, who wished to enrich the life and thought of Australasian Methodism by original contributions from scholars, preferably British. In the early months of the war, indeed until the autumn of 1940, Flew was still hoping that he might be able to keep the original date. He had received invitations to lecture or preach on the way out from places as disparate as

Capetown and Hawaii. In his excitement, he wrote to his mother in 1940:

> By the next post I shall expect an invitation from the Emperor of Japan to address his harem in Tokyo; and after that an invitation from some Paramount Chief in the neighbourhood of Fiji to offer myself as the most succulent morsel in the chief Boiled Meat Festival of the Year – since he has heard of my generous proportions. I really cannot accept all these invitations.
>
> Hear the shouts from Honolulu! hark! the cries of Uraguay!
> The desires of Matabeles and the longings of Cathay!
> Do you hear them calling, Mother, from the depths of old Peru?
> "We want Faith and we want Order!
> We want Robert Newton Flew!"
>   Yours in overwhelming modesty ...

It was not to be. Even as late as the Michaelmas term of 1947, Professor F. S. Marsh was enquiring of his Wesley House pupils 'When is your Principal going to Australia? I shall believe it when he has actually left.' He did leave, at last, with Mrs Flew, by RMS *Orion* from Tilbury, on Thursday evening, 25th March, 1948, and the next morning watched with emotion the receding outline of the Isle of Portland as 'the old country' was left behind.

He enjoyed Australia, learned the vocabulary and was able to say 'Good oh!' at appropriate moments, and, in a sermon, to translate the Greek *axios* by 'You beaut!'. The programme was alarmingly crowded. The Flews arrived at Fremantle towards the end of April and in the next fourteen days he kept thirty engagements between Perth and Melbourne. His children's addresses, especially an old one, (OWNERUPERER), which involved writing on an invisible blackboard, 'the kind you see in an Arab tent because there isn't one', and his sermons, were hailed with enthusiasm. In Adelaide, he was interviewed on the radio as Chief Personality of the week and asked by the

Lord Mayor to inaugurate a new 'Food for Britain' Campaign. There were politicians and dignitaries to meet and also academic occasions and lectures to students. The Cato itself, delivered to a crowd during the General Conference, 'went off as well as could be expected'.

The book, however, was nowhere near completion. It was not destined to be finished in his lifetime. This has been a puzzle to some. Certainly, at this stage his health was good and there was no waning of his powers. It has been suggested that perhaps, after all, ethics was not so congenial a subject as spirituality and ecclesiology and demanded a rigidly philosophic investigation of moral judgements, which was not so much in his line as the more theological aspects. But there is probably no need to be so sophisticated. The writing of learned books, which are to influence the scholarship of a generation, demands all the time a man has. He must eschew all other pursuits and deny not simply pleasures but duties. This was made impossible by the direction Flew's life had taken for many years. It might have been different had he been elected Norris-Hulse Professor. Instead it was decreed that he should be a scholar, but also an evangelist, a theologian, but also a statesman, using his learning and his acumen in the arduous work of Christian reconciliation. And although, by 1948, he was an ex-President of the Methodist Conference and had no more big books of his own to give to the world, the harvest of his ecumenical labours was still to be reaped.

The Presidential Address to the
Ministerial Session of the Methodist
Conference, July 1946

The President, addressing the Conference, spoke as follows:
All the work of the Church may be summed up in two words – Evangelism and Worship. To bring others to know the

God revealed in Jesus Christ, and with them to worship – these are the all-inclusive ends. By worship I mean what the New Testament writers mean, the response of the whole personality to the mercies of God. The word includes what we do in daily life, the work of man, as well as the prayers we say, although only One Life has ever been true worship right through its course. *I beseech you, brethren, by the mercies of God to present your bodies a living sacrifice – and this is our reasonable worship.* The word *body*, as often in St. Paul, means the individual personality as an active concrete whole, and all its activities are meant to be worship. St. James says the same thing in his picturesque way about pure and undefiled worship. St Paul and St James did not always agree. But here there is no argument between them, and when we interrogate St Peter as to what he means by 'spiritual sacrifices', we discover that, on this point of theology, there is no need for St Paul to withstand him to the face.

But there is a narrower sense in which we use the word worship, of the prayers of the individual, or the devotions of the community. It is 'worship' in this sense of which I would fain speak today. Here it is, in our prayers, that we draw on the resources of God for our work of bringing others to Him, and for that even greater task of transforming the common life of mankind. We have an altar, a secret shrine, a holy of holies, where we replenish our scanty stock of love. As my old friend, Alfred Whitham, used to say: Our religion begins as a domestic affair, and ends as a foreign policy; it first accepts a gift and then proceeds to distribute it. It is first a homely lamp, and then a public beacon. It is the homely lamp which we are tending now.

Nearly twenty-five years ago, some little time after I had gone into a new circuit, a girl of twelve wrote me a letter, asking me to teach her how to pray. She had come from a home of the modern kind, where the parents do not believe in bringing up the child in any particular faith. But she had strayed into our church, and then asked to be baptised, and became a member. And that letter was the result. It was a shock for me to realise that never in that church had I preached a sermon telling people how to pray. So I began to rebuild on the ruins of my failure. It does seem to me now that, wherever else we may fail, we ought not to fail in this realm. Most of you,

I expect, have your own schemes of giving others 'first aid in prayer'. As a brother among brethren I will share my own with you.

Here is the first. Get some regular habits. Whenever a man says to you, 'I only pray when I feel like it', you are fearful for him. His soul is in deadly peril, for he is at the mercy of his moods. Why this need for regular habits? Why not be 'spontaneous', as they call it? Well, in the ordinary business of life we have certain fixed times for meals – or fixed times for work, fixed times for recreation. And for private prayer, no fixed times at all? That means removing prayer clean out of the category of the serious business of life. But prayer is an art; it must be learnt and practised, as that little girl of twelve knew very well.

Secondly, I would say to the enquirer, after you have appointed your regular time for private prayer, get quietness of mind. We have to be quiet enough to receive the great gift which God will give. 'Wherefore stand still in thy mind', says an old director of souls. Or as the more modern George Tyrrell said of prayer, 'God does not like fidgets'. All the highest gifts of life are costly in reception. It needs more of you to listen to Beethoven than to jazz, to read *Macbeth* than to read the newspaper headlines. Some kind of sustained effort is needed to overcome our restless mood, our incurable reluctance to commune with God. 'Put pressure on thyself', says Thomas à Kempis. Everyone of us knows, or has to learn, how most swiftly to enter into the inner shrine, after the settled time of praying has begun. One brother minister told me out in Mesopotamia that whenever he thought of his home he could begin to pray at once. And as we learn the ways of our heavenly country, there are certain avenues which draw us thither by their own spell. For Methodists, brought up in our tradition, there are hymns which mean immediate quietness of mind whenever we begin to repeat them. I know a man who has only to say:

> *Open, Lord, my inward ear*
> *And bid my heart rejoice,*

and he must have fallen very far from grace if, after a few lines, the strain and heat haven't left him, and the healing streams are not washing his soul clean.

Another prescription in our first aid is that there is a variety in prayer. I know that more than ever my brethren in their directions to beginners include a sight of the map of the prayer life. And they find that for many people in our churches the rich domains and spacious provinces of prayer are as mysterious as the mediaeval maps of Africa. Our traditions help us here. Thus, there is a fine tradition in Presbyterian worship that the first prayers in the service should be confession and adoration, mingled in the New Book of Common Order with supplication; and the second period is devoted to Thanksgiving and Intercession. A glance at the page of 'Contents' in our own hymn-book ought to tell our people that there is a great width in prayer. I wonder if the lesson is getting home. But we do tell beginners at least that prayer is more than 'I want', and more than 'Thank you'.

From an older minister, who is present in this Conference, I learnt many years ago that one of the directions most needed was the simplest: *Tell it all to God.* The other way of putting it is, 'Just as I am'. This counsel comes right out of the heart of the Gospel. Take the common sentence that we hear, 'I've tried praying and it's no use. It's like talking to a brick wall.' I always say, 'Have you told Him that?' 'Well, no,' the man says, 'not exactly that.' And I say, 'Well, He is there, whatever you feel. Tell Him that, and you will soon be ashamed, and your shame will be His answer.' Of course, this simple counsel is based on the most characteristic promise in the Christian faith. There is some difficulty to be told to God. And the promise is that *God is to be found in the hard place.* It was in Gethsemane that the greatest victory was won. When St. Paul unveils his heart, and says that his trouble, unknown to us, was as a stake lacerating his flesh, and knocks thrice at the door, the answer comes, though he does not get the answer he wanted. *My strength is made perfect in weakness.* As a living master of the art of the cure of souls has said: 'We want people to come to God, but they do not come to God in general. They come through the sharp challenge with the call of God in it that is meeting them in daily life, or through some decision in practical things which throws open the choice between the darkness and the light.'

We are meant to take the practical work of life into the sanctuary. Our religion ought never to be escape, unless it be escape from sin. Wilfrid Moulton used to tell how in one of his circuits a certain man used to pray in the vestry with him before the service, and every Sunday came the words: 'We thank Thee that today we can escape from the unwelcome labours of the week.' But if we cannot find God somewhere in the labours of the week, we shall end by losing Him. It is in the hard place that He is.

There is an unfathomable depth in this characteristic promise of our Lord. *My grace is sufficient for Thee, for my strength is made perfect in weakness.* It means that faith is to be exercised in face of a particular difficulty, a mountain in view. It means that when we are asked, 'How can I find God?' we shall not merely answer, 'In this Book', even if it is the Book of Books. That may be an evasion. And we shall not necessarily say that the questioner will find Him in the beauty of the earth, or deep in the human heart. There is one answer that is never unreal or irrelevant. We shall say: 'Please look at that which you dread most, or with which you are most concerned; that problem which has been weighing you down the most, which is always besetting you. Go boldly up to that closed door and knock and you will find God at the opening of the door.' Is there any other parallel in all the religions of the world to the Christian preacher who dares to grasp the nettle of suffering with words such as these? *Wherefore I take pleasure in weaknesses, in injuries, in necessities, in persecutions, in distresses, for Christ's sake; for when I am weak, then am I strong.* In a word, God has planted the Cross at the very heart of the prayer life.

These four directions for beginners do not lose their urgency when we come to the consideration of our public worship. They imply, as we have already seen, far more than they say. Regular habits of private prayer carry with them habits of corporate worship, or else religion tends to become refined self-centredness. The prayer for interior quietness, for the attentive ear, implies a God who speaks, a God who inspires the very prayer that He accepts, a God who gives. The rich variety of prayer points to the height, and breadth, and length and depth, of the salvation which He gives. And the fact that He always succours us in the hard place brings us at once to the incarnation and the Atonement and the Life Everlasting, for He has come to meet us in this life just where we are. Here, then, are four principles which should govern our public worship.

Why should we have serious and regular habits of public worship as of private prayer? Because of the very nature of the Christian life. It springs out of an infinite indebtedness to Christ, in which all His people share. In a sentence we may say, 'Our religion is grace, our worship is gratitude'. But grace is no private privilege, and the gratitude is shared. Take the saying which might seem to be the most highly individual and personal of all expressions of worship. *He loved me and gave Himself up for me.* Set it in its context of Galatians two and three, see how the writer in his emotion changes his pronouns almost recklessly – We, a man, I – we, and it is the pronoun 'we' which is victorious in the end. That passage is entirely characteristic of Christian spirituality. God deals with us as sons, and we know Him as Father. There is nothing in the world more personal than this relationship, and nothing less private. It runs out into social reform, international service, and yet in its essence it is a personal relationship for which every man was created, and without which he must go blinded and hungry all his days. But it is always gloriously shared.

Take that lovely hymn, 'Thou Shepherd of Israel, and mine' – there are the two elements, individual and social, in the very first line. Then four lines of personal longing, so entirely individual that if you didn't know the verse off by heart you would say, 'This is the flight of the alone to the Alone, of which Plotinus wrote. But no!' before the end of the verse, in the sixth line, he is thinking of all 'who their Shepherd obey'. The crowd is always present, there are multitudes continually thronging their way into the devotions of Charles Wesley. Away he goes in the second verse:

> *Ah! show me that happiest place,*
> *The place of Thy people's abode,*
> *Where saints in an ecstasy gaze,*
> *And hang on a crucified God;*

and so on, to the end of the adoring gratitude of that passionate hymn. Father Hebert agrees that the mediaeval mysticism of the Catholic Church is often a solitary flight, and that much of

Reformation piety is nearer to the shared and corporate life of the New Testament. Contrast the saying of Newman that he knew only two luminously self-evident beings, the soul and God – with verse after verse of our hymns:

> *Come let us, who in Christ believe,*
> *Our common Saviour praise.*

But this is a hymn under the heading of 'The Gospel Call'. It is an appeal to the worst of sinners. But the Lord is a common Saviour, and experience of Him is gloriously scattered abroad. Every service we conduct should have this gratitude at the heart of it, a gratitude to be shared.

The second principle of Christian worship, of the gratitude which is shared, is that the worship itself is the gift of God, the product of grace. Christian worship is *in the Spirit*, on a new supernatural level. In his little book, *Prayer in Christian Theology*, that great theologian, Canon A. L. Lilley, first sets down the distinguishing quality of Christian prayer as contrasted with the ideas of the natural man. The natural man prays for visible material benefits. But the Christian view is that mere man cannot pray at all, and that no mere desire of his can constitute real prayer. It is God in us who prays. It is our nature, penetrated by the Divine Spirit, and assisted by the Divine grace, that is alone capable of true prayer, in the full Christian sense.

Somehow, through every service which we conduct, there should be pulsating the conviction that we are working the work of God; that He is inspiring the worship which we present; that we are offering a gift to the congregation, and not merely making fresh demands. If only Methodists would join in persevering prayer that their corporate worship should be God's gift, inspired by Him, there would be no more powerful means of Evangelism and the mountains would begin to flow. It must be the aim of every service to proclaim how near God is, and how good He is, and what an amazing power He has over those who yield themselves to His adorable will.

The third principle of public worship is that every worshipper should catch at least a glimpse of the rich variety of the life of prayer; and in consequence be made ready for the fresh bestowal of the wealth of God. Here I think we are confronted with the greatest obstacle in the way of re-vivification of the Free Church type of worship. This Puritan type has been dominated by the long prayer. Never was any title more appropriate. But the only occurrence of the phrase in the New Testament is an unfortunate precedent, and when our Lord gave a model prayer it was miraculously brief. It is not my desire to gird at the past, or to decry any genuine worship. I must remember the words of the prophet Malachi to critics of divine service: 'Ye said also, Behold, what a weariness is it! and ye have snuffed at it, saith the Lord of Hosts.' But I will also quote from one who cannot be accused of lack of reverence for the Puritan tradition, my friend, the lamented Bernard Manning. The year before he died, he wrote a paper for our Cambridge Ministers' Fraternal. Let us consider his criticisms so as to avoid the faults he detects in our Free Church worship. 'Too long,' he said of our prayers, and 'too woolly, too wordy, too voluble, too casual.' Our common prayers are not often enough what our prayers (in the language of Jeremy Taylor) should be – intense, solemn and affectionate. 'I speak', he said, 'as a lay preacher who has tried for a quarter of a century, and failed utterly. Consider the ordinary dangers of extempore speech; and add the peculiar difficulty of that sort of extempore speech which is common prayer. How can we gather Confession, Thanksgiving, Intercession, Adoration, Dedication, into two or three prayers? And too often we try to combine them all in one.'

The remedy suggested by Bernard Manning was to plan the whole service – the call to worship, the lessons, the hymns, the prayers, and sermon, so as to give an appropriate place, and not always the same place, to the various elements of prayer. We have, I believe, almost endless liturgical possibilities in our hymn book. There are hymns of adoration, confession, dedication, thanksgiving, intercession. The Old Testament lesson, which preachers often find a difficulty, can be so chosen as to reduce the burden carried by the prayer. Both lessons, indeed, can be used, sometimes, either for supplying a meditation on the nearness and the power of God, or for Confession, or even Intercession. If only the congregation is helped to understand what is being done, and why, there is no need to cover the same ground again. But nothing will be of any avail unless the minister knows the needs of the congregation, and

unless he knows people how can he pray on their behalf, and
not merely for them? Provided that the minister knows how
frail and wayward these minds of ours can be at the hour of
prayer, the pastoral heart, which is the gift of Christ to His
under-shepherds, is the best guide in public prayer.

This brings us to the 'hard place', which is daily life. Somehow the men and women of our time must find God and His
purpose for them in the ordinary work of life. I cannot resist the
conviction that this task is hardly begun. This means, I think,
a widening, or 'outering' as Dr Lidgett expressively calls it, of
religious experience; it ought to be possible, but is not yet
common, to find Christians everywhere who know what it is,
not merely to do their daily work and then be glad to have
done with it, not merely to be Christians as they do it, but to see
God's meaning in the very work itself. That is one of the 'hard
places' where God can be found. He is the author of nature as
well as of supernature. Indeed, an old minister of the Wesleyan
branch of our Church used to say, 'Every man needs to be
converted twice, once from nature to grace, and then from
grace back again to nature.' *We have an altar* – Christ Crucified,
Living, Reigning. We take our problems there, and Christian
spirituality has found it possible to take pleasure in distresses for
Christ's sake.

A minister of God whom I greatly admired used to say,
'Meet suffering, when it comes, with joy. That is the Christian
way!' Ah, yes, it is, but how far above these frail hearts of ours
does that truth soar. Yet I can see that living under the Cross
means exactly that. There is a member of this Conference
whose sister was told that she had only a few months to live.
When he hurried to her room of suffering, he found her eyes
shining with divine radiance. 'How thankful I am', she said,
'that at last I have a chance of bearing my witness for our
Lord!' Edward Lyttelton, headmaster and cricketer, used to
say that when we say the General Thanksgiving everyone of us
ought to remember that Bishop Reynolds of Norwich wrote it
in 1662 in the course of twenty years of continuous physical
suffering. Scott Holland was a man who spread joy around
wherever he went. Yet for thirty years he was never free from
headaches. And you and I, God forgive us, are ministers of a
religion which can produce men who thus can meet suffering

with joy. Who are we that we should ever whimper about the steepness of the way, or appeal for self-denial or stress the heaviness of the Cross – when we know the Great Companion who bears it with us, and has opened to us the vastness of eternity, and the illimitable possibilities of growth and service?

How dare I say this? I do not know. I take refuge now in the words of that great seventeenth-century commentator on First Peter. Leighton was writing to the clergy of his Synod of Dunblane. 'But you will possibly say, What does he himself that speaks these things to us? *Alas, I am ashamed to tell you.* All I dare say is this: I think I see the beauty of holiness and am enamoured of it, though I attain it not; and howsoever little I attain, would rather live and die in the pursuit of it, than in the pursuit, yea, in the possession and enjoyment of all the advantages that this world affords. And I trust, dear brethren, that you have the same opinion, and have the same desire and design, and follow it both more diligently and with better success.' And to Leighton's words let me add that, in very truth, we know some at least of the proffered benefits of public and private worship, some fragments of the plenitude of Gospel grace:

> *A pardon written with His blood,*
> *The favour and the peace of God.*

ometimes at least we know:

> *The genuine, meek humility,*
> *The wonder – Why such love to me?*
> *The o'erwhelming power of saving grace,*
> *The sight that veils the seraph's face;*
> *The speechless awe that dares not move,*
> *And all the silent heaven of love.*

7

The Ecumenist

ON 22ND AUGUST, 1948, Flew walked in procession with the 1400 delegates, alternates, consultants, youth representatives and accredited visitors to the Nieuwe Kerk in Amsterdam for the inaugural service of the First Assembly of the World Council of Churches, which was brought into official existence the next day. Thus the vision, seen afar by some prophetic eyes from the sad days of the earliest schisms in the Body of Christ, and greeted as nearer by the Edinburgh Conference of 1910, came to reality after decades of consultation and two world wars. Flew wrote to his mother:

> The days are so full that I cannot tell you one-hundredth part of the interest of this city and this World Assembly. Tis delightful to meet more and more authors of the books I've read – e.g. Karl Barth, who has been vigorously nodding his assent to some forthright speeches I have made in the discussion on the 'Universal Church in God's design' in the 'section' of about 100 people who are entrusted with this topic. Other new friends are Bp. Martin of USA who called on us, the Archbp. of Sydney and his wife who often sit with us at dinner or breakfast, Professor Jacques Courvoisier of Strasbourg whose books on Bucer I have read, Huxtable, a very pleasant and able young Congregational minister from Palmers Green, Professor Devadult, a Baptist from Serampore College Bengal, whom I invited to have luncheon with us today, Prof. Pauch of Chicago. The old friends side

by side with whom I sit on committee are Principal William
Robinson (The Disciples of Christ) and Martin Niemöller.
The most gorgeously dressed person last Monday at the
RIJKS MUSEUM when the Minister of Justice gave a reception
to us, introduced himself to me as an old student of mine at
Bangalore. He is now the Metropolitan Bishop of the Mar
Thoma Church of Travancore of South India, known to me
as C. M. John but to all S. India as the Metropolitan
Juhanon! He was very proud when I introduced him to the
Archbp. of Canterbury as an old pupil of mine! Geoffrey
said 'Why yes I know him Flew, he came to visit me at
Lambeth'. Putting his arm round my neck, Geoffrey turned
to the Metrop. Juhanon and said 'I thought there was
something wrong with your Theology – it must have been
because you've been trained by Flew'. This was precisely the
kind of humour which Indians love! The Archbp. proceeded
to tell him how once he was *proxime accessit* to me in 1913 for
the Ellerton Prize!!

We are just off to the Burgomaster's reception in the Royal
Palace.

. . . .

We saw the Princess Juliana and Prince Bernhard last
Monday. They came to hear Karl Barth. Next Sunday we
go to communion in the Nieuwe Kerk by invitation of the
Reformed Church of Holland. Benson Perkins our President
is taking part in the celebration.

Flew had arrived at Amsterdam after a lifetime's
journey via Merton, Marburg, Rome, Bangalore and
Cambridge. We must examine some of the milestones,
trace some of the parallel and tributary roads, and see
how the route continued in the years that remained when
the Assembly was over.

But first we must destroy a myth, to which much of
what we have so far recorded, such as W. F. Howard's
induction speech, may have given credence. The letter
from Amsterdam shows what was probably evident in
his Oxford days, that Flew enjoyed to be recognised by
dignitaries and to talk on equal terms with them. He did

not discourage the inevitable jokes at his expense and told Ian White-Thomson, successively Chaplain to Lang, Temple, and Fisher, and later Dean of Canterbury, of the friend who had re-punctuated Isaiah 6:6 to read 'Then Flew, one of the seraphim, . . .'. He might have found an apocryphal story, which derived from a bowdlerised version of a remark of Howard's and went the rounds in Methodism, rather less to his taste. It was said that one day he inadvertently changed the *Sanctus* in the Communion Service so that it ran 'Therefore with *bishops and archbishops* and all the company of heaven . . .'.

He generally appreciated this kind of humour. One day in September 1950, when he was at Christ Church, Oxford, engaged in the talks which produced the Report *Church Relations in England*, he was anxious to show a former pupil Wolsey's cardinal's hat. He was not quite sure of the way to the place where it was kept and asked guidance of Canon A. S. Reeve, then Vicar of Leeds, later Bishop of Lichfield, whom he and his student happened to meet in a corridor. Reeve expressed surprise. 'I should have thought, Dr Flew, that you, of all people would know where there was a Cardinal's hat!' 'No, my dear Canon,' Flew retorted, 'only the Papal tiara interests me!'

This was the image, which, far from resenting, he was inclined to build up himself. But we must not be beguiled. He venerated the Anglican tradition and loved Anglican culture and company, but this did not make him a smooth-tongued negotiator prepared to sacrifice Christian truth as he saw it for a gaitered calf. His whole ecumenical life was knit together by an unwavering consistency of principles. He could never bring himself to recognise the historic episcopate as of the *esse* of the Church. He gave of his scholarship, his powers of heart and mind, his time and his physical strength for the healing of the broken Body of Christ, not for its interment in the imposing tomb of what he regarded as a false and unevangelical catholicity. This was an immolation no less real because it reinforced the ebullience of his nature and gave him excitement, prestige and association with great and kindred spirits. He was not to see any completion of his own distinctive work and it may have been more than illness which made him somewhat despondent at the last. We must not grudge him the Archiepiscopal *bonhomie*, or his proud place in the Amsterdam Procession. He had an exodus to accomplish, though undramatic and unnoticed.

Flew was thus a leading champion of the Free Churches as well as of his own Methodism. The Moderatorial dignity of 1945–6 was no less than his due, though perhaps his greatest services to the Reformed tradition came in the years which followed.

All this comprises the thesis of this account of Flew the ecumenist. It will frequently be illustrated in the story of his manifold inter-Church activities.

Where he came in

When Flew was drawn into the ecumenical stream, the historic Letter 'To All Christian People' from the Lambeth Conference of 1920 was still dominating discussion in England. The noble sentiments of that appeal, which owed much to Cosmo Gordon Lang, then Archbishop of York, to E. J. Palmer, Bishop of Bombay, and to the initiative of George Bell in suggesting that it be drafted by an informal group of younger bishops,[1] make it one of the great documents of Church history.

> We acknowledge this condition of broken fellowship to be contrary to God's will, and we desire frankly to confess our share in the guilt of thus crippling the Body of Christ and hindering the activity of His Spirit. . . .

[1] See R. C. D. Jasper, *George Bell, Bishop of Chichester* (Oxford 1967), p. 57.

The vision which rises before us is that of a Church genuinely Catholic, loyal to all Truth, and gathering into its fellowship all who profess and call themselves Christians, within whose visible unity all the treasures of faith and order, bequeathed as a heritage by the past to the present, shall be possessed in common and made serviceable to the whole Body of Christ.[2]

But while the letter marked a great victory for Anglican ecumenists, its claims for episcopacy – 'it is now and will prove to be in future the best instrument for maintaining the unity and continuity of the Church'[3] – disappointed many non-Anglicans, who were committed in principle to the unity of all Christian people.[4] The immediate outcome in England 'was the series of joint conferences lasting until 1925 between representatives of the Church of England and the Free Churches'.[5] But these, though a great achievement in their very existence, foundered on the question of the validity of Free Church orders and were 'brought to a *pause*'. The Free Churches could not accept conditional ordination; the Anglicans did not favour a form of solemn episcopal authorisation.[6] The conversations were resumed after the Lambeth Conference of 1930, with William Temple, then Archbishop of York, and A. E. Garvie, the Congregational leader, as conveners. Lidgett and Lofthouse were the two most eminent Methodists on the Free Church side. By 1938, these talks had produced the *Outline of a Reunion Scheme for the Church of England and the Free Churches in*

---

[2] The Lambeth Letter III, Iv, G. K. A. Bell *Documents on Christian Unity* (1920–24) Oxford (1924).

[3] *Ibid.*, VII.

[4] For the effects in India see Bengt Sundkler, *The Church of South India: The Movement Towards Union* 1900–1947 (Lutterworth 1954), pp. 131 ff.

[5] Jasper, *loc. cit.*

[6] Cf. J. G. Lockhart, *Cosmo Gordon Lang* (Hodder and Stoughton 1949), pp. 273 ff.

England.[7] This was in fact the adoption of the proposals of an unofficial group under Canon Tissington Tatlow, meeting between 1931 and 1936. The Scheme is remarkably detailed even to its devising a constitution and Church courts. The influence of the South India negotiations is strong. The ideal of the proposers is 'one of unity with variety'. Episcopal ordination must be the rule for the future, but there is full acceptance of existing ministries. But the Free Churches, who replied at great length in 1941, effectively damned the Scheme by a combination of Scripturally-phrased tribute, high-sounding assertion of their evangelical principles, and a summary of their constituents' doubts.

In the judgement of the *Methodist Conference* the Scheme 'does not sufficiently allow for the free exercise of those differing forms of government and organization which have been granted to the various churches in their separated existence', and suggests that 'such of the uniting communions might at first be recognized as semi-autonomous within the united Church, each with its own discipline and form of government, but each submitting to and honouring the authority of the whole body (expressed in some way yet to be determined) as controlling the aims and developing life of every part'. We believe that this statement would find general support in all the Free Churches.

There is still among many Churches a strong aversion to episcopacy for which the history of the past offers some justification; and even if on other grounds an episcopate should be agreed to as one organ of the United Church the replies generally are very definite in rejecting the doctrine of Apostolic Succession as defined above. The *Methodist Conference* insists that there must not be any such application of the doctrine in practice as would exclude communion with non-episcopal churches, nor must episcopacy be regarded as so essential to the existence of the Church that

[7] G. K. A. Bell, *Documents on Christian Unity* Third Series 1930–1948 (Oxford 1948), pp. 71–101.

it would not be free to follow the guidance of the Spirit to a change of polity.[8]

The Convocations of Canterbury and York proceeded no further than to commend the documents for study.

In spite of this stalemate, Church relations in England had been revolutionised since 1914. Personal friendships began to flourish across the divides, but, far, far more, in 1941, the Archbishop of Canterbury (Lang) led a deputation of both Anglican and Free Churchmen to the President of the Board of Education (R. A. Butler) on the subject of Christian teaching in schools. So soon was the bitterness of the early years of the century forgotten. All the same, Free Churchmen were still made to feel that most Anglicans regarded them as second-class Churchmen, if not citizens, and it often seemed as if, for many in the English Church, union with almost anybody else in the world counted for more than the healing of the old conflicts with their nearest neighbours. Of course, there were important cultural differences, perceptible even in a Flew, despite Christ's Hospital and Merton, but perhaps these were best secularised and left to the lonely battle of F. R. Leavis in the English School at Cambridge. Episcopacy was the main matter of theological principle.

In the wider world, there had been the Stockholm Life and Work Conference in 1925 and Faith and Order at Lausanne two years later. The latter ran into difficulties in its Section VII – 'The Unity of Christendom and the relation thereto of existing Churches'. There were at least three conflicting points of view. There was the spiritual ecumenism of Nathan Söderblom, with its awareness that the goal of true unity was distant, but which sought intercommunion, confessional groupings and linguistic understanding on the way. There were the

---

[8] *Loc. cit.*, pp. 102–19.

younger Churches of Asia and their criticism that
Lausanne was a conference of old men, with Bishop
Palmer of Bombay insisting that the matter of corporate
reunion required haste. And there were the Anglo-
Catholics of Britain and America vociferously com-
plaining of 'pan-Protestantism' and being rude to
Söderblom in the process. But nearly all the reports were
accepted *nem. con.*, and the controversial VII was
referred to the continuation Committee.[9]

In the 1930s in England, the Friends of Reunion was
formed. It was a remarkable group in that it included so
many Church leaders – Temple, E. S. Woods, Lofthouse, Hugh Martin (of the SCM Press, a Baptist),
Leonard Hodgson, and the young Oliver Tomkins (later
Bishop of Bristol). The Anglo-Catholics were chary and
inclined to opt in and out according to the fluctuations of
their consciences. Flew belonged from the beginning.
Early on, the minutes record that he reminded the Committee that 'lay people soon tire of mere discussion about
unity and would very soon want something more to be
done'. Later he besought committee members to read the
Church Times regularly that they might be 'in a position
to deal with opposition' to the plans for unity in South
India 'directly and at once'.

The Church of South India

It took almost thirty years of travail before union in
South India was achieved in 1947 by its own special
method of the unification of ministries over an interim
period of thirty years and a Pledge.[10] The Wesleyans were

---

[9] See Bengt Sundkler, *Nathan Söderblom: his Life and Work*
(Lutterworth 1968), pp. 404–13; Ruth Rouse and Stephen
Charles Neill (eds.), *A History of the Ecumenical Movement* 1517–1948
(SPCK 1967 second edition), pp. 420–5.

[10] The Pledge runs as follows:
'They therefore pledge themselves and fully trust each other that
the united Church will at all times be careful not to allow any

hesitant at first, but once convinced, they were steadfast to the end. J. Stirling M. Hooper was probably their greatest advocate of union in the sub-continent itself, though due to his mistrust of the Anglicans, he had been converted slowly. It was the patience of Bishop Palmer which won him for the cause. In 1932, Hooper became the first General Secretary of the British and Foreign Bible Society in India, Burma and Ceylon. He turned to Lidgett and Flew, and to a lesser extent Lofthouse, for advice from home.

Lofthouse toured India in 1934 and his report was a decisive factor in the declaration of the Methodist Conference that year that 'The Scheme of 1934, taken as a whole, was not contrary to the principles of Methodism.' This particular revision had emphasised liberty of interpretation about the 'historic episcopate' which it had been agreed, would have to be accepted if unity was to be consummated.

Flew had been seized of the necessity of Church union in India since his Bangalore days. One of his ablest and most devoted pupils, Marcus Ward, went out to the Madras District in 1932 and became one of the younger architects of the South India Church. Though a member of the Methodist Sacramental Fellowship, which Flew was not, Ward always enjoyed Flew's confidence and the two kept in close touch throughout the years. But

---

over-riding of conscience either by Church authorities or by majorities, and that it will not in any of its administrative acts knowingly transgress the long-established traditions of any of the Churches from which it has been formed. Neither forms of worship or ritual, nor a ministry, to which they have not been accustomed or to which they conscientiously object, will be imposed upon any congregation; and no arrangements with regard to these matters will knowingly be made, either generally or in particular cases, which would either offend the conscientious convictions of persons directly concerned, or which would hinder the development of complete unity within the united Church or imperil its progress towards union with other Churches.'

Flew was always a little more reluctant than some of his
colleagues to concede to the high Anglican position.
Flew wanted to press for presbyteral participation in
all ordinations, as in the Methodist rite, but the Methodist
missionaries in India felt that this was asking for too
much and born of an exaggerated idea of the power of
Bishops. He fought very hard in 1933 and the early
months of 1934 against an Anglican interpretation of the
famous Pledge of 1929, which would make its 'conscience
clause' a cover for the non-acceptance of non-episcopal
ministries. In 1944, he was tepid about a proposal for
supplemental ordination, which had been suddenly
produced by the Indian Anglicans to relieve their
continuing fears about the Pledge in some such terms as
these:

> Receive the Holy Ghost for the work of a presbyter in the
> Church of God, both for the continuance of that work which
> thou hast done hitherto, and for the performance of that work
> which is now committed unto thee by the laying on of our
> hands. Take thou authority to preach and teach the word;
> to fulfil the ministry of reconciliation and to minister Christ's
> sacraments in the congregation, where unto thou shalt be
> further called or lawfully appointed . . .

Lidgett, Lofthouse, Harold Roberts and others of the
Methodist Faith and Order Committee were in favour
of this, but Flew thought that some less offensive name
should be given such as 'An Extended Commission with
the laying on of hands', and that it should be made very
clear that it was prospective not retrospective. He would
have no truck with any hint of re-ordination and
pointed out that should this proposal form part of the
basis of union, the whole scheme would have to be
presented again to the Methodist Conference. In the end,
the proposal was defeated by the Joint Committee in
India, to the disappointment of Marcus Ward as well as

of the Anglicans. It could not overcome Presbyterian and
Congregationalist suspicions that it meant re-ordination
by the back door. Its ambiguity savoured of the dis-
honest. It is significant that Flew was less enthusiastic
than his former pupil on the field and than several in
England whom popular opinion might have deemed less
Catholic than he.[11]

On the other hand, when, in 1935, there was a
reaction on the part of the left-wing representatives of
the Reformed tradition, who felt that the South India
proposals were a 'sell-out' to sacerdotalism and demanded
that provision be made for lay administration of the
Lord's Supper, Flew opposed the idea. He gave one of
his memorable judgements: 'If the doctrine of the
Priesthood of All Believers can only be represented by
Lay Administration, this is magic sacerdotalism all over
again.'

Flew thus occupied a central position between Anglo-
Catholics and the extremer Protestants. He was always a
resolute advocate of South India unity, not only in the
Methodist Conference, but in public meetings, notably
one in Cambridge Town Hall during the war, when the
vigour of his refutation of criticisms made by the
Revd Frederic Hood, Warden of Pusey House, Oxford,
reverberates still in the memories of some who heard it.

The Road to Lund

In 1934, Flew became a Methodist member of the World
Faith and Order Continuation Committee set up at
Lausanne. His first meeting was at Hertenstein on Lake
Lucerne in September. Like its parallel organisation
which had resulted from 'Life and Work' in Stockholm,
the Committee was planning a further full-scale Con-
ference. It was attended by the notorious German Bishop
Theodor Heckel, fresh from the controversies of the

[11] See Bengt Sundkler, *Church of South India*, pp. 305 ff.

Universal Christian Council at Fanø, Denmark, and his
protest at the condemnation of the Nazi Church policy.
But at this stage the theological discussion did not result
in political disputes, and Heckel seems to have been
received more favourably at Hertenstein than at Fanø.
The Committee formed three Commissions on the
Church and the Word; the Ministry and the Sacraments:
the Church's Unity in Life and Worship. Flew was a
member of the second under A. C. Headlam, Bishop of
Gloucester. The next year, he was at Hindsgaul,
Middelfart, Denmark, when it was decided to hold the
World Conference at Edinburgh in 1937. In connection
with Hindsgaul, F. L. Wiseman wrote in *The Methodist
Recorder*:

> The crux of the whole matter is probably the question of
> Intercommunion. Shall it precede or follow the formal union
> of the Churches? Shall it lead to it, or be the joyful sign of a
> union now at last happily achieved? At present many,
> probably the majority hold the latter view – in the interest
> of unity itself. Yet to some of us the other seems the better
> and the more natural way. The principle of *solvitur ambulando*
> is applicable to many situations and to none more usefully
> than this. To do a great right it may be more than pardonable
> to do a little wrong.

Before Edinburgh, Flew was a delegate to the Life and
Work Conference on Church, Community and State at
Oxford in July 1937. The atmosphere was heavy with
the sense of world crisis, made more grave by the absence
of the official delegation from the German Evangelical
Church, which had been forbidden to attend by the
Nazi government. Niemöller was already in prison. It
was sad that a German Methodist should protest against
the dispatch of a message of sympathy to their absent
brethren, on the grounds that genuine evangelicals now
had full liberty to proclaim the gospel and that God 'in

his providence' had 'sent a leader who was able to banish the danger of Bolshevism in Germany'.

The Flews enjoyed the social life surrounding the Conference. There was a particularly exciting luncheon party at the Cadena Café:

> Behold your daughter in law presiding. . . . On her right Canon Raven, Regius Professor of Divinity in the Univ. of Cambridge. On her left Rev Rektor Julen, head of the theological College at Gothenburg, Sweden. . . . Also there – Pastor Henrikson once at Stockholm, now of Gothenburg; and Professor Bela Vasady of Hungary, with whom I became friendly last August when we were colleagues at the Palace at Gloucester. . . . We are going to entertain the Archbishop of York (Temple) soon.

But there was richer food than this:

> The service on Sunday morning at 8 a.m. is the most marvellous Eucharist I have ever known. Negroes, Chinese, Japanese, Mexicans, Indians, Frenchmen, Dutchmen, Danes, Swedes, Norwegians, Latvians, Poles – all whether Lutherans or Calvinists, Anglicans or Methodists met at the Table of the Lord. When Winifred and I went up to the Table in *Newman's* Church, I was kneeling next to the Archbishop of Uppsala, Dr. Eidem; we received the wafer from the hands of the Archbishop of Canterbury (Lang) and the chalice from the hands of another bishop. The Bishop of Dornakal, Azariah, the first Indian to be made a Bishop was also serving with Leslie Hunter, Archdeacon of Northumberland, who stayed with us a few years ago. The mixture of men and races sounds like the day of Pentecost. Winnie and I were so deeply moved by it all that we could not speak for the time of our journey back to breakfast.

The Faith and Order Conference at Edinburgh was Flew's especial milieu. He was appointed to preside over a section on 'The Nature of the Sacraments' because of his experience of the ecumenical movement and 'mastery of the subject'. It will be observed that next to the Ministry this was likely to be the most prickly subject of all. He found his team, some thirty strong, a formidable one. On one occasion he had to call the Great Archimandrite Constantinides to order, when the latter in the course of someone else's speech, began to hurl a protest at R. Lee Cole, the Secretary of the Irish Methodist Conference, for something he had said the day before. Flew rose and remained standing till the Great Archimandrite sat down. He seemed confident that a little gentle humour from the Chair could banish all acrimony.

His great supporter was Canon Oliver Chase Quick, whom Flew regarded, for that season at any rate, as 'the leading Church of England theologian'. At that time van Mildert Professor at Durham, Quick was destined to succeed Goudge at Oxford in 1939 and to die, in the fullness of his powers, in 1944. Flew probably did not overestimate Quick's pre-eminence. Alec Vidler has said 'I do not remember anyone who struck me as so formidably acute in argument'.[12] Quick had written a philosophico-theological study of *The Christian Sacraments* and he shared the drafting of the section report with Flew. He also submitted an important note on *validity*. The two clearly worked together in great affability, concord and mutual admiration. Flew felt that it was 'wonderful to get such a heterogeneous crowd agreeing together on so much' and, bearing in mind that poor chairmanship is the greatest single cause of the unsatisfactory nature of many ecumenical reports, we may conclude that neither the congratulations he received nor his own self-satisfaction were misplaced. The report is a most lucid

[12] Alec R. Vidler, *20th-Century Defenders of the Faith* (SCM 1965), p. 65.

and constructive exposition of basis sacramental theology.[13]

The Edinburgh Report as a whole marked a considerable advance on Lausanne. There had been better preparation and there was a truer interchange of minds. Theologians were beginning to trust one another and to learn to speak the truth in love. The Conference approved in principle the formation of a World Council of Churches, but A. C. Headlam would have voted against the Report had it not included the sentence 'Some members . . . desire to place on record their opposition to this proposal'.

Once again Flew delighted in the company. There was little time for a conclave of Methodists, though Ryder Smith and Jacob Walton were in the same hotel. Bishop Whitehead, formerly of Madras, and one of the South India pioneers, a rigid high Anglican, who had altered his views in Indian conditions, wanted him to conduct a retreat for Anglicans and Nonconformists at Reading. He writes 'I have returned a prudent answer!' He had to address meetings and to broadcast with Dr William Adams Brown, Dean Brilioth, Dr Adolf Keller and Bishop Palmer. He met Gustav Aulèn and Professor Timothy Tingfang Lew of Yenching, Dean Willard Sperry and Azaraiah of Dornakal, and his old teacher, H. N. Bate, Dean of York, whose dog was called William Ebor!

William Ebor, the man, was, as President, the outstanding personality of the Conference, which rallied to the skill, humour and impartiality of his Chairmanship. The Flews gave a luncheon party for the Temples, with Professor Goudge, Dean Brilioth, Dean Bate, the Methodist Calvert Barber of Melbourne, and the Watkin-Joneses also present. The Temples reciprocated. The Archbishop was extremely affable to the young

---

[13] *Vide* Bell, *Documents*, Third Series, pp. 261–7.

Antony Flew, walked with him arm-in-arm and never failed to enquire after him whenever he met his father in the future.

An African Methodist Episcopal Bishop and his great-niece were turned out of their Edinburgh hotel on colour grounds. The Temples immediately invited the two to stay with them. By this time the Africans had been made very comfortable in another hotel, so they refused with simple and dignified thanks. Flew 'said what I thought of W. T. and his missus and they looked embarrassed'.

Flew attended the Continuation Committee at Clarens the following year. This began to consider the draft constitution of a World Council of Churches. It also gave Flew his great ecumenical assignment for the next fourteen years by making him Chairman of the Commission on the Church. Dr G. W. Richards was to preside over an American Theological Committee on the same subject. Flew asked Kenneth Riches to be Secretary.

Before long, the war had interrupted these hopes and plans. The Flews were at Clarens again in August 1939. Canon Leonard Hodgson, the Secretary, urged the postponement of further meetings of the whole Continuation Committee because he wanted to save money for the Commissions. But news of the Nazi–Soviet pact and of the blackout in Britain, sent members scurrying to safety. Back in Oxford, Hodgson felt that he ought not to have left in such disarray and wrote penitently to Flew in his neat hand. The Flews themselves travelled to Dieppe and lingered there until the last possible moment. As they crossed the Channel, a stewardess seemed to relish telling them that they were sailing under sealed orders.

William Temple became Archbishop of Canterbury in 1942. Flew wrote:

I've only met one opinion so far among Nonconformists, about William Temple's nomination to Canterbury. But

Anglicans are curiously divided. A great many dignitaries think that he will commit 'indiscretions', and that an Archbp. of Canterbury should never commit indiscretions! I fancy that this means that they don't like his Labour political views, and his Malvern programme, or his distinction between retribution and vengeance and the like. Some say that he hasn't 'sound judgment'. If this means that he isn't always a sure judge of men, I think that it's true of him, as it certainly is of Wiseman. But all the same if you want real leadership you have to put up with a man who is courageous enough to make mistakes, and who can trust men even if some of those whom he trusts turn out to be unreliable. . . .

I met W.T. at Sion College on the Embankment last Friday. He came up to Dr. Garvie and myself before the meeting (a Faith and Order one).

Garvie said: 'You look too young to be the Archbp. of Canterbury.'

W.T. gaily: 'Yes, I shall look younger still next week, because I'm going to have my hair cut on Monday.' He then turned to me and said how sorry he was to miss seeing Tony at Oxford, and hoped to see him the next time!!

Flew maintained contact with British ecumenism during the war, and had consultations with Leonard Hodgson whenever possible. The British Council of Churches was inaugurated in September 1943. Just over a year later, William Temple died. Flew attended the funeral at Canterbury.

On 9th February, 1945, Flew was one of twelve British theologians meeting at Presbyterian Church House, Regent Square, London. As they dispersed, the building was hit by a V2 rocket. Five of them were either seriously injured or killed. The dead included W. T. Elmslie, the Presbyterian Church Secretary and Reginald H. Tribe of the Society of the Sacred Mission. Leonard Hodgson received severe head injuries, Flew himself was badly shaken, but otherwise unharmed. He placed the loss of W. T. Elmslie (at 48) in the same class as that of William Temple and William Paton, the great missionary statesman, whom that same cruel winter had also removed.

The aged A. E. Garvie passed from the scene too, and when the Continuation Committee met again, after the ravaged years, at Clarens in August 1947, it made Yngve Brilioth, who was, of course, Nathan Söderblom's son-in-law, and a historian of the Holy Eucharist and the Oxford Movement, its Chairman in succession to Temple, and Flew its Vice-Chairman in place of Garvie.

Earlier than that, in February 1946, he had been present at Geneva for the first post-war meeting of the Provisional Committee of the World Council. This was the tense and historic occasion at which those whose ecumenical partnership has been ruptured by the enmity of their countries met again. Flew saw Bishop Berggrav of Oslo, who had been interned during the German occupation, greet Martin Niemöller in Christian brotherhood, and heard his sermon in the Cathedral of St. Pierre in which he said that 'the surprise of that meeting was that it was no surprise to find the sense of fellowship so real among those who had but lately been political and military enemies'; and also 'In these last years we have lived more intimately with each other than in times when we could communicate with each other. We prayed together more, we listened together more to the Word of God, our hearts were together more.'[14]

To translate the spiritual unity, which the war had deepened, into action in the 'new order' in which the iron and bamboo curtains were to replace the Nazi blitzkrieg and barbed wire, was to be the task of the World Council. Flew was mostly concerned with the theological aspect, but he was too much of a Christian humanist to be silent when the issues of relief arose, with

[14] Rouse and Neill, *A History of the Ecumenical Movement* 1517–1948, pp. 715, 708.

their political ramifications, and he was anxious that the Council should have an organisation efficient enough to mobilise Christian opinion and co-ordinate Christian action on global scale. Thus, at the first meeting of the Central Committee after Amsterdam, held at Chichester in July 1949, he urged the duty of the World Council to speak quickly on matters of Church policy. This was the meeting at which inter-Church aid, which had already great achievements to its credit in the aftermath of war, was recognised as 'a permanent obligation'. Meanwhile he had been gathering together the threads of the work of the Commission on the Church.

Flew had two gifts which are rare in senior theologians, or indeed, in leaders of any kind. He was able to delegate responsibilities and share out work, to co-ordinate theological discussion and writing; and he was always eager to bring in younger men. Thus at Clarens in 1947, he proposed that Ernest Payne, the Baptist, and John Marsh, the Congregationalist, then both in their early forties, which was young for those days, should be appointed to the Continuation Committee which, after Amsterdam, became the Commission on Faith and Order. He also involved Ernest Payne in the Commission on the Church, for which, years before, he had made the young Kenneth Riches secretary, and, after the war, called in the advice of the young Chaplain of Trinity Hall, Owen Chadwick.

The plan for the Faith and Order Conference, the successor to Edinburgh 1937, which was eventually to meet at Lund in Sweden in 1952, was ambitious, not least for the Commission on the Church. A memorandum prepared by Flew during the war, outlines the scope and organisation of the work:

The most encouraging part of the work on 'the Church' is to be found in the series of meetings held by the America committee. Conditions in Europe make such meetings impossible here. Most theologians on this side are busy on other work in addition to their normal teaching functions, but the desire for the kind of study which was proposed at the Continuation Committees at Clarens in 1938 and 1939 remains as strong as ever.

It will be remembered that the accepted plan of study consists of four sections. Each section is called for the sake of convenience a 'volume'. But it may well prove that the word carries too portly associations with it. Certainly it does not follow from the use of the word that each 'volume' will be as massive as 'The Doctrine of Grace' or 'The Ministry and Sacraments', the two tomes produced in preparation for the Edinburgh Conference. The four sections are:

I. Biblical.

II. Historical.

III. Confessional; i.e. Modern statements as title beliefs held by each of the great traditions today.

IV. Systematic or Constructive.

It is hoped that work for the first three 'volumes' will proceed simultaneously, and that the fourth 'volume' will appear only after some time has been allowed for study of the first three. But that does not mean that ardent spirits may not run ahead of the programme. Indeed it is greatly to be desired that work should be proceeding, both in the USA and elsewhere, with an ultimate synthesis in view.

The greatest possible importance is attached to the production of Statements for Volume III. Such Statements ought to carry greater authority than would attach to the utterance of any single theologian, however representative of his communion he might be. It is therefore desirable that the production of every such document should be preceded by some corporate work, such as the two years' study given by British Methodists which in 1937 resulted in 'The Nature of the Christian Church, according to the Teaching of the Methodists.' (Epworth Press, London.) The pioneer document on the other side of the Atlantic has appeared this year: 'The Nature of the Church according to the Teaching of the Congregationalists.' (The Commission on Interchurch Relations, 287 Fourth Avenue, New York.) Comments on this statement are earnestly desired by the theologians who have worked on it, and may be sent to Dr. Hachiro Yuasa at the above address. 'In its present form' the statement must be regarded as provisional; and as such it is now sent out for criticism and correction to Congregationalists in many parts of the world, in order that, when finished, it may represent the widest possible consensus of Congregationalist thought.' This quotation proves how admirably the group which drafted the Statement have interpreted their task, and may point the way to the production and circulation of such provisional Statements from the communions represented in the Faith and Order Movement. It would be of the greatest possible help to the work of this Commission if similar groups could be formed in each of those communions, and if every such group, whether in the USA, or in Australia or India or any of the countries at present severed from us by the war, could publish its results for future consideration by the other members of that communion throughout the world.

It has been a great help and relief to me that the American Committee under the chairmanship of the Rev. George W. Richards, D.D., has taken charge of the task of producing the American material for Volume III. The initiative of Dr Richards in securing the co-operation of a group of Congregationalists has already been gratefully acknowledged in the document mentioned above. It is further most desirable that some distinctively American work should be produced which would reflect the national and psychological differences between America and Europe and the younger churches in Asia and Africa. Similarly the younger churches have their own distinctive contribution to make. Any documents produced with this end in view would not necessarily be published in Volume III, but they would be most valuable in guiding my Commission when it is able to meet after the war. Our aim should be to enrich our studies by the full consideration of those many differences.

The work on Volumes I and II is proceeding, though no catalogue of results is possible at this stage. In the course of time, with fresh experience to guide us, modifications and improvements will doubtless be made in the original plans. But there is also no doubt that the four sections of work originally proposed are all necessary, if our preparation for the next World Conference is to be accomplished with the thoroughness of Christian scholarship and the insight and imagination which also are the gifts of the One Spirit of God.

After the war, the Commission was able to meet, sometimes at Cambridge. It was truly international for its time and included Orthodox Representatives, among whom was the Oecumenical Patriarch, Archbishop Germanos, though Professor Hamilcar Alivasatos made the outstanding Orthodox contribution. Prominent in the discussions were Edmund Schlink of the Evangelical Church in Germany, K. S. Latourette, the historian of missions, G. D. Henderson of the Church of Scotland, William Robinson of the Churches of Christ, and A. M. Ramsey, later Archbishop of Canterbury. There was no Roman Catholic representative. This was the period of post-war ultra-montanism. The Edinburgh volume on *Ministry and Sacraments* contains two chapters by Roman Catholics, but the Pope, Pius XII, forbade Roman Catholic attendance at Amsterdam and so frozen were official relationships in spite of much friendliness and interest on the part of individual Romans, that Flew could not obtain any Roman Catholic theologian to share in the discussions or the resulting publications. The chapter on 'The Church of Rome' in the Lund preparatory book *The Nature of the Church*, a work of comparative ecclesiology, which consists largely of authorised statements, is therefore written by Flew himself, as he says '*non ut diceretur, sed ne taceretur* – lest silence should be interpreted as forgetfulness or culpable neglect of the great place which the Church of Rome must occupy in the thoughts of all who are sorrowfully aware of the tragedy of disunity'.[15]

He presented it in its first draft to a meeting of his

[15] R. Newton Flew (ed.), *The Nature of the Church* (SCM Press 1952), pp. 17–40.

Commission held at Wesley House in July 1949. It opens with an acknowledgement of his debt to von Hügel and Mandonnet, at Fribourg, and is a 'classic' instance of the strength of his theological method, which we have earlier described. He has completely mastered his sources and summarises them under point-headings, with a fine sensitiveness of selection, so that the essay is perfectly balanced and judicious enough to have gained the *imprimatur*. The doctrine of the Church promulgated by the first Vatican Council in its developments to the end of the fifth-decade of the twentieth-century is lucidly presented. He will not have the Roman doctrine caricatured; but neither will he allow non-Roman Christians to delude themselves as to its severity. In the end to be saved means to belong to the Church, and there is only one Church – that over which presides the Bishop of Rome. The 'Branch theory' so beloved of Anglo-Catholics and expressed in a wider form in the Doctrinal Basis of the Free Church Federal Council of England and Wales (1917; reaffirmed 1941) is totally repudiated. Unity can only be attained by a return to the Vicar of Christ.

Today Roman theologians would gladly join in the discussion and state their own case. *The Dogmatic Constitution on the Church* promulgated by the Second Vatican Council has helped to transform the ecumenical movement and to make it possible to talk with Rome and not simply listen to her. The *Schema* lifts ecclesiology into a new dimension by treating of the Church as a mystery, recognises that 'in some real way' Christians outside the Roman obedience 'are joined with us in the Holy Spirit', and has a far less static conception of the people of God, to whom those who have not yet received the gospel are in some way related. Flew would rejoice in the prestige of the American Methodist, Albert C. Outler, whom he met and admired at Springfield, as an interpreter of Roman Catholic theology. But it would be interesting to have a completely revised version of his essay in the light of Vatican II.

His Commission also published a report, 'a slender, paper-clad volume', entitled simply *The Church*. This seeks honestly to state both the agreements and disagreements between the various traditions. The purpose is not synthesis but reconciliation:

> For it is not that Christians can themselves piece the broken fragments of truth into one, but that God can expose those errors and lead them to see in unity what at present they see only in fragmentariness resulting from centuries of divisions.

Lund – the Anti-Climax

Flew came to Lund as one of the respected seniors of the ecumenical movement. He was, by then, sixty-six and had been at the heart of Faith and Order discussions for eighteen years. Few days had gone by in all that time when he had not had to give his mind to some aspect of the work, and, since the war, in spite of all his other preoccupations there had been constant correspondence, committees and conferences. At the very beginning of the Lund proceedings it was he who moved that Yngve Brilioth, now Archbishop of Uppsala, should take the Chair. He had also to read prayers in the principal Conference service in the romanesque Cathedral. The letter inviting him to do so had somehow gone astray and he was not aware of his assignment until he was robed and waiting to join the procession.

> Fortunately I had a solitary meggezone (Boots Cash Chemist product) in my waistcoat pocket and so was fortified for the immense task of getting myself heard in such a vast cathedral.

He was presented with twenty other leaders to the King and Queen of Sweden. He was third after the Orthodox Archbishop Athenagoras and the German Bishop Wilhelm Stählin.

We were presented by Brilioth, who laid great stress on my
tireless work as Chairman of the chief Theological Commission. The King said to me in his private talk with me that
he had noticed my work in the big Book (meaning I suppose
on *The Nature of the Church*).

He himself had to present Dr G. W. Richards to the
Archbishop in full session of the Conference. Richards
was the oldest delegate and Flew paid tribute to all that
he had done to keep the Faith and Order programme
alive during the war.

May I tell you his secret? If you want to see his face light up,
ask him what is the best first question and best first answer
of any Christian catechism in the world, and he will recite to
you the opening sentence of the Heidelberg catechism.[16]

There were four of Flew's own pupils at Lund –
Marcus Ward, Rupert Davies, Irvonwy Morgan and the
Metropolitan Juhanon of the Ancient Syrian Church –
and many who hailed him as the author of *Jesus and His
Church*. It was at Lund that he met Mother Margaret,
the Prioress of the Order of the Holy Paraclete from
Whitby. He discovered that they were born in the same
year and had been contemporaries at Oxford. The Flews
kept in touch with her until her death. He also exulted
in the friendship of the Bishop of Derby, whom he had
got to know well in England, and Mrs Rawlinson, while,
as ever, the Flews and the Watkin-Joneses were close
companions.

The thorn in the flesh is that there are no hot baths to be had

[16] The opening sentence of the Heidelberg Catechism 1562 is as
follows:
'What is thy only comfort in life and in death?'
'That I, with body and soul, both in life and in death, am not
my own, but belong to my faithful Saviour Jesus Christ, who with
His precious blood has fully atoned for all my sins.'

except by violent means. I did not go on the 'Expedition' yesterday when most of the Conference (except officials) went gallivanting on a charabanc ride. I went to the Municipal *Bad huset* and spent two kroner on a glorious hot bath.

There were, however, other difficulties. The ecumenical movement is perhaps inevitably, more prone than most large organisations to charge its committees with tasks and then complain because they have fulfilled them and not done something else. This sounds outrageous but it must be remembered that the problems of one period are not necessarily those of the next and so by the time an answer has been worked out over the years, it may be felt especially by newcomers that the original question was not the right one. The preparatory work on the Church for Lund had been done over a term of thirteen years, which included a world war and its aftermath, and therefore it is not astonishing that there were those – and this has become the accepted opinion – who felt that it marked a monument to the past, rather than a signpost for the future.[17]

Their spokesman at the Conference itself was the massively learned Edinburgh Barthian, T. F. Torrance. He has made most of his contemporaries among British theologians look pigmies. It will be interesting to see what his creative contribution will in the end be judged to have been, though we hope that the time for such assessment will be long delayed. In 1952, he had entered ecumenical discussion with characteristic enthusiasm and persistence. (He has rather withdrawn from it in recent years.) He proceeded to try to change the whole basis of the discussion and Flew, feeling that the work of his

---

[17] See Meredith B. Handspicker in Harold E. Fey (ed.), *The Ecumenical Advance: A History of the Ecumenical Movement* 1948–68 (SPCK 1970), pp. 151 ff.

Commission was being ignored, was, naturally, uneasy. The two were not *en rapport*.

Torrance embodied the criticisms he had voiced in the Conference in an article the following year in his *Scottish Journal of Theology*.[18] He argued that Lund marked the end of an era. He wrote of 'the great value and ultimate failure of the old procedure of *Faith and Order*' evidenced in the preparatory volumes.

This continual comparison and contraposition of different ecclesiastical traditions in frank discussion of their widest and deepest differences can actually help to harden the differences. . . . What was wanted was a theological method whereby we could think together our one faith in the one Christ, beginning with the very centre with Christ Himself, and proceeding on this Christological basis seek to think through our differences in regard to Church, Worship and Sacrament. Already the character and results of the preparatory volumes make this a clamant necessity, for in trying to adopt the traditional conference procedure as theological procedure, they had failed to provide any real basis for discussion at Lund, and there was a good deal of anxiety on the part of the Old Guard and even accusations of despair when it was found that theologians had at times to start almost from scratch. That was most apparent in one of the commissions on the Church which found that the Report on *The Church* even under the *Mode of its Definition* had failed to define the nature of the Church in terms of its essential relation to Christ as His Body.[19]

Torrance was quite certain of what should be the starting point. 'Because we believe in Jesus Christ we believe also in the Church as the Body of Christ.' Biblical studies had forced the churches back 'to deeper

[18] 'Where do we go from Lund?' *Scottish Journal of Theology* Vol. 6, No. 1, pp. 53 ff.
[19] *Op. cit.*, pp. 54–5.

appreciation and fuller understanding of the classical Christology of the Ecumenical Councils'.

> The attempt to formulate a doctrine of the Church as part of the doctrine of Christ is not new, for it was made in the fifth century, though the first great attempts had to wait till the Reformation when it was Calvin particularly who sought to give thoroughgoing expression to the doctrine of the Church in terms of the analogy of Christ. . . .
>
> When we speak of the Church as the Body of Christ we do not mean a relation either of identity or difference between Christ and His Church but an analogical relation in which there is no relation of proportion but only of similarity (and dissimilarity) of proportion. . . .
>
> The Church is not the Body of the Trinity, nor the Body of the Holy Spirit. . . . The relation of union between the Church and Christ is grounded on the consubstantial communion of the Holy Spirit between the Father and the Son, but the material content of that relation of union is given by the Incarnation of the Son of God. . . . Thus the doctrine of the Church must be thought out in terms of a triangular relation between the Church and the historical Christ, the risen and ascended Mediator, and the Christ who will come again in His full Humanity as well as Deity.[20]

Torrance refers appreciatively to the Roman Catholic theologian Hans Urs von Balthasar, who has so great an understanding of Barth and the Reformed dialectic, and the learned reader will be aware of what fruitful ground for future discussion with Roman Catholics is here prepared. At Lund, Torrance seems to have gained the day. In its message to the Churches, the Conference wrote:

> We have seen clearly that we can make no real advance towards unity if we only compare our several conceptions of the nature of the Church and the traditions in which they are

[20] *Op. cit.*, pp. 57–8.

embodied. . . . We need, therefore, to penetrate behind our divisions to a deeper and richer understanding of the mystery of the God-given union of Christ with his Church.[21]

In the years since 1952, all parties may be said to have won – and yet none of them. There has been a great deal of high theological discussion, aided by the participation of Orthodox and Romans and by the disciples and successors of Bultmann. Yet the comparative study of traditions has proved more rather than less necessary, because the World Council is now far less dominated by American and European Churches, or by Orthodox Protestants. Pentecostalists and Seventh Day Adventists seek to gain admission as well as the innumerable sects and churches of Africa. The patience and sensitiveness of a Flew are still required and revealed, in some cases by Flew's old pupils, as their understanding of the nature of the Church is brought in as a catalyst of more orthodox notions. On the other side, there is an ever-increasing activism and a radical theology, which challenges some of the credal assumptions, which it was thought held Christians together even in the times of darkest separation.

All this was hidden from Flew as he returned from Lund, after 'a most interesting world Conference' in 'a most friendly place'. In 1953, as England were winning the Ashes for the first time since 1933, he was at the Working Committee at Bossey, championing, so he said, the Eastern Orthodox. (He had to interrupt his subsequent Swiss holiday for Morgan's funeral.) But he had ceased to be Vice-Chairman of the Faith and Order Commission after Lund, and, by the next summer, illness had terminated his long and pioneer part in World Council affairs.

---

[21] Report of the Third World Conference on Faith and Order (1952), p. 5.

Church Relations in England

The second war had seen much practical co-operation between the Churches in England, but the *Outline Scheme for Reunion* was as good as buried. Although the loss of William Temple was immeasurable, Geoffrey Francis Fisher came to the primacy with a resolve to break the deadlock and the advent of his fresh and vigorous – though less philosophic – mind made speedy impact.

Fisher spoke to the Free Church Federal Council at Westminster Chapel, Buckingham Gate, in April 1946. Flew had just concluded his Moderatorship. He was afflicted with fluid on the knee and was walking with a stick. Fisher spoke with his usual vivacity and humour. At one point he said that he thought that discussions between the Churches should be confined to those under fifty and over ninety, since Dr Lidgett must never be left out. Lidgett, who had perhaps only half-heard, interrupted to say, 'I'm ninety-two'. Fisher also jokingly speculated as to the consequences if Dr Flew's trouble were not water on the knee but water on the brain. Whereupon, Flew took up his stick and shook it at the Archbishop!

It was all very relaxed and good humoured. One cannot imagine such mirth had Cosmo Lang been the visitor, although Flew used to say that the Baptist leader, M. E. Aubrey, maintained that he was the greatest Archbishop of all. Fisher disclosed something of his own vision of the future in another pleasantry. He hoped that the day might come when it would be possible to walk around a town centre and see the various Church buildings each with notice boards – Church of England (Baptist), Church of England (Congregationalist), Church of England (Methodist), Church of England (C. of E.)!

The *jeu d'esprit* is worth a moment's pause. Clearly the revolution of the town centres was not then foreseen and it was assumed that the pattern of Church life would not radically change. But the whole rationale of Fisher's new approach was that schemes for organic union were not likely to succeed and that what was wanted was intercommunion, to make possible the free flowing of life among the members of Christ's Body.

This was the theme of Fisher's Cambridge sermon on 3rd November, 1946. He invited the Free Churches to consider taking episcopacy into their systems as a step towards making possible common sacraments and a commonly accepted ministry.

> The Church of England has not yet found the finally satisfying use of episcopacy in practice: nor certainly has the Church of Rome. If non-episcopal Churches agree that it must come into the picture, could they not take it and try it out on their own ground first? . . . As it seems to me, it is an easier step for them to contemplate than those involved in a union of Churches; and, if achieved, it would immensely carry us forward towards full communion, without the fearful complexities and upheavals of a constitutional union.

The following year the Churches began conversations to try and discover where this new approach might lead. The Archbishop himself appointed a panel of representative Anglicans under the Bishop of Derby, Dr A. E. J. Rawlinson. It is significant that they were not official delegates of the Church of England, whereas the Free Church consultants were appointed by the Council itself and included Henry T. Wigley, the Secretary, a Methodist, who, said Flew, 'grows in stature every week'.

Dr Nathaniel Micklem was elected joint Chairman with the Bishop of Derby, but, says E. A. Payne, 'it was Dr Flew who in effect directed and led the Free Church representatives. The Conversations lasted until September 1950 and throughout I was impressed by the mastery Dr Flew showed, and felt he had stepped into the position of leadership in such discussions which had formerly, according to what I have read and been told, been occupied by Dr Carnegie Simpson and Dr Garvie.'

The conversations were tough, but very good humoured. Free Church participants always remembered the saintliness of Philip Loyd, Bishop of St. Albans, formerly of Nasik, India, and Dom Gregory Dix's great gifts as a *raconteur*. Nor would they ever forget Dom Gregory's meditation one night on the Name of Jesus. They remarked that when Free Churchmen took prayers they tended to be rather formal in the style of *The Book of Common Order*. The Anglicans were often more free and from the heart.

A. E. J. Rawlinson, who had been Bishop of Derby since 1936, became a close friend of Flew from henceforward. Rawlinson was a scholar, who may be considered unfortunate not to have obtained an Oxford or Cambridge Divinity Chair. He was a liberal Catholic, who had contributed to *Foundations*, done a book on *Dogma, Fact and Experience* (1915), and written a remarkable Commentary on *St. Mark* in the 1920s, which was possibly the most advanced English work on that Gospel until Dennis Nineham's Pelican in 1963. He also gave the Bampton lectures on *The New Testament Doctrine of the Person of Christ*. He knew more continental and especially German theology than most Anglo-Catholics, and, as an ecumenical statesman, his liberalism and learning made him a mediator. A Catholic at heart, he knew well that it would be intolerable both on grounds of scholarship and of faith to make the acceptance of any one theory of Episcopacy a condition of union. While he agreed that official Anglicanism had to assert that the proper minister of the Eucharist must be an episcopally ordained priest, he recognised 'the liberty sanctioned by precedent' of individual Anglicans to communicate, in certain circumstances, at non-episcopal celebrations. He had already in 1946 presided over the committee, set up by Archbishop Fisher, which gave cautious and critical approval to the South India Scheme in the so-called 'Derby Report'. The extremist Anglo-Catholics mistrusted him and spoke of him with great bitterness. Flew and he were kindred spirits and not dissimilar in physique, both short of stature and ebullient, though Rawlinson had the habit, which Flew had not, of pacing his study when engaged in conversation or interview – his 'caged lion act'.[22]

Parallel with this work there was another, also due to the initiative of the Archbishop of Canterbury. In November 1945, in the first months of his primacy, Geoffrey Fisher asked Dom Gregory Dix to convene a group of Anglicans of the 'Catholic' school of thought with the following terms of reference:

(i) What is the underlying cause – philosophical and theological – of the contrast or conflict between the Catholic and Protestant traditions?

(ii) What are the fundamental points of doctrine at which the contrast or conflict crystallises?

(iii) Is a synthesis at these points possible?

(iv) If a synthesis is not possible, can they co-exist within one ecclesiastical body, and under what conditions?

The group was remarkably distinguished in its membership. Canon A. M. Ramsey, then van Mildert Professor at Durham, was elected Chairman, and of the others apart from Ramsey himself, three have become Bishops (H. J. Carpenter, R. C. Mortimer and Ambrose Reeves) and one a Dean (E. S. Abbott), while V. A. Demant, A. M. Farrer, A. G. Hebert, Charles Smyth and L. S. Thornton have each in different ways made outstanding contributions to twentieth-century Anglican thought.

---

[22] For Rawlinson's views on the matter under debate in Church relations see his *Problems of Reunion* (Eyre and Spottiswoode 1950).

The solitary layman was T. S. Eliot – no less. The resulting pamphlet, *Catholicity*, was one of the most provocative and, in its way, profound documents of religious discussion in our time.[23]

Together with *Catholicity*, which appeared in 1947, must be mentioned the vast symposium, published the previous year under the editorship of the Bishop of Oxford, Dr Kenneth Kirk, called *The Apostolic Ministry*. If *Catholicity* emphasises that the Church is prior to individual discipleship, *The Apostolic Ministry* has to own that the ministry is theologically prior to the Church. Both these publications, the pamphlet and the tome, represent Anglo-Catholicism in what now seems to be its last united and assured initiative. They are learned, literary, confident, ingenious and withal strangely perverse and, despite their scholarship, so ignorant of the Protestant tradition as to misrepresent it to the point of caricature.

Flew never had very close associations with Kenneth Kirk, but for much of his life the shadow of the formidable bishop was across his path. Kirk had been one of his examiners for the Oxford B.D. *The Vision of God* is a parallel work to *The Idea of Perfection* as we have seen. Kirk refused Flew permission to preach at Kenneth Grayston's marriage in an Oxfordshire village church, thus provoking, so Flew had been told, one of William Temple's rare outbursts of wrath. Flew was appalled by 'the blasphemy' of Kirk's ordination rite, when he attended it in Christ Church Cathedral in September 1950, with its introit, *Ecce sacerdos magnus*!, 'a title (High Priest) reserved in the New Testament for Our Lord'. He wondered whether his conscience would allow him to attend Kirk's University sermon at Cambridge that year, but he went – doubtless he would say that 'the natural

---

[23] *Catholicity* A Study in the Conflict of Christian Traditions in the West (Dacre Press, Westminster, 1947).

man was overcome' – and listened with admiration and a good deal of approval.[24]

The two might not have found personal contact easy. Kirk was a large man, Flew small. Kirk had once been a Methodist and tried to forget the fact, so much so that his own son did not know of it until after his death. Flew was for ever talking of his father and the communion 'to which he owed his soul'. Flew might well have irritated Kirk as much as he delighted Rawlinson.

In some ways this is a digression, yet in those days Kirk was the Anglo-Catholic leader, even though he was neither a participant in conversations with the Free Churches nor a member of the *Catholicity* group. He was himself the symbol of the position for which he fought – a bishop and canonist, a fine scholar, gifted with an enviable lucidity of expression which served as well at a village induction as in a university lecture or Diocesan Conference address, so possessed by Catholic spirituality that any good thing in Protestant seemed to him exceptional and uncovenanted, stiff for the rigours of Church law and hating such abominations as the Church of South India, women in Holy Orders and exchanges of pulpits! He carried his controversy with those who did not share his interpretation of Catholicity to the limits. Stephen Neill wrote in a devastating critique that 'those of us who reject the doctrine of Church and ministry set forth in *The Apostolic Ministry* reject it, not on grounds of minute differences on points of archaeological interpretation, but because we cannot recognise as Christian the doctrine of God, which seems to underly this imposing edifice'.[25] Kirk was delighted. At least,

---

[24] The sermon is reprinted in K. E. Kirk, *Beauty and Bands* and other Papers prepared by E. W. Kemp (Hodder and Stoughton 1955), pp. 256 ff.

[25] *The Ministry of the Church*, a review by various authors of a book entitled *The Apostolic Ministry* reprinted from 'The Record' with

such a critic recognised by implication that a systematic theologian's doctrine of the ministry must colour and be coloured by his doctrine of God. These questions of the ministry were not matters of indifference on which a variety of opinions might be held, in creative tension, or whatever was the jargon of 1950. They were matters of true faith or false.[26]

It looked then as though there might be a debate on the grand scale. From the Free Church point of view, Gordon Rupp wrote in similar vein to Kirk:

> Behind *The Apostolic Ministry* and *Catholicity* lies a coherent interpretation of Christian truth and its development which needs to be met at the highest level of exact and profound scholarship and careful theological argument. Really to come to grips about that might bring about a discussion of classic importance, worthy of the great centuries of theological discussion.[27]

The trouble was, as Professor Rupp has stated elsewhere and so staunch an Anglican Catholic as Professor Mascall has recognised, that, in spite of its courteous and eirenic tone, so free from arrogance, and its resources of scholarship, *Catholicity* outraged Protestants by its misunderstanding of the doctrines of the reformers and the life of the Protestant Churches.[28] The pamphlet republishes all the high Anglican ignorance of Protestantism that was current in its day – the belief that

---

[26] Cf. Kenneth E. Kirk, *The Coherence of Christian Doctrine*, A Lecture delivered on the Charles Gore Memorial Foundation on 9 November 1949 in Westminster Abbey (SPCK 1950), p. 4.

[27] *Theology* LI, p. 264.

[28] See E. L. Mascall, *The Recovery of Unity* (Longmans 1958), pp. 37 ff. Also Gordon Rupp, *Protestant Catholicity* (Epworth 1960), pp. 40 ff.

---

corrections and a preliminary chapter by Bishop Stephen Neill (The Canterbury Press 1947), p. 28.

Protestantism neglected the doctrine of creation, failed to take the visible Church with due seriousness, despised reason and 'with certain partial exceptions has produced very little ascetical or mystical theology'. There is also the frequent contemporary Anglican 'howler' which sets Cranmer over against Luther and the continental reformers, in ignorance that the very works of his which are cited are closely dependent on continental sources at the very points at which they are supposed to show the distinctiveness and the Catholic insights of the English Reformation. In addition there is a somewhat romantic view of the primitive Church and the historic episcopate.

Archbishop Fisher had not intended that his four questions should be answered by Anglo-Catholics alone. He wished for an Anglican evangelical contribution, and had already suggested to Flew that a Free Church group might be convened with a similar mandate. The appearance of *Catholicity* made a rejoinder essential. The heirs of Luther, Calvin, Bunyan, Baxter and the Wesleys could not keep silent. Flew secured money to finance the enterprise from Mr R. Wilson Black, the Baptist layman who was treasurer of the Free Church Federal Council, and, in 1948, called together a representative company which included several younger scholars. Flew was Chairman and the leading parts were played by Ernest Payne (Baptist), Lovell Cocks (Congregationalist), Philip Watson (Methodist), who gave his original Luther research unstintingly to the work, and Rupert Davies (Methodist), who as Secretary and co-editor took a great deal of the burden from Flew's shoulders.

Flew found the meetings of the group, held at Regents Park College, Oxford, a great inspiration. He would sometimes return to Wesley House, obviously tired, but able to preach a brief extempore sermon of great power from some aspect of the discussion. Once, at the Lord's Supper, he pointed out how wrong it was to talk of 'making one's communion', how altogether Pelagian and false to the doctrine of grace, and gave a positive interpretation of Free Church sacramental customs, such as 'the table spread' and the Methodist reception of the bread and wine in small groups. One of his great concerns during these years was to demonstrate what became the title of the Free Church report – *The Catholicity of Protestantism.*

This was published in 1950. The *Church Times* was unconvinced and patronisingly dismissive, but the Protestant religious press felt that never again would certain travesties be possible among educated and honest men. The full orthodoxy of the great Protestant communions had been vindicated with a wealth of illustration. Far from being anarchical and individualistic, they had been shown to have Church polities, which could claim greater warranty of Scripture and possibly of the primitive tradition than episcopacy.

Perhaps it was unfortunate that the inaccuracies of *Catholicity* had necessitated a defence of the Protestant tradition rather than an unfettered exploration of the terms of reference. But this seemed to be the need of the hour. It was Flew's lot to be occupied in clearing the ground of prejudice rather than in raising the edifice of unity. He was pressed to the task of comparative ecclesiology, however great the clamour for new methods.[29] And two decades and a Vatican Council later, there seems to be a groundswell of feeling that true Catholicity is an ideal laid up in heaven towards which we must unceasingly strive, but meanwhile, *in via*, we must recognise that our differences about the Gospel are very great and always liable to appear in new mutations. The achievement of Flew and his contemporaries was to

---

[29] There is also the fact that the Anglo-Catholics were apt to change their ground. Refuted by the appeal to history they themselves first demanded, they would then say, 'Ah, but it is theology we need', or 'We have been appealing to the wrong period of history'.

help us to learn to receive God's judgement and salvation through one another, and to speak the truth in love.

Flew was a great defender of evangelical Catholicity, to use Lidgett's term. This is evident in an interesting exchange of letters with Bishop Neville Talbot in 1939.

> The Right Reverend
>   Bishop Neville Talbot, D.D.
> St. Mary's Vicarage,
> Nottingham.
> 16th March, 1939.

Dear Brother Flew,

I am venturing to send you my little book. There are some rather bad misprints in it I am afraid. There are some things in it that people have sat up and taken notice of. But how hard it is to judge of one's own stuff.

I am deadly keen on what I have tried to say about the preaching of the Incarnation, and I also burn I must say with hope about there being great deep fundamental reconciliation on Scriptural grounds about the Eucharist. I just indicate that on page 130 ff. At any rate I send you the little book with all best greetings.

> Yours sincerely,
> N. S. TALBOT, Bp.

My Dear Bishop,

Please accept my heartiest thanks for the gift of your book, 'Great Issues'. I am in the middle of it now, and in essential agreement with it. And I believe that there need not be controversy over the Eucharist. But I do not know of any one of the great Evangelical Churches of Christendom which holds the view ascribed to Evangelicals in the quotation (p. 135) from Brabant. Zwingli himself did not hold the view attributed to Evangelicals by Brabant – see e.g. *Christian Worship* (ed. Micklem), O.U. Press 1936, pages 149–50; and the famous phrase of Zwingli, *Hospes atque epulum.*

> Once more, my heartiest thanks!
> Very sincerely yours,
> R. NEWTON FLEW

He also refused to be party to any attempt on the part of high Anglicans to detach Methodism from her Nonconformist associations and give her favoured treatment as a body which was somehow less infected with the Protestant virus than the others. On 23rd June, 1950, this vigorous letter appeared in the then extant Church newspaper, *The Guardian*:

Sir – Nonconformists are frequently given fresh surprises when Anglo-Catholics inform them what Nonconformists believe. But surprise mounts into dismay and bewilderment when Mr. Hugh Ross Williamson declares: 'What the adherent of classic Nonconformity (by which I exclude the Methodists) believes is that there is no such thing as sacraments. That is why he is a Nonconformist'. Indeed! And from what document of 'classic Nonconformity' does Mr. Williamson derive this item of news? Surely a gentleman whose letter is given the place of honour in *The Guardian* of June 16 might have phoned to the Secretary or even the Moderator of the Free Church Federal Council at 27 Tavistock Square to verify his egregious statement. He would have then been provided (free of charge) with the 'Declaratory Statement' which forms the doctrinal basis of the Federal Council composed of fully accredited representatives of the Free Churches of England and Wales. This document was drawn up on March 26, 1917. It was re-affirmed in 1941 when the former National Council of Free Churches became amalgamated with the Free Church Federal Council.

The following is one paragraph of that Declaratory Statement, headed 'The Sacraments of the Gospel':

'The Sacraments – Baptism and the Lord's Supper – are instituted by Christ, Who is Himself certainly and really present in His own ordinances (though not bodily in the elements thereof), and are signs and seals of His Gospel not to be separated therefrom. They confirm the promises and gifts of salvation, and, when rightly used by believers with faith and prayer, are, through the operation of the Holy Spirit, true means of grace.'

The doctrinal basis of the Federal Council was drafted by the late Professor P. Carnegie Simpson. Does Mr. Williamson really think that the Presbyterian Church of England believes that there is no such thing as sacraments? I would recommend the study of the book edited by R. Dunkerley and A. C. Headlam (the former Bishop of Gloucester) and entitled *The Ministry and the Sacraments*, or Ernest A. Payne's books.

If Mr. Williamson were to read in some Free Church periodical that Anglicans (with certain exceptions) 'believed that there is no such thing as sacraments', he would justly feel that something infinitely precious to him had been calumniated. We feel like that now. As a Methodist, I congratulate Mr. Williamson on his knowledge that by Methodists the sacraments of the Gospel are diligently valued and honoured, and (as our Deed of Union declares) of divine appointment and perpetual obligation. But I am not to be separated from my fellow Free Churchmen. *Sit mea anima cum illis*! As one who has been given the great privilege of joining with the Baptists in Cambridge, in one of the historic homes of 'classic Nonconformity', and of marvelling at the traditional order of the Lord's Supper, so strangely akin to that of the *Didache*, I do appeal to those who think like Mr. Williamson to take the trouble to learn something about the 'classic Nonconformity' of their fellow-Christians. I ask Mr. Williamson to do what he can to atone for and refute this travesty of the truth.

R. NEWTON FLEW

Meanwhile the conversations of the inter-Church group reached their end in September 1950 and the report *Church Relations in England* was published shortly after *The Catholicity of Protestantism*. Nothing had occurred to reassure Flew about the dangers of episcopacy. In August 1949, he had written to Ernest Payne:

In my bones I feel and with my mind I see the dreadful corruption of the Episcopate in Church History. But one can hardly say in these conversations that we fear Episcopacy because it at once sets up a clerical race in the 'cursus honorum' especially in a State Church!

He had not seen the Methodist 'brotherhood of the ministry' in the Church of England.

The report had this to say about the main issue of the Archbishop's Cambridge Sermon:

> The Free Church would 'take episcopacy into its system' by the acceptance of an episcopate consecrated in the first instance through Bishops of one or more of the historic episcopal Churches, and thus linked with the episcopate of the past, and would adopt episcopal ordination as its rule for the future. The Church of England would acknowledge that the Bishops and episcopally ordained Presbyters were from the outset duly commissioned and authorized for the same offices in the Church of God as its own Bishops and Priests.
>
> The Church of England would agree to admit to communion baptized and duly commended communicant members of the Free Church in good standing, and would officially authorize duly commended communicant members of the Church of England in good standing to receive the sacrament of Holy Communion at the hands of such Ministers of the Free Church as had been either consecrated to the episcopate or episcopally ordained or further commissioned to the Presbyterate.
>
> It would be recognized that the Free Church, though itself episcopal, or in process of becoming episcopal, would yet continue to maintain the relations of fellowship and intercommunion which it at present enjoys with non-episcopal Churches; and the Church of England, though not able to adopt the like policy for itself, would yet not regard the matter as one which should stand in the way of the achievement of intercommunion between itself and the Free Church.

Difficulties were frankly recognised – some Free Churches would find the acceptance of episcopacy in any form intolerable, some Anglicans could not contemplate their Church being in communion with any episcopal Church which itself was in communion with non-episcopal Churches, while a Free Church which became episcopal would have two classes of ministers within its ranks, one acceptable, the other unacceptable to Anglicans. Even so:

> All the members of the Conference would plead that no Communion should refuse this way towards closer unity except under an inescapable sense of obligation.

As is well known, the Methodist Church alone among the Free Churches, having obtained certain, perhaps not entirely unequivocal, assurances, entered into negotiations with the Church of England in these terms. When Dr Harold Roberts proposed, at the Methodist Conference of 1955, that conversations should take place, Dr Flew attending for the last time as an *ex officio* member, rose simultaneously with Dr Norman Snaith to second the motion. Dr Snaith caught Dr Weatherhead's eye first, but on seeing Dr Flew, the President said, 'Bless him! we'll let him third it!'. Flew was not able to take part either in the talks themselves or in any public debate. On one occasion in the Methodist Faith and Order Committee he deprecated an attempt to foment opposition in the wake of the *Interim Statement* of 1958. Yet what he heard of the likely proposals disturbed him. It was not that he was against discussions about intercommunion turning into negotiations for organic unity. He felt somehow that the Methodists were prepared to make too great concessions to episcopalian claims while the proposed Service of Reconciliation revived the ghost of the discarded South India scheme for Supplemental Ordination.

The letter has been lost, but in his last years, while still he was able, he wrote to Kingsley Barrett, the most forceful and scholarly of the Methodist dissentients, and told him that of all his old pupils, he was the one who most faithfully maintained his views about Church relations.

8

The Last Years

In April 1949, Flew was elected a member of the
Athenaeum. Although he claimed to be embarrassed by
the announcement in the personal columns of the
Methodist Recorder, probably inserted at the instigation of
his old friend Bardsley Brash, he regarded this as a very
great honour and savoured it with undiminishing relish
for the rest of his life. His sponsors were the Archbishop
of Canterbury and Canon J. A. Douglas, the first
secretary of the Church of England Council on Foreign
Relations.

He was delighted when the students' Chairman of
Wesley House managed to unearth Scott Holland's
comments on Randall Davidson's membership of the
Club and quoted them against him, attempting to mimic
something of his own accents, at the appropriate places:

> Bishop Davidson's point of danger is not the Court. He has
> survived its perils with singular simplicity. Rather it is to be
> sought at the Athenaeum. There dwell the sirens who are apt
> to beguile and bewitch him. They have ceased to be mer-
> maids with harps and have adopted the disguise of elderly
> and excellent gentlemen of reputation, who lead you aside
> into corners and, in impressive whispers, inform you what
> will not do and what the intelligent British public will not
> stand. The Bishop has a deep veneration for the judgement
> and the wisdom of important laity of this type. Yet the

Athenaeum is not the shrine of infallibility. Its elderly common sense has no prophetic *afflatus*.[1]

He would continue to love the company of high ecclesiastics and the eminent in various callings and his letters are sprinkled with the famous names of the time, either talked to or seen at the next table. For Archbishop Fisher he had the greatest affection and respect, regarding him as, among other things, a realist, who had none of the romantic Anglo-Catholic illusions about the true place of Anglicanism in the world Church.

When King George VI and Queen Elizabeth, with Princess Margaret, visited Cambridge in April 1951, Flew was given an excellent seat in the choir of King's College Chapel:

Elmslie and I sat together, almost next to the Head Master of Eton and his lady, but I couldn't get a word with him. I know him of old. Behind us sat Sir Will and Lady Spens and the Master of St. Johns. Across the way sat the civic dignitaries and the MP for the City. Mrs. Mellish Clark looked at me long and gloomily as if she would like to reform me or send me to a Home for the Aged. . . .

The King sat in the Provost's seat and the Queen in the next stall and Princess Margaret in the next. I could not see their dresses at such a distance. The Archbp of Canterbury and the Bishop of Ely were there and walked in procession to the Altar. The Archbp did a charming thing on his return march after the service. On the way up he had spotted me, and deliberately on the way down the aisle as he passed within two feet, he gravely gave me a gentle bow and I returned it and saw just a twinkle in his eye which said: 'If only this finery were doffed, I'd pull your leg about the mischief you made in Australia' – or something equally characteristic. I told no one about it and did not think that any one else had noticed. But I dined at Ridley Hall on

---

[1] G. K. A. Bell, *Randall Davidson, Archbishop of Canterbury* (Oxford, Second Edition 1938), p. 407.

Friday night and the new Principal (Bowles)[2] said to me:
'I saw a very charming bow given by the Archbp to a friend
of mine'. He spotted it! And I said I didn't expect it but it
was just like the friendliness of the man.

Similarly his heart was warmed when at the Methodist
Conference of 1955, the Bishop of Manchester (Dr
W. D. L. Greer, formerly Principal of Westcott House)
who was being welcomed with the customary ecumenical
delegation, noticed him seated in the front row of the
auditorium, and saluted him from the platform.

There were sorrows and anxieties as well as exultations
and comforts. His sister had lost one son in the war and,
in 1947, her husband died. This brought consolation in
that she and his mother, who remained amazingly alert
and lively through the years, moved house to Cambridge.
In 1952, he had to give the address at the memorial
service in Oxford for Bardsley Brash. Only eighteen
months later, he was at Headingley, Leeds, performing
the same sad office for Howard Watkin-Jones. Both
friends had died with unexpected suddenness. He was
inevitably saddened and tortured in spirit by his son's
rejection of the Christian faith. He could never forget
that his own father had 'led him to Christ' and wondered
where he had failed. But he rejoiced in his boy's academic
achievements, and respected his intellectual honesty,
while the bonds of family affection were in no sense
weakened. Antony Flew's pride in his father and filial
solicitude never faltered.

In 1953, he gave the annual lecture of the Wesley
Historical Society, the last of his books to be published
in his lifetime. It is on *The Hymns of Charles Wesley: A
Study of Their Structure*,[3] and, although slight, is full of
characteristic discernment and by no means an in-
appropriate consummation of his literary work. The

[2] C. W. J. Bowles, now Bishop of Derby.
[3] Epworth Press 1953.

hymns had meant so much to him and had so often illustrated his theology that it would have been almost a defiance of natural law had he not gathered something of his lifelong meditations and discoveries into a book.

If the following pages, with their attempt to enter into the purpose, the doctrine, and the structure of the hymns of such a man, could induce twelve Methodists to begin and continue the habit of meditating on one of the great hymns of Charles Wesley every day, I should have my reward. But if the analysis of the hymns they study does not convince them that there is a 'normal pattern', I must beg them to remember that to recover the original pattern they will often have to refer to the thirteen volumes of the *Poetical Works of John and Charles Wesley*. Alas, these volumes are rare. But I think it is true to say that Charles Wesley has an orderly mind beyond all others of the great hymn-writers. One doesn't perceive it at first. But when the hymn is studied, the order is there. In the Church of St. Mary at Hitchin, there is an 'Angel Screen' to which men come from afar to admire. At first the screen seems beautiful, and delicately wrought, but confused and intricate. Is there a key to the meaning? Yes, if you look at one place – the upper part of the carvings. There are angels with intertwined wings, and each angel has one of the material things which were used at the Crucifixion. There is the wooden cross, the crown of thorns, the spear which pierced His side, the nails, the hammer, the scourge, the sponge, and the seamless robe. At last you see the design of this work of art. Each one of those material things is held by an angel, as it were in adoration, and they are bearing to heaven these emblems of the world's redemption, in wonder and praise.

As I have considered hymn after hymn by Charles Wesley for many years now (I began the habit as a boy away from home at school) I have often been puzzled at first, but now I see more clearly their meaning. Meditation has a way of ending in adoration; and all the time you are not alone, even in the secret place with door shut. You find yourself murmuring:

Ah! show me that happiest place,
  The place of Thy people's abode,
Where saints in an ecstasy gaze,
  And hang on a crucified God;
Thy love for a sinner declare,
  The passion and death on the tree,
My spirit to Calvary bear,
  To suffer and triumph with Thee.[4]

The little book has a double purpose – to help Methodists and others to learn the art of meditation from the treasury of the Wesley hymns, and also to teach them by these examples how to bear a clear and convincing witness to their Lord:

> The main thesis, which I submit with diffidence to those with greater knowledge of hymnology than I possess, is that Charles Wesley's hymns can be analysed; that they have a coherent and intelligible structure of thought, and that this habit of orderly composition is due to his desire to teach Christian doctrine to ordinary people. Their counterpart in prose would be orderly sermons with the divisions clearly marked, as contrasted with sermons destitute of divisions.[5]

There speaks Flew the homileticist, straight from the Wesley House sermon class.

The Hymns of Charles Wesley was received by Hendrik Kraemer at Bossey with great interest. John Rawlinson quoted from it in the Annual Sermon of the Church Missionary Society in 1954. His subject was *Episcopacy and the Anglican Tradition* and he was referring to a phrase, which in 1935, Stephen Neill had seized on to provide a formula for the South India Scheme: 'The uniting Churches recognize that Christ has bestowed His grace *with undistinguishing regard* on all their ministries. . . .'

[4] *Op. cit.*, p. 13.
[5] *Op. cit.*, p. 18.

Anglo-Catholics who disapproved of the sentiments vented their spleen on the construction. Rawlinson, with Flew's help, cited the original context in Charles Wesley's hymn 'Father, whose everlasting love':

> Thy *undistinguishing* regard
> Was cast on Adam's fallen race;

on which Flew comments: 'The word "undistinguishing" is a reminiscence of Acts 11:12, where Peter says: "The Spirit bade me go with them making no distinction."'[6]

Work at Wesley House continued and the members of the college venerated him as 'the old man', a title which amused him, but which had echoes of his schooldays when to a certain circle he was known as 'old Flew'. Lectures caused him no trouble, but by 1954 the amount of administration had quadrupled since his early days as Principal. He wrote to Roderick Macleod:

Owing to the utter confusion of practice among Local Education Authorities, every man presents a fresh financial problem when he appears on the scene and tells us that he has grants, or that they will not give him a grant because it will be used for denominational purposes! Of course, the Church of England and the Free Churches have agreed together that they will accept no money for denominational training of the ministry. It is only for the major scholarships, which are awarded to men of ability, irrespective of the subjects they are studying, that we will accept State grants.

All this, together with the toil and travels of the post-war years, had tired him, and yet it was a man, who had recently been assured by his doctor that his heart was as strong as in his days on the running track, who cycled to Cambridge station for the London train on

---

[6] *Op. cit.*, p. 50. For the South India discussions see Bengt Sundkler, *Church of South India*, pp. 268 ff.

16th March, 1954. In the train he was attacked by an
unwonted breathlessness, so he took a taxi to his
committee at Westminster Central Hall. He called in at
his brother, the accountant's, office. Howard Flew was
alarmed and ordered him into another taxi bound for
the casualty ward of Westminster Hospital. There
coronary thrombosis was diagnosed and he had to
remain for eight weeks. He did no more work at Wesley
House until Michaelmas.

Once he had emerged from the full force of the attack,
he began to enjoy hospital life. He received visitors,
including the Archbishop, read detective stories and
made friends with his fellow patients, especially Sir
Lionel Fox, the authority on prisons and the penal code.

He had already decided to retire on 31st August, 1955.
His recovery was such that he did not need to advance
the date and was able to do a final year's teaching. In
December 1954 he maintained his unbroken record of
almost thirty years attendance at the Varsity match at
Twickenham, in spite of having been told to take great
care about all excitement. 'We both went up to it and
had a glorious time even though Oxford was beaten and
deservedly beaten. I found that particular form of
excitement did me great good!'

Frank O. Salisbury was commissioned to paint Flew's
portrait. Maldwyn Hughes had sat for him in 1937, at
Flew's instigation. The unveiling and farewells at Wesley
House were fixed for Thursday, 26th May, 1955, a date
which happened to coincide with a General Election.

Cambridge was bathed in May sunshine as the
audience, which filled the large lecture room to capacity,
assembled. They came from the University and from the
Methodist Church. W. J. Noble, Chairman of the
Governors, presided, 'scared', as he said in a private
letter, 'to my toenails of the academic audience'. The
Bishop of Ely, Edward Wynn, was there, and many
tributes were paid, perhaps the most notable both in

phrasing and temper being that of the Lady Margaret Professor of Divinity, C. F. D. Moule.

Flew liked the portrait and expressed his relief that Frank Salisbury was an artist of different idiom from Graham Sutherland, whose controversial study of Churchill had been unveiled in Westminster Hall a few months earlier. Flew's portrait hangs, with Hughes, Gutteridge, and Fletcher of Madeley, in the Hall at Wesley House.

For some time, the Flews had owned a house in Cambridge, at 49, Glisson Road, 'Glover's old road', with an attic view of Fenners. There Flew retired, withdrawing in most exemplary fashion from all affairs of Wesley House, and devoting himself to a large correspondence, much of it by way of guidance to old students. He had many visitors, especially Americans, many of whom came to see him because of his work on Christian Perfection, though not all described him in the identical terms of an American bishop, who had called during his latter days at the House and said, 'I guess you're the focal point of holiness in this country'.

Dr Alan Kay invited him to succeed Ryder Smith as the review editor of the *London Quarterly and Holborn Review*, a task he fulfilled until 1961. As infirmity advanced, he sometimes found it a struggle to keep his copy dates, but his own reviews, *From My New Shelf*, show an altogether lovable septuagenarian – 'on ticket of leave' as he put it, quoting an old Portland woman – with his scholarship unimpaired and in some ways enriched as he recollected his emotions in tranquillity. Nearly always he praises the volumes he has read. Once he sniffs old battles and takes an Anglo-Catholic theologian to task for learning his Protestantism from Father Louis Bouyer and not going to the Reformers themselves. He is not altogether happy with C. S. Lewis's *Reflections on the Psalms*, especially on the twenty-third Psalm. Every now and then some light is shed on the great ones of the past,

Maltby, Lidgett, von Hügel, while he can still coin a memorable *mot*: 'I am left with an uncomfortable feeling that if Pelagius had to be condemned and turned out of the Holy Places, a very frightening proportion in some modern congregations ought to share his fate!' Or of one author: 'He is less at home with his Luther references than with his Bible. But Luther himself would have preferred him like that.' Or, quoting von Hügel's judgement on Kierkegaard, 'Christ's self-renunciation is here, but not his expansive tenderness'.

He was regular in attendance at the University Sermon and happy if the preacher was someone, like Kenneth Riches, whom he had known in his active days. Towards the end the preachers were sometimes saddened to see him looking old and frail. But for some years, he preached occasionally himself. As we have mentioned earlier, he was Hulsean preacher at Cambridge in 1956. At the start of the University autumn term in 1957 he went to Manchester to preach in the Cathedral. He preached to the German Lutheran Congregation in Cambridge as late as 1961 on the New Testament word *Makrothumia* (patience, endurance) without which, as he kept saying, the New Testament and our world would 'grow cold'. He maintained his membership of the London Society for the Study of Religion, though in later years would ask to be excused from taking part in the discussion.

In the autumn of 1957, he went at the invitation of the Presbyterian Professor Haire to give fifteen lectures on Christian Ethics, in Belfast. He visited Dublin en route, and promptly succumbed to 'Asian 'flu', as did his wife two days later. The Regius Professor of Divinity at Trinity College, R. R. Hartford, whom he had met at Lund and Clarens, saw that he had good and generous medical attention, and he was able to go on, a little late, and fulfil his course in the North. He was intrigued by the Catholic maids and their interest in the married priest and his wife.

But the great feature as well as the chief joy of his retirement became his annual visits to Rome. All the time, he was working on *Jesus and His Way*, shaping material collected and used over almost twenty years, trying to conform to certain stipulations of the Oxford University Press, whom he hoped would be his publishers. He was anxious to avail himself of the Roman libraries, the Dominican Library at the Collegio Angelico, where in those days not even nuns were allowed, and his wife could not accompany him, and, above all, the unrivalled library of the Facolta' Valdese in Via Pietro Cossa, which had books not possessed even by the University Library in Cambridge.

For four successive years, from the spring of 1958, he and his wife would stay with Signorina Morelli in the Via delle Mura, Gianicolensi. The Signorina had turned her family villa into a *pensione*. Everything belonged to the culture of the pre-Fascist era in Rome. She loved the 'Fleurs', as she called them and they would stay for six weeks or even twelve at a time. They went everywhere by public transport. Newton would do the daily shopping and in Panama hat, alpaca jacket and with his disarming smile has been described as the typical English don in Italy.

They found a home, too, with Rex and Elizabeth Kissack, the Methodist Missionary Society representatives, in their flat at Ponte Sant' Angelo, just as the young Newton Flew had done years before with William Burgess, who hoped he might succeed him.

Says Rex Kissack:

On Sundays they would be in the English language congregation. . . . If he could not follow the sermon for any reason, he quietly read. At first he was able to preach himself. . . . He found friends among the Salvation Army in Rome, and revealed his life-long love of them and their worship. He would come with us to remote Italian Methodist

Churches and spent some weeks at Casa Materna in Naples.
He was quite at home in the cosmopolitan fellowship of
Methodism in Rome, especially in his quiet contacts with the
children.
Successive years found him weaker. This showed chiefly in a
loss of words. But the telepathy between Winifred and
himself was wonderful. He would look at her and she would
read the thought in his eyes and frame the word for him.

'Rome is inexhaustible', said Flew to James Stevenson
of the Cambridge Faculty of Divinity, the last time they
talked together. The Flews saw it all on their visits – the
churches, the galleries, the classical remains, the
catacombs, the house where Michelangelo lived, the
vestiges of the exiled Stuarts, the tomb-stone of his first
cousin, Harold Harrison Burdess, one of Rex Kissack's
predecessors, who had died in 1937, aged fifty-two.

Flew felt that for restfulness and beauty the Dominican
cloisters were unparalleled. It was there, at the Collegio
Angelico, that he enquired if Garrigou-Lagrange, whose
lectures he had attended in 1916, were still alive. The old
monk was sent for and was glad to meet one whom he
had taught so long before. As they parted, Garrigou-
Lagrange said slowly, in hesitant English, 'And I will
pray for you'.

The great Roman Church had for him then, as always,
its ancient lure. When he visited Santa Croce in
Gerusalemme, he declared that the 'title of the Cross',
which the Empress Helena, Mother of Constantine, had
brought from Jerusalem was more likely to be authentic
than any other relic he had seen. In Rome, he developed
a greater appreciation of the part relics, saints' days and
holy places have in the very real devotion of humble
Roman Catholics.

On his first return visit, in 1958, Pius XII was still
alive. Flew was curious to know if there had been any
official Roman Catholic reaction to his essay on the

Catholic doctrine in the Lund volume on *The Nature of the Church*. He had heard somewhere a rumour that His Holiness had read it and approved. Suddenly, he was dazzled by the thought that there might be possibility of an audience. Rex Kissack had no influence at that stage, but knew that Bishop Bell, recently retired from Chichester, who was in Rome at the time, had been received by the Pope. Kissack telephoned Bell and put Flew on the line. Kissack heard him explain his hopes in a bright and expectant voice, but then the tone grew flatter. It was clear that Bell was either unwilling or unable to help. After some minutes of wistful enquiry, the receiver was replaced, with heavy disappointment. Kissack tried to console him. A formal interview with an Italian pontiff might have been an anti-climax. 'Yes,' Flew reflected, 'that is so. After all, one could not hope to get far with His Holiness in a mere half hour.'

He was aware before his visits ceased that John XXIII was revolutionising Church relations. A German Lutheran Pastor, who knew him in Cambridge, remarked on the postcard portrait of the Pope which came to adorn the mantlepiece at Glisson Road and 'enjoyed the rights of a sort of family friend'. One night, he accompanied the Kissacks to one of the humble soirées, given by Father Meura, a disciple of the Abbé Couturier, 'and his redoubtable wit of a housekeeper', Mme Couster. Perhaps that was one occasion when he saw and greeted the *aggiornamento* from afar, for later it was Father Meura who brought Methodism into its first official contact with Monsignor (now Cardinal) Willibrands of the Secretariat for Promoting Christian Unity.

In the autumn of 1961, he had a mild heart attack, when out on the Gianicolo. Appropriately, it was a passing car of a Cardinal which stopped and took him to hospital. Afterwards, he was advised not to return to the Signorina Morelli's villa, which had many steps, so the

Flews went to the Manse at Ponte Sant' Angelo, where they stayed until just after Christmas. He would see Rome no more.

There were times throughout these years when he was not far from despair. News of the Anglican–Methodist conversations depressed him. Rawlinson's death in 1960 recalled the South India controversy and made him say, perhaps too harshly, 'The Anglicans have not learnt a thing'. And his book could not get finished.

He would quote the words of the Charles Wesley hymn which opens the Methodist Conference:

> What troubles have we seen,
> What conflicts have we passed,
> Fightings without and fears within. . . .

Sir Barnes Wallis saw him for the last time at a Christ's Hospital dinner in London, and afterwards drove him to the Athenaeum. He described himself as 'a poor old Methody'.

Benjamin Drewery, one of his first generation of post 1945 students, came to his aid over *Jesus and His Way*, and with characteristic generosity and enthusiasm, sorted out the now rather confused masses of material, and began to weld them into a book, which was in the press by September 1962. Flew, who found speech increasingly difficult, was deeply moved. He dropped into a verse from a Doddridge hymn, 'What wonders love can do!'

On the 5th September, 1962, he took tea with his mother and sister. The three of them were together for a particularly happy two hours. After tea, his sister read from Sir Charles Petrie's book, *The Victorians*, passages about the monarchy, a subject which had always fascinated him, and he was so delighted, that Mrs Strong made a mental note to do the same on his next visit. But it was not to be. The next day, descending the stairs at Glisson Road, he stumbled and fell. Four days later he died in Addenbrooke's hospital on his mother's ninety-ninth birthday.

A Memorial Service was held on 15th September, in the Hills Road Church, Cambridge, where he had worshipped since retirement. The Reverend Alfred Binney, the Superintendent Minister, officiated, and the Reverend Benjamin Drewery gave the address. It was a simple Methodist service, with some of the characteristic Wesley hymns – 'Give me the faith which can remove and sink the mountain to a plain' (*Methodist Hymn Book* 390), which he had chosen in almost every place during his Presidency, and, at the end 'Captain of Israel's host' (*Methodist Hymn Book* 608), which customarily concludes the Conference each year. At the start, they sang this, a rollicking sea-shanty of triumph, rarely heard in our cautious and inhibited times:

> Rejoice for a brother deceased,
>   Our loss is his infinite gain;
> A soul out of prison released,
>   And freed from its bodily chain;
> With songs let us follow his flight,
>   And mount with his spirit above,
> Escaped to the mansions of light,
>   And lodged in the Eden of love.
>
> Our brother the haven hath gained,
>   Out-flying the tempest and wind,
> His rest he hath sooner obtained,
>   And left his companions behind,
> Still tossed on a sea of distress,
>   Hard toiling to make the blest shore,
> Where all is assurance and peace,
>   And sorrow and sin are no more.
>
> There all the ship's company meet
>   Who sailed with the Saviour beneath,

With shouting each other they greet,
  And triumph o'er trouble and death;
The voyage of life's at an end,
  The mortal affliction is past;
The age that in heaven they spend
  For ever and ever shall last.

Jesus and His Way was published in 1963 by the Epworth Press. The proposed chapter on *Hebrews* had to be excluded and also the careful examination of 'conscience' in the New Testament, which the author desired, but the work bears all the marks of the scholar-evangelist and proclaims as with a trumpet that the ethics of Jesus is an ethics of grace – 'We love because he first loved us'. In some ways, it unifies all Flew's abundant labours. He was too great a penitent to have thought it credible, but he would have coveted as his epitaph, words which he quotes about his Lord:

At every step of his life he let loose another secret of God's love.[7]

He would have insisted on adding:

What hast thou, that thou didst not receive?[8]

[7] *Jesus and His Way*, p. 31n. The words are attributed to a Scottish writer, R. W. Barbour, but no reference is given.
[8] I Corinthians 4:7.

9

Epilogue

My Master was so very poor –
And with the poor He broke the bread,
So very rich my Master was
That multitudes
By Him were fed.

My Master was so very poor
They nailed him naked to a Cross;
So very rich my Master was
He gave his all
And knew no loss.

HARVEY LEA
(Written at the beginning
of RNF's petty cash book)

THE YEARS pass more relentlessly than ever, most of
Flew's contemporaries have gone, his name is treasured
by diminishing numbers of those who remember his
Methodist Circuit ministry and his 'children's talks', the
youngest of his surviving pupils turns grey. *Jesus and His
Church* has about exhausted its reprints (although a
recent traveller in North America met several students
who were occupied with it), theology has passed from
liberalism through Barthianism to radicalism, and the
liberal orthodox Protestantism with Catholic sympathies,
which was Flew's position, is rather at a discount.

Ecumenism, thwarted of organic unions, turns to politics. Perhaps it is thus fulfilling its destiny, though at risk to its mission of peace. Ours could pass into an age of extremists, with the establishments ever more conservative and the dissenters throwing home-made bombs to destroy social systems, rather than becoming the architects of theological systems.

Flew's name is good for a couple of mentions in a five-hundred-page history of the ecumenical movement, but it is easy to think of him as a period piece whose time is now past. A new world is at hand, bright and brittle with technology and the birth of nation states, unheard of when he talked of the 'new order' after Hitler's war.

He lived to see very little of what he worked so hard to accomplish. Church unity happened in South India but not in England, and in ecumenical theology it is easy to dismiss him as one of the 'old guard', whose ways are not our ways, and who have been found expendable by the Churches, if not by God.

But this is a superficial view to be treated with the contempt he sometimes showed for theories which he thought inadequate. He would not be displeased to have his biography end with three points and we may discern three elements of permanence in his life and work.

(1) His interest in *theologia spiritualis* needs to be maintained and extended. He understood that *lex credendi* is *lex orandi* and the only theology which is likely to satisfy our world is one that begins with reason and sound scholarship and ends in mysticism as Flew understood it, Christ-mysticism, which does not evade the 'scandal of particularity', which is expressed in metaphors of *commun*ion, not union, and of which the joys are 'social' and must be shared.

(2) He was an exact scholar, who verified his quotations, and could rarely be accused of misrepresenting his sources. But his main concern was always people. He was a very human theologian – human in his

foibles and eccentricities, human in the self-consciousness
of his reactions and regard, human in his love of sport
and interest in women's clothes, human, essentially,
because all his true life derived from the humanity of the
Son of God. He loved the saints and thinkers he interpreted, as people; he enjoyed to talk with the great ones
of the earth and to discover that they were human too.
But he had respect for the lowly. His gospel was for
Oxford, Cambridge, Edinburgh, Amsterdam, Lund and
the Athenaeum, but also for Portland quarrymen,
Fenland farmers and Indian and Italian peasants, for the
actress on the stage, the soldier at the front, the 'boozer'
in the pub.[1], and, in our world, for the nuclear research
worker, the computer operator, and the disc-jockey. He
made friends everywhere, among young and old. He had
to resist what he regarded as the pretensions of Anglo-
Catholicism, but many Anglo-Catholics he dearly
loved – Hoskyns, Goudge, Michael Ramsey, the Prioress
of Whitby among them. He believed that laymen were
more likely to be saints than the ordained. 'The cleric
may be very useful, amiable, business-like, eloquent even!
But someone in his flock is the saint. That has been the
story, not in *every* committee or church or college in which
I have lived, but in very many.'

(3) His ecumenism, unfulfilled in his lifetime, and
misunderstood by those who thought of him as willing
to give up everything for a super-Church, is precisely
what the future requires. It was a patient, scholarly study
of the beliefs of others, free of all arrogance, humble
before the truth, yet tenacious for what it regarded as
the heart of the gospel. Its method was 'dialogue' and
fidelity to sources, not imposed solutions concocted from

---

[1] Cf. Charles Smyth, *The Genius of the Church of England* (SPCK
1947), p. 40, and his claim, which Flew loved to repeat, that
Methodist hymns got home to the 'converted old boozer' in the
eighteenth century.

the clever philosophising or surface impressions of those who would not trouble to listen to their fellow Christians. Yet, the immovable foundation was that the gospel is not something we invent or earn, it is all, as von Hügel said, 'of givenness', 'of grace'.

He seems to have become disillusioned with Anglicans. Perhaps in his old age he did not sufficiently reckon with the change in the hearts of many Anglo-Catholics. At least three of the surviving members of the *Catholicity* group became ardent supporters of the Anglican–Methodist *Scheme*, whose terms they might well have repudiated in 1947. But he may have suffered sometimes from that inveterate Anglican superiority, which has been apparent again, at least in Methodist eyes, since the Vatican Council and which would seem to ignore or spurn Methodism for the glamours of rapprochement with Rome.

Such an attitude overlooks the fact that Rome is anxious for a new understanding with Methodists too.[2] Perhaps, in the end, Anglicans and Methodists will be completely reconciled only as they find, either separately or together, a new relationship with that great communion which is at once the apotheosis and the nadir of institutional Christianity and which, though a mystery and a problem still, has within its vast and complex life so many of the marks of the Crucified. Of this, Flew's life was in some sense prophetic and although he did not live to taste more than the first-fruits of the *aggiornamento*, there is poetic justice in a trivial yet moving incident barely a month after his death.

When he said farewell to Rome for the last time, Flew inadvertently left his umbrella behind in Ponte Sant'

---

[2] For an account of Methodist-Roman Catholic relationships from 1966–71 see *Anglican–Methodist Unity*, Report of Joint Working Group (Church Information Office and Epworth Press 1971), pp. 32 ff.

Angelo. One Saturday evening, at the beginning of the Second Vatican Council, John XXIII gave a reception for non-Catholic observers. As Rex Kissack and two other Methodists set out, it started to rain. Kissack remembered Flew's umbrella, and under it they went to meet the Pope.

Index